OF
VICTORIA AND
ADJOINING AREAS

Leon Costermans

Costermans Publishing

By the same author:
Native Trees and Shrubs of South-eastern Australia
(published by Lansdowne Publishing, Sydney)

Costermans Publishing
1/6 St Johns Ave
Frankston, Victoria 3199

Trees of Victoria: an illustrated field guide
First published 1966; reprinted 1966
Second edition 1967; reprinted 1968, 1970
Third edition 1973; reprinted 1975, 1977, 1978
Fourth edition 1981; reprinted 1983, 1986, 1990, 1992
Fifth edition as *Trees of Victoria and adjoining areas*
  (this fully revised edition) 1994

National Library of Australia
Cataloguing-in-Publication data

Costermans, L. F. (Leon F.), 1933– .
  Trees of Victoria and adjoining areas.

  5th Ed.
  Includes index.
  ISBN 0 9599105 2 2.
  1. Trees - Australia, Southeastern - Identification. I. Title.

582.160994

Design, typesetting, illustrations and photographs by the author.
Printed in Australia by Rolls Printing, Seaford, Victoria.

Contents

Preface

When *Trees of Victoria* was first produced in 1966, the public response to it revealed an interest in our native vegetation far greater than expected. Even so, it was never imagined that a continuing demand for the book would cause it to be still in print more than twenty-six years later.

Although numerous additions and modifications were made during that time, it remained essentially the same book, its basic illustrated format and pocket size having found popular acceptance.

However, some significant changes within the community for whom the book was written have now brought about the need for what is, in effect, a completely new book. It is worth explaining here some of those changes, and the ways in which this new edition is a response to them.

Initially the book was conceived as a simple practical introduction for 'bush explorers', especially younger ones, at a time when there were no other local field guides of this type. However, it became much more widely used, including prescription as a university reference. At the same time, numerous outdoor programs and group activities, as well as more accessible literature, have led to a much greater level of environmental knowledge in the community overall. For these reasons, it was decided to raise the level of 'botanical sophistication' in this edition, with expansion of the ecological and geographic aspects, and greater precision in some of the more formal aspects of classification and description, while still retaining, it is hoped, the book's essentially introductory character.

The earlier editions of *Trees of Victoria* were restricted in species coverage largely for the sake of simplicity of presentation and reduction of cost. The species originally included were mainly the commoner ones of the more populated and frequently visited bush areas—the treatment for remoter areas was somewhat limited. In particular, quite a few tree species of East Gippsland were omitted, but it should be remembered that it has only been in relatively recent years that the unique natural attractions of that area have come to be widely recognised. This edition is greatly expanded to include virtually all trees (and some larger shrubs) native to Victoria and adjoining areas of New South Wales and South Australia—about 250 species in all.

In recent years, there has also been a marked increase in activity in the taxonomic field, leading to the recognition of some new tree species, and quite a few changes in botanical names (often for reasons somewhat puzzling to the general population!). This edition incorporates such changes, but in a way that can accommodate botanists' differences in interpretation, as well as inevitable further changes.

As a result of its history of periodic modification, the book itself was showing its need for totally updated typesetting. Modern desktop publishing techniques have made it possible for the author to type and set up the complete book in virtually ready-to-print form—a far cry from the cumbersome metal-setting processes of the first printing.

With all these changes, however, the book's field guide format has been retained, as have its basic aims, namely –

- To help beginners in particular, but indeed anyone who enjoys out-door exploration, to find greater understanding of the Australian bush. While this book focuses mainly on trees, it is hoped that the observer will also become more perceptive of the other essential components and inter-relationships of natural environments.

- To introduce and explain some of the botanical characteristics of our more conspicuous woody plant groups, as well as some practical techniques which can be used for identification in field situations.

- To encourage the book's users to find satisfaction not just in naming plants, but also in using greater understanding as a basis for action—to preserve the constantly threatened remnants of native bush, and to revegetate with local indigenous species, where appropriate.

Assistance from two particular sources must be acknowledged here: firstly from the staff of the National Herbarium, Melbourne, who cheerfully make available to me the full resources of that institution; secondly, from countless people who used the earlier editions, especially on walks and field activities—their reactions and suggestions have provided me with the stimulus and encouragement to produce yet another edition.

LEON COSTERMANS
Frankston, 1994

Peppermint—messmate foothill forest: the most common association in moderate rainfall areas south of Divide

Common and widespread species

- Common coastal trees
- Trees of moister areas from plains to ranges (especially south of Divide)
- Trees of drier areas from plains to ranges (especially north of Divide)

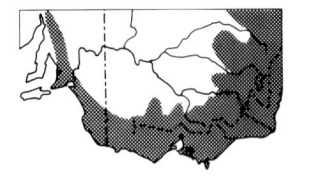

Page 9 ➤

Tall forest of Mountain Ash, with dense understorey of wattles, Hazel Pomaderris, treeferns, and other species

Mountain forests and moist valleys

Forest trees mainly in higher rainfall areas in ranges of central-east Victoria to NSW, also in South Gippsland and Otway ranges

- Tall trees of the top storey
- Smaller trees of middle and lower storeys

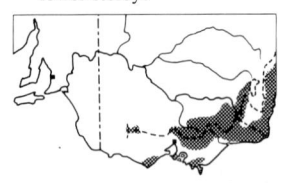

Page 13 ➤

East Gippsland and South Coast NSW

- Trees of the coastal fringe
- Various eucalypt forests
- Warm temperate rainforests
- Cool temperate rainforests
- Pine–box woodlands of the Upper Snowy River valley

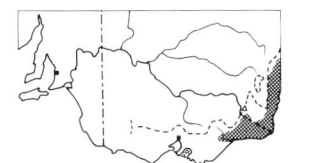

White Cypress-pine and White Box along the Upper Snowy River valley—an area with spectacular beauty

Page 24 ▶

Black Box in foreground on occasionally-flooded grey soils; mallee species on brownish sands in background

Western and northern areas

- Trees by rivercourses, lakes; Wimmera and northern plains
- Mallee eucalypts on reddish loams of 'Murray Mallee'
- Mallee eucalypts on pale sands of 'Lowan Mallee'
- Pine–belah woodlands
- SW Vic to SE SA

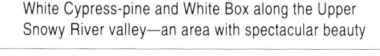

Page 33 ▶

Blue Gum (*E. bicostata*) – page 63

'Gum' eucalypts   **Page 51 ➤**

Bark smooth, peeling in large flakes or ribbons on most of trunk; leaves often long and narrow.

Silver-leaved Stringybark (*E. conspicua*) – page 77

'Rough-barked gums'   **Page 74 ➤**

'Gum-type' leaves etc., but rough bark on most of trunk; juvenile leaves often greyish, opposite.

'Box' eucalypts   **Page 83 ➤**

Bark flaky-scaly on trunk; leaves often small and greyish; buds, fruits in compound clusters.

White Box (*E. albens*) – page 89

'Peppermint' eucalypts   **Page 92 ➤**

Leaves peppermint-smelling; bark short-fibred, finely fissured (upper trunk sometimes smooth).

Broad-leaved Peppermint (*E. dives*) – page 94

Alpine Ash (*E. delegatensis*) – page 99

Red Stringybark (*E. macrorhyncha*) – page 106

Tall 'ash' eucalypts ▸ Page 97

Mostly 'half-barked'; other adult characters can resemble stringybarks or peppermints.

'Stringybark' eucalypts ▸ Page 102

Mostly 'stringy-fibrous' bark on whole trunk; adult leaves thick, broad, curved, asymmetrical.

Some other rough-barked eucalypts ▸ Page 111

- **Red Bloodwood**: bark tessellated; leaves paler green beneath, with widely spreading veins.
- **Mahogany**: bark thick fibrous on trunk, smooth on limbs; leaves thick, paler green beneath.
- **Woollybutt**: bark greyish, subfibrous on whole trunk, flaking irregularly; leaves long.
- **Ironbark**: bark hard, black, deeply fissured.

Red Bloodwood – p. 112   Red Ironbark – p. 115

'Mallee' eucalypts ▸ Page 116

Multi-stemmed small trees in drier inland mallee areas, NW Vic to SA and NSW, and 'outliers'.

White Mallee (*E. gracilis*) – page 118

Prickly Tea-tree (*L. continentale*) – page 126

Scented Paperbark (*M. squarrosa*) – page 129

Tea-trees (*Leptospermum*) | Page 124 ➤

Small leaves; 5-petalled flowers; fruit capsules (mostly woody) irregularly scattered.

Melaleucas (*Melaleuca*) | Page 127 ➤

Small leaves; small soft 'bottlebrush' flower-spikes; sessile woody capsules in groups.

Wattles (*Acacia*) | Page 132 ➤

Wattles with *'feathery'* (bipinnate) leaves; globular flower-heads; pods.

Wattles (*Acacia*) | Page 135 ➤

Flat-leaved (phyllodinous) wattles with *cylindrical* flower-spikes; pods.

Silver Wattle (*A. dealbata*) – page 132

Coast Wattle (*A. sophorae*) – page 135

Coast Banksia (*B. integrifolia*) – page 149

Banksias (*Banksia*)   Page 148 ➤

Stiff leaves, white or pale green beneath; large flower-heads; large wide-valved woody cones.

Black Sheoak (*Allocasuarina littoralis*) – page 152

Sheoaks and Bulloaks   Page 151 ➤

Slender 'jointed' green branchlets; multi-valved cones on female trees; male trees separate.

Wattles (*Acacia*)   Page 138 ➤

Flat-leaved (phyllodinous) wattles with *globular* flower-heads; pods.

Mountain Hickory Wattle (*A. obliquinervia*) – page 139

Cypress-pines (*Callitris*)   Page 154 ➤

Cypress-like fine green branchlets; rounded woody cones with six segments.

Scrub Cypress-pine (*C. verrucosa*) – page 155

'The Amphitheatre' on the Mitchell River (East Gippsland), an area of particularly interesting relationships between plant communities and the physical environment. Dry eucalypt forest (mainly *E. sieberi*, *E. globoidea*) at the top of the escarpment; dry rainforest (bright green, including *Pittosporum undulatum*, *Acmena smithii*, occasional *Brachychiton populneus*) on the slope of loose talus rock; *Tristaniopsis laurina* and riparian shrubs close to river level.

GETTING TO KNOW THE BUSH

From the time that eighteenth century white explorers first set eyes on the Australian continent, this land has commonly been seen as one of curiosities, contrasts and contradictions.

Of course, the Aboriginal people had come to know it intimately in more than fifty thousand years of occupation, and their understanding and explanations of the land and life became an integral part of their traditions and culture. They had learned to manage, respect and conserve nature in order to survive as part of it.

But to many European eyes, the Australian bush was wild and unruly, superficially monotonous, yet at the same time bewildering in its great diversity of strange plants and animals. In Victoria, a few early settlers took interest in the plants and sent specimens to England, but it was a young German migrant pharmacist and botanist, Dr Ferdinand Mueller, who was to pioneer the serious scientific study of our plants. Mueller was appointed as first government botanist in 1853, and immediately set out on his remarkable collecting expeditions, traversing the length and breadth of Victoria. By 1868, his herbarium collection exceeded 300 000 specimens, many of them representing species new to science.

To the great majority of newcomers, however, the subtle values and botanical curiosities of the bush meant little. With first the gold rush, then the clearing of vast tracts of land for farming and grazing, ruthless onslaughts were made on what seemed to be endless forest and scrub. The main value of trees was seen in terms of their timber.

It has only been in recent decades that we have witnessed a wide-spread change in community perceptions of the Australian bush, and in attitudes towards it. There is now a greater understanding of ecological processes—the interactions of all the living things and the physical elements of a natural environment. A healthy ecosystem is seen as one which can maintain itself and adjust to natural pressures—this largely depends on diversity of species with mixed ages. By protecting remnant natural vegetation, and replanting as appropriate, we can aid diversity and provide habitat for a range of native animals, including birds and insects. Even in farming areas, the presence of native species, including birds, when coupled with good agricultural practices, can have benefits, especially in pest control. We are now coming to appreciate the wisdom of the Aboriginal philosophy by recognising that our survival too depends on seeing ourselves as a part of a great ecosystem, not separate from it.

With this heightened environmental concern, many people are keen to know more about their natural vegetation, but still find it difficult to know how and where to start. What follows is just one possible approach for coming to understand the plants of 'the bush' as a whole, and one of its important components in particular—the trees.

Start by trying to gain an overview . . .

It is worth taking a lesson from film-makers. They often start with a wide view to provide a context, then zoom in to medium views and close-ups for the critical details. (See, for example, the photo opposite page 1.)

If you are able to view your area from a high vantage point (or to examine an aerial photo of the locality), look for *variations* in hue and texture in the vegetation, especially in relation to topography. Seeking the *causes* of such variations can give more purpose to bush study, and clues to bush dynamics. The following are some possibilities.

1. *Well defined vegetation changes related to geology.* Vegetation can vary with changes in soil characteristics and topography because of geological transitions; marked differences in land utilisation can also be evident. Some easily observed examples of geological influences –

*   Granite adjoined by the sedimentary rock into which it intruded when in its original molten state. The Mt Buffalo and Mt Baw Baw outcrops illustrate this contrast well.

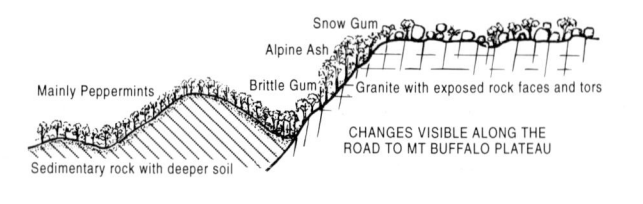

Snow Gum
Alpine Ash
Brittle Gum — Granite with exposed rock faces and tors
Mainly Peppermints
Sedimentary rock with deeper soil

CHANGES VISIBLE ALONG THE
ROAD TO MT BUFFALO PLATEAU

- Volcanic soils (derived from old basaltic lava flows) overlying and adjoining the exposed sedimentary rock. This is clearly exemplified north-west of Melbourne (e.g. Malmsbury–Daylesford area) where the basaltic land is open compared with the forested sedimentary country, and in Gippsland (e.g. Neerim South–Noojee area) where the more fertile soils from the Older Basalt are cultivated, while the surrounding sedimentary and granite areas mostly remain forested.

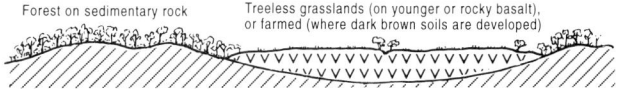

Forest on sedimentary rock   Treeless grasslands (on younger or rocky basalt), or farmed (where dark brown soils are developed)

- In north-west Victoria, pale infertile sands of the undulating 'Desert' dunes (bearing small mallee eucalypts such as *E. costata* and shrubby understorey) overlie older reddish clay-sands (with taller mallee such as *E. gracilis* and rather sparse understorey). Abrupt transitions of this type are exemplified along the Calder Highway near Hattah Lakes, the taller open mallee type having largely been cleared for wheat. It is one of the apparent contradictions of the Australian environment that poorer (low-nutrient) sandy soils usually carry a richer and denser array of native plant species, especially in the form of heathlands.

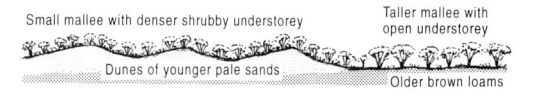

Small mallee with denser shrubby understorey   Taller mallee with open understorey

Dunes of younger pale sands   Older brown loams

2. *Localised areas of vegetation change.* Irregular patches of different vegetation or regrowth can indicate areas burnt by earlier bushfire, or sometimes previous heavy clearing. The different types of response of eucalypts to fire are explained on page 43; plants of other groups have similar survival mechanisms. Some are killed by fire, but the seeds they drop can produce dense regrowth (e.g. in leguminous plants, such as wattles, or proteaceous plants such as hakeas). Others can sprout from the rootstock or trunk. The nature of such regrowth can indicate a great deal about fire history and the various plant species' responses to it.

3

3. *Changes in vegetation types related to aspect and position on slopes.* Because north-facing slopes receive more direct sun-radiation, soils tend to be drier and shallower. As an illustration of this effect, Silvertop Ash (*Eucalyptus sieberi*), which prefers drier soils on ridges, usually extends to lower elevations on a hill's north-facing slope than on its southern side.

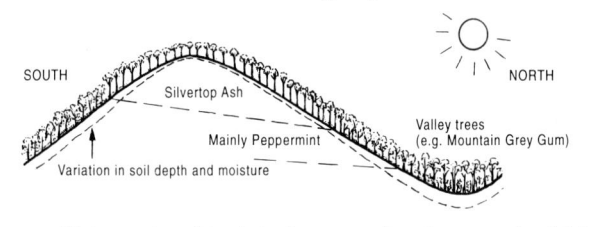

4. *Changes with increasing altitude in the mountains.* An example of this is given below (with further details of species on page 8). Such changes result mainly from increasing precipitation with increase in altitude, together with decreasing mean temperatures and longer periods of snow.

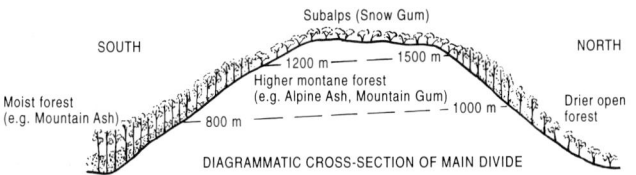

Move in to look more closely at each identifiably different area . . .

1. Examine the characteristics of the rock, soil or general substrate. Is the soil
- heavy and clayey, or light and sandy or gravelly?
- deeply developed, or shallow and rocky?
- free-draining, or poorly-drained and prone to periodic waterlogging?

2. Look at the whole vegetation formation from top to bottom. Consider the trees of the *top storey* –
- Look for colour, density and textural characteristics—are the leaves

4

fine, weeping, broad, shade-giving, dark green or grey-green, glossy or dull? Stand underneath to see how much light is let through the canopy. Do the crowns of the trees touch?

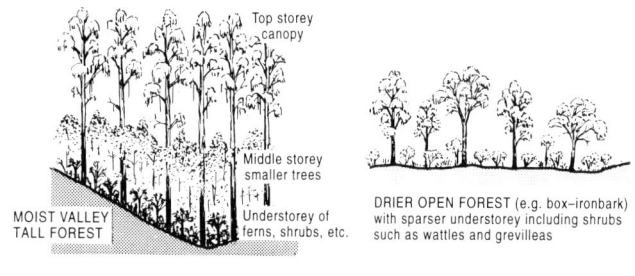

MOIST VALLEY TALL FOREST

Top storey canopy

Middle storey smaller trees

Understorey of ferns, shrubs, etc.

DRIER OPEN FOREST (e.g. box–ironbark) with sparser understorey including shrubs such as wattles and grevilleas

For the *understorey*, consider these possible differences –

- In moister tall forests (e.g. of Mountain Ash), the top storey canopy is usually quite open, but thick growth of broad-leaved large shrubs or small trees in a lower storey can make the forest appear much denser.
- In drier forests, the top storey trees are not so tall, and the understorey is sparser, usually composed of shrubs with leaves which are smaller, narrower and 'harder' (sclerophyllous).

3. Look for evidence of fire or clearing—blackened bark, or dense, even-height regrowth of a few kinds of shrubs.

4. Look at the bush formation as a habitat for animals. For example, particular bird species tend to occupy specific strata in a forest.

Now try to identify particular species in each community . . .

1. Before focusing on one particular tree, look around to get an idea of the likely number of clearly different species in the area, by considering an *aggregate* of each tree's characteristics, rather than one attribute such as bark. This will help to give some idea of the degree to which variation can occur in each species (e.g. in growth form or bark characteristics).

2. When attempting to identify a particular tree, look for as many of the parts—buds, flowers, fruits and leaves (adult and juvenile)—as are

5

present. If these are too high on the tree, there will often be bits of branches, or most certainly single parts (e.g. fruits), on the ground. With a little detective work, and a process of matching and elimination, it is usually possible to work out which sample comes from which tree.

3. Even if inflorescence buds are immature (e.g. months before flowering in wattles), their shape, grouping and numbers will usually give clues to the likely mature form, and should therefore aid identification.

4. For identification of understorey shrubs, refer to *Native Trees and Shrubs of South-eastern Australia* by the same author. This is designed to be used by applying the approaches outlined above.

Using this book for identification

Users of the book who are not familiar with the basics of botanical naming, description and grouping will find a glossary of descriptive terms and an explanation of classification and naming on pages 157–8.

The four sections in Part 2 (pages 7–38) have several purposes: to compare natural aspects of some broad regions and environments, to list for each region the most significant tree species from the major genera treated in Part 3, and to describe trees of other genera whose principal occurrence is in each area. Where possible, species are grouped to reflect common associations, as explained in each section's introduction.

The great majority of trees fall into the seven main groups or genera treated in Part 3 (pages 39–156). It is relatively easy to recognise these groups, and the key photos in the front of the book should provide a quick lead. Once a tree is placed in a group, its species identity can be established with the help of the explanations at the start of each section.

It should be noted that within all the species descriptions, features given in *italics* are those most useful for differentiating each species from otherwise similar ones. On the diagrams, the scale of the illustration is shown thus: [× 1] = natural size, [× 1/2] = half natural size, and so on.

If a tree doesn't appear to match any of the descriptions in relevant sections, it could be a species from elsewhere which has been planted or otherwise introduced, or it could possibly be a hybrid (see page 50).

2 SOME BROAD NATURAL REGIONS AND ASSOCIATED VEGETATION

These sections of the book . . .
- identify in broad terms some regions and natural environments, with particular reference to their characteristic vegetation types;
- list, for each environment, the more common species described in Part 3, indicating their most frequent associations;
- describe other tree species for each region or environment (most being the sole tree-sized members of their genera in this book's area).

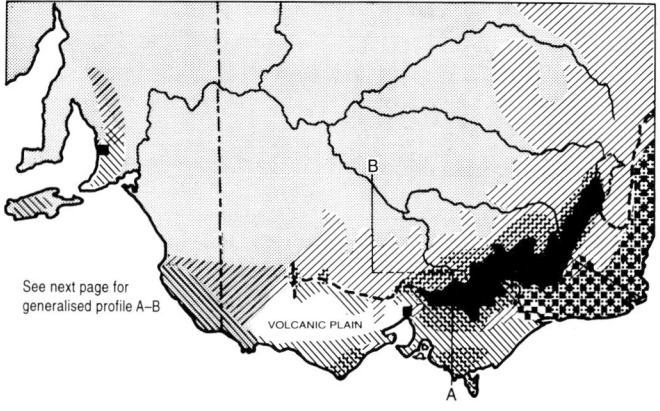

See next page for generalised profile A–B

VOLCANIC PLAIN

GENERALISED PROFILE OF VEGETATION TYPES
Coast—Main Divide—Murray River
SOME TYPICAL ASSOCIATIONS AND THEIR RELATIVE LEVELS

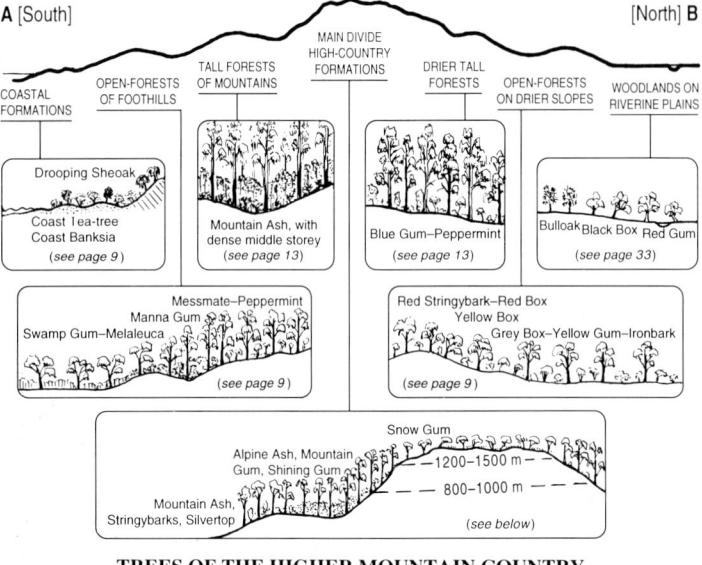

TREES OF THE HIGHER MOUNTAIN COUNTRY

In the mountains of the Main Divide, tall forest species such as Mountain Ash, Messmate, Peppermint and Silvertop Ash occur mainly up to about 1000 m. Above this, two zones (as below) can be recognised, related to the duration of annual snow cover. The transitions are generally lower on cooler south-facing slopes (see page 4).

- **Montane forests of tall trees, between about 800–1000 m and 1200–1500 m**

Alpine Ash (*Eucalyptus delegatensis*)	99	Brown Barrel (*E. fastigata*)	104
Shining Gum (*E. nitens*)	61	Catkin Wattle (*Acacia dallachiana*)	137
Mountain Gum (*E. dalrympleana*)	57	Montane Wattle (*Acacia frigescens*)	144

- **Subalpine woodlands, from 1200–1500 m to treeless levels (about 1900 m)**

Snow Gum (*Eucalyptus pauciflora*)	64	Spinning Gum (*E. perriniana*)	69
Black Sallee (*E. stellulata*)	65	Tingaringy Gum (*E. glaucescens*)	70
Buffalo Sallee (*E. mitchelliana*)	65	Kybean Mallee-ash (*E. kybeanensis*)	73

8

COMMON AND WIDESPREAD SPECIES

COMMON COASTAL TREES

Coast Banksia (*Banksia integrifolia*) – on sands, east from Port Phillip Bay area 149
Coast Tea-tree (*Leptospermum laevigatum*) – on sands, east of Otways 125
Coast Beard-heath (*Leucopogon parviflorus*) – mainly on sands, throughout coast 10
Boobialla (*Myoporum insulare*) – on various coastal sites 10
Moonah (*Melaleuca lanceolata*) – mainly on limy sands, west of Western Port ... 128
Drooping Sheoak (*Allocasuarina verticillata*) – on cliffs and old dunes 152

COMMON TREES OF RANGES, HILLS AND ASSOCIATED PLAINS

• In higher rainfall areas or on damper soils, especially south of Divide

Manna Gum (*E. viminalis*) – mainly in moister valleys; on some plains and hills 56
Rough-barked Manna Gum (*E. pryoriana*) – near-coast sands, Pt Phillip–W Gippsl'd 76
Narrow-leaved Peppermint (*E. radiata* etc.) – widespread, coast to ranges 93
Messmate (*E. obliqua*) – widespread, especially in taller moister forests 103
Brown Stringybark (*E. baxteri*) – coast to ranges, esp. on poorer sandy sites 108
Silver-leaved Stringybarks (*E. cephalocarpa* etc.) – poorly-drained infertile soils 77
Swamp Gums (*E. ovata, E. camphora*, etc.) – poorly-drained sites, coast–ranges 54
Swamp Paperbark (*Mel. ericifolia*) – poorly-drained sites, E half S Vic–NSW coast 128
Scented Paperbark (*Melaleuca squarrosa*) – esp. wet peaty sands, coast–hills ... 129
Prickly Tea-tree (*Leptospermum continentale*) – esp. moist areas, coast–ranges 126
Woolly Tea-tree (*Leptospermum lanigerum*) – esp. moist gullies, coast–ranges .. 126
Blackwood (*Acacia melanoxylon*) – esp. on deeper soils with clay, coast–ranges 144
Silver Wattle (*A. dealbata*) – esp. near streams and in forests, E from Grampians 132
Black Wattle (*A. mearnsii*) – widespread, coast to ranges, mostly on drier soils .. 132
Black Sheoak (*Allocasuarina littoralis*) – various forests, S of Divide, esp. east ... 152

• In lower rainfall areas or on drier soils, especially north of Divide

River Red Gum (*E. camaldulensis*) – along rivers, N and W plains; also S of Divide 52
Yellow Box (*E. melliodora*) – mostly lower slopes of foothills, N and S of Divide ...86
Apple Box (*E. bridgesiana*) – east Vic–NSW, lower slopes, often with Yellow Box 78
Long-leaved Box (*E. goniocalyx*) – on poor dry shallow soils, N and S of Divide 79
Red Box (*E. polyanthemos*) – dry shallow soils, E of Melb, N of Divide, Gippsland ..84
Grey Box (*E. microcarpa*) – common, plains to foothills, mostly north of Divide 88
White Box (*E. albens*) – mainly NE Vic–NSW, esp. with Grey Box; also E Gippsl'd 89
Red Stringybark (*E. macrorhyncha*) – dry shallow soils on hills, N and S of Divide .. 106
Broad-leaved Peppermint (*E. dives*) – mainly on shallow soils, foothills–ranges 94
Candlebark Gum (*E. rubida*) – mainly on shallow soils, foothills–ranges 57
Red Ironbark (*E. tricarpa/sideroxylon*) – mainly 'goldfields country'; also S of Divide 115
Yellow Gum (*E. leucoxylon*) – west half, plains–hills; also E of Melbourne (Kew) ..67
Drooping Sheoak (*Allocasuarina verticillata*) – widespread, esp. on rocky hills 152
Lightwood (*Acacia implexa*) – widespread, on drier shallow soils of hilly country 145
Golden Wattle (*Acacia pycnantha*) – widespread on drier shallow soils 138

Some further common small trees are described on pages 10–12 following.

Coast Beard-heath

Leucopogon parviflorus

Shrub–small tree, 1–5 m; bark firm, dark, finely fissured; *new foliage bright green.* Common *along coast,* mainly on sands. LEAVES broadest above middle, to 3 cm long, tip acute (but *not pungent*), veins fine, parallel, numerous on *pale green* underside. FLOWERS (July–Nov) small, white, 5 corolla-lobes *hairy inside* (*'leuco-pogon'* means 'white beard'), in clustered spikes 1–3 cm long. FRUIT small white bead-like drupes.

Family EPACRIDACEAE (Australian heaths)

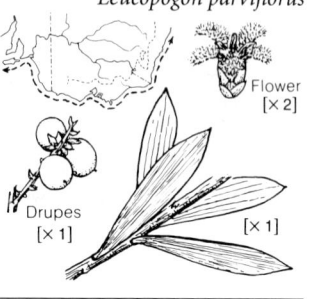

Flower [× 2]

Drupes [× 1]

[× 1]

Tree Broom-heath

Monotoca elliptica [A]
Monotoca glauca [B]

Shrubs or small trees, 2–6 m, in scrub or forest *near coast.* Two very similar species: [A] *M. elliptica* most extensive; [B] *M. glauca* in Otways; both in Wilsons Prom. area. LEAVES to about 3 cm long, *smooth dark green above, whitish beneath with many fine veins,* a fine *pungent* point. FLOWERS small, white, *without* hairs on corolla lobes; [A] usually in compound terminal structure of *stalked* flowers (July–Oct); [B] in *short* single axillary spikes of 2–9 *sessile* flowers (Dec–Mar). FRUIT red or yellow drupes.

Family EPACRIDACEAE (Australian heaths)

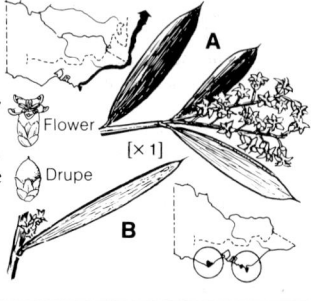

Flower

Drupe

A

B

[× 1]

Boobialla

Myoporum insulare

Leafy shrub or small rounded tree, 1–6 m; bark corky, fissured. Common *on and near coast* throughout area. LEAVES to 10 cm long, smooth, green, glabrous, thickish but not stiff (fleshy close to sea), *edges ± toothed towards tip.* FLOWERS (Oct–Dec) about 1 cm across, 5 petals, white with purple spots. FRUIT globular green-purple small drupes.

Family MYOPORACEAE

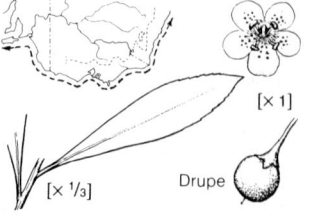

[× 1]

Drupe

[× 1/3]

Sweet Bursaria

Bursaria spinosa

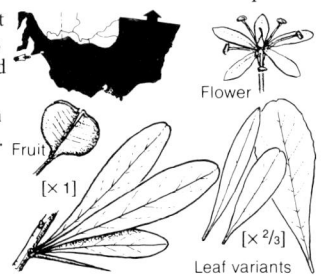

Usually a stiff erect shrub on drier sites, but sometimes a small tree, especially in gullies and on some coastal dunes (e.g. large-leaved form on road to Wilsons Prom.); *often has 'thorns'*. LEAVES in clusters, very variable in size (8–40 mm long), green (paler beneath). FLOWERS (*summer*) creamy, 5-petalled, small but numerous giving showy clusters. FRUIT CAPSULES flat, thin, dry, becoming brown and *purse-like* (hence *Bursaria*).

Family PITTOSPORACEAE

Flower

Fruit [× 1]

[× 2/3]

Leaf variants

Cherry Ballart, Wild Cherry

Exocarpos cupressiformis
(*Exo-carpos* means 'outside fruit')

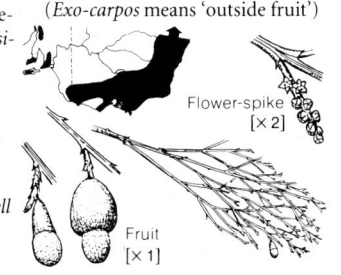

Distinctive small tree (to 8 m), green, sometimes bronzy, ± cypress-like (hence *cupressiformis*); bark hard, grey, finely fissured. A root-parasite, scattered in various forests, especially on shallow soils. BRANCHLETS *green (acting as leaves), fine, faintly ribbed.* FLOWERS (Dec–May) green, *minute*, in spikes < 6 mm long. FRUIT hard, green, ovoid, on a *stout green stalk which may swell to fleshy orange-red* (the edible 'cherry').

Family SANTALACEAE

Flower-spike [× 2]

Fruit [× 1]

Golden Spray

Viminaria juncea

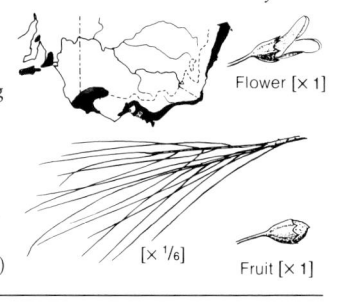

Erect shrub or small tree, 2–5 m, many slender branchlets 'spraying' outwards. Fairly common, especially near coast, on *poorly-drained sandy soils*, often emerging above damp heaths. LEAVES reduced to *soft and flexible green 'needles'* (8–25 cm long). FLOWERS (Oct–Feb) *pea-type*, yellow, numerous towards the ends of drooping branchlets, producing a golden 'spray'. FRUIT small soft ovoid pods.

Family FABACEAE (have pods/pea-flowers)

Flower [× 1]

[× 1/6]

Fruit [× 1]

Tree Everlasting

Ozothamnus ferrugineus
(formerly *Helichrysum dendroideum*)

Erect shrub or small tree, 2–6 m, with rather open crown and often grey-brown firm fissured bark. Common and widespread, mostly in scrubby understoreys on moist or poorly-drained sites, coast to mountains.

LEAVES: Flat, but margins tending to turn down and often wavy, variable in length (2–7 cm × 2–7 mm), shiny dark green above, *greenish-white beneath (thinly felted with minute white-cottony non-glandular hairs which also occur on small branchlets).*

FLOWERS (Nov–Feb): In many headlets (*greenish in bud*), with tiny white petal-like 'rays' on opening; these are compounded into *large round-topped clusters* (to about 8 cm across) at the ends of branchlets.

Family ASTERACEAE (the 'composites')

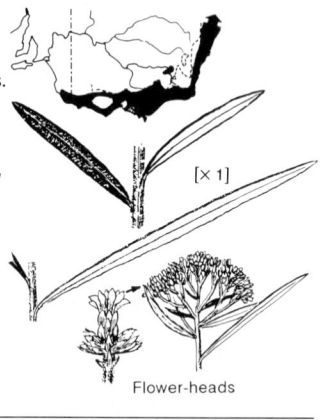

[× 1]

Flower-heads

Sweet Pittosporum

Pittosporum undulatum

Wholly hairless densely-foliaged small tree, 4–14 m. Original natural occurrence was in valleys and rainforests east of Western Port, but now widely naturalised and a trouble-some weed, with the seeds spread largely by introduced birds in populated areas where a lack of hot fires allows its free regeneration.

LEAVES: Radiating terminally, *thin*, glabrous, shiny dark green above, paler green beneath, to 14 cm × 5 cm, *often with wavy margins.* New terminal leaf growth bright green.

FLOWERS (Sept–Nov): 5-petalled, creamy-white, fragrant, in terminal clusters.

FRUIT: Globular (10–15 mm), smooth, hard, becoming orange, opening in two valves to expose the sticky brown seeds.

Family PITTOSPORACEAE [See also pp. 20, 35]

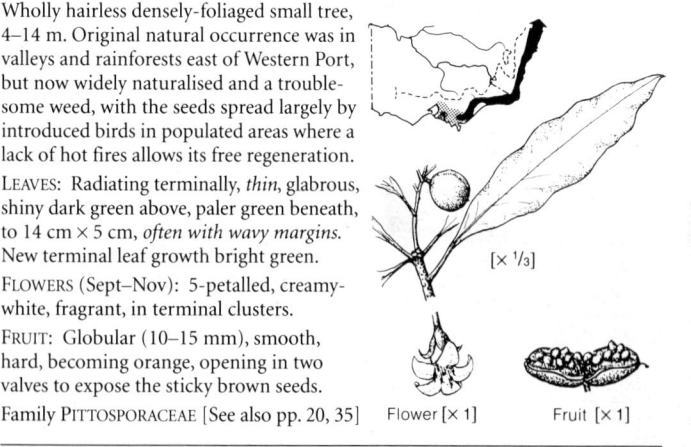

[× ⅓]

Flower [× 1]   Fruit [× 1]

MOUNTAIN FORESTS AND MOIST VALLEYS

In the ranges of the Main Divide, the Otways and Gippsland, where annual rainfall exceeds 900 mm, eucalypt forests are commonly tall (more than 30 m), and usually have a dense understorey of tall shrubs or small trees, especially in sheltered valleys.

The giant of Victorian forests, Mountain Ash (*E. regnans*), occurs in higher rainfall areas mainly south of the Divide at altitudes of about 500–1000 m, and often exceeds 60 m in height, with understorey trees (especially wattles) sometimes reaching a third of this. Other dominant trees in tall moist forests include stringybarks (particularly Messmate, *E. obliqua*), Mountain Grey Gum (*E. cypellocarpa*) and Shining Gum (*E. nitens*). Silvertop Ash (*E. sieberi*) can grow tall even on drier slopes and ridges, while Alpine Ash (*E. delegatensis*) usually forms pure stands above about 900 m altitude, where snow lies for several weeks of the year.

Although some mountain forests can appear dense, the canopy of the tall eucalypts is actually quite open, allowing a moderate amount of light to reach the understorey. It is this understorey which gives the feeling of

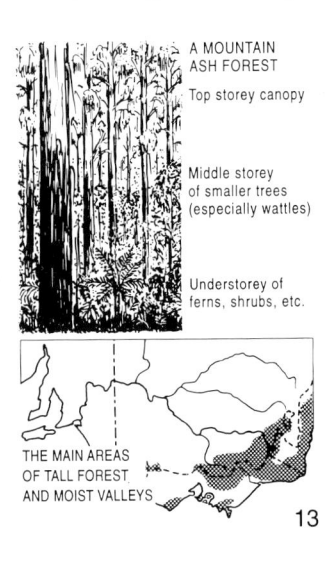

A MOUNTAIN ASH FOREST

Top storey canopy

Middle storey of smaller trees (especially wattles)

Understorey of ferns, shrubs, etc.

THE MAIN AREAS OF TALL FOREST AND MOIST VALLEYS

13

density: in moist valleys many of the component species have broad, soft leaves, and little light can reach the near-ground plants. At the same time the level of humidity increases nearer the ground—ferns, mosses and other moisture-loving plants grow in abundance, and decomposing organic matter helps form a deep humus-rich soil. Here we can find a complex web of interactions between parasitic plants, their hosts, and many animal organisms which depend particularly on decomposition.

Although this section focuses on mountain forests, some of the tall shrub or small tree species described on pages 17–20 (e.g. Christmas Bush and Hazel Pomaderris) can occur in sheltered gullies in otherwise drier foothill country where forests are more open and not so tall.

Still more species have their main occurrence in the tall forests of East Gippsland and South Coast NSW, in upper storeys and understoreys. These are treated in the next section (pages 24–32).

COMMON DOMINANT EUCALYPTS IN TALL FORESTS

Messmate (*E. obliqua*) – in moister forests throughout area 103
Peppermints (*E. radiata, E. dives,* etc.) – often with Messmate and gums 93–94
Mountain Grey Gum (*E. cypellocarpa*) – in Grampians, Otways, eastern ranges 60
Blue Gums (*E. globulus* in south; *E. bicostata* mainly north of Divide) 62–63
Mountain Ash (*E. regnans*) – usually in pure stands, mostly south of Divide 98
Alpine Ash (*E. delegatensis*) – at higher montane levels, often in pure stands 99
Shining Gum (*E. nitens/E. denticulata*) – at higher levels in C–E Vic 61
Mountain Gum (*E. dalrympleana*) – at higher levels in eastern ranges 57
Silvertop Ash (*E. sieberi*) – on drier ridges and slopes, mostly eastern ranges ... 101

SOME LOWER-STOREY TREES DESCRIBED IN PART 3

Blackwood Wattle (*Acacia melanoxylon*) – very common in most moister forests 144
Montane Wattle (*A. frigescens*) – restricted occurrences at higher levels, E Vic .. 144
Silver Wattle (*A. dealbata*) – very common throughout ranges, esp. after fire 132
Mountain Hickory Wattle (*A. obliquinervia*) – common in higher level forests 139
Mountain Wattle (*A. kettlewelliae*) – north-east Vic to NSW 141
Catkin Wattle (*A. dallachiana*) – localised in NE Vic mainly with Alpine Ash 137
Narrow-leaved Wattle (*A. mucronata*) – common with Messmate S of Divide 135
Cinnamon Wattle (*A. leprosa*) – ranges of E-C Vic, mainly in messmate forests .. 142
Varnish Wattle (*A. verniciflua*) – small tree form esp. in messmate–gum forests . 142
Mountain Tea-tree (*Leptospermum grandifolium*) – by streams at higher levels ... 126
Some common species of other genera occurring in moist forest understoreys are described on pages 15–23 following, and on pages 24–32 for East Gippsland.

14

Myrtle Beech

Nothofagus cunninghamii

Densely-foliaged dark green tree, 6–40 m. In gullies and on sheltered slopes in *cool higher rainfall areas* of ranges of E–C Vic, Otways and S Gippsland, often montane with (e.g.) Alpine Ash; common in Tas. [The three Australian *Nothofagus* species, of cool high-rainfall areas, are considered remnants from previously extensive rain-forests before eucalypts became dominant.]

LEAVES: Small (6–18 mm × 6–15 mm), *in large flat fan-like sprays*, dark green above, paler green beneath, margins with small 'teeth'; young growth often bronzy pink.

FLOWERS (Nov–Jan): In axils, small and inconspicuous, male and female separate.

FRUIT: Small nuts, in bristly 4-valved body.

Family NOTHOFAGACEAE

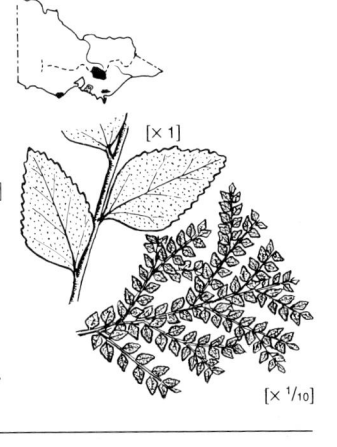

[× 1]

[× 1/10]

Southern Sassafras

Atherosperma moschatum

Straight-trunked tree of 10–25 m, usually *conical*, bark smooth, grey-green; most parts *nutmeg-scented when handled*. In cool moist valleys in ranges from Dandenongs eastward, S Gippsland, and Errinundra area of E Gippsland (under Shining Gum).

LEAVES: *Opposite, aromatic*, margins often toothed, 4–9 cm × 15–35 mm, shiny green above, *whitish* beneath (venation visible).

FLOWERS (July–Sept): Scented, about 2 cm across the creamy petal-like segments (8 in two whorls of 4); usually hanging in pairs (one from each of adjacent axils); separate male and female flowers.

FRUIT: Plumed 1-seeded achenes in a cup-shaped receptacle about 1 cm across.

Family MONIMIACEAE

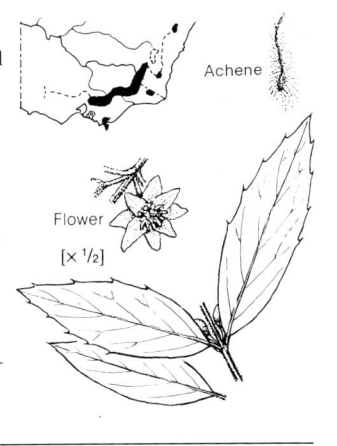

Achene

Flower

[× 1/2]

Lilly-pilly

Acmena smithii

Dense, glabrous, dark green tree, 8–30 m, with fairly smooth grey bark. The main component of 'jungle' pockets (*closed canopy rainforests*) which occur in some stream valleys eastwards from Mitchell R area (where its proximity to dry forest is remarkable); also on Wilsons Promontory.

LEAVES: *Opposite*, elliptic, contracting to an extended tip, 4–9 cm × 1.5–4 cm, glossy dark green above, paler green beneath, with fine widely-spreading lateral veins.

FLOWERS (summer): Small, creamy, in open terminal compound clusters (panicles).

FRUIT: Stalked *globular berries* to about 15 mm, *white, often becoming pink or lilac*.

Family MYRTACEAE [*Acmena smithii* is the only *berry*-bearing member in Victoria]

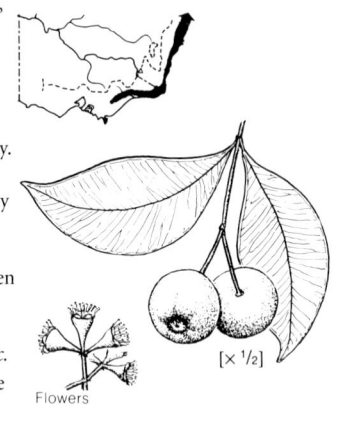

[× ½]

Flowers

Blanket-leaf

Bedfordia arborescens

Slender-trunked small tree, 3–7 m, with *white-woolly young branchlets*; bark pale brown and fissured. Common in moist forest gullies, near-coast to montane levels, mainly in ranges of east Vic and SE NSW.

LEAVES: Soft, often wavy-edged, 15–24 cm × 2–4.5 cm, glabrous dark green above with main veins impressed, *underside felted with white woolly hairs* (hence common name); radiating around the ends of branchlets, often with dead leaves hanging beneath.

FLOWERS (Nov–Jan): Tiny yellow florets in white-coated tubular heads in clusters (panicles) arising from terminal leaf axils.

FRUIT: Single-seed achenes with bristly projections at top, released from heads.

Family ASTERACEAE (the 'composites')

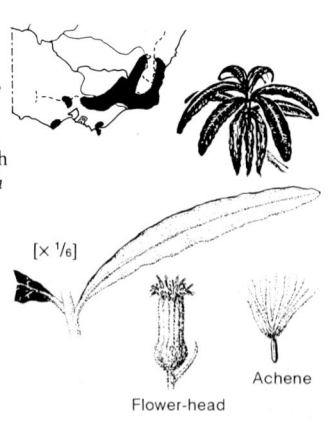

[× ⅙]

Achene

Flower-head

Musk Daisy-bush

Olearia argophylla

Tall shrub or small tree, 3–8 m, with *large* musky-smelling leaves and grey-brown fissured bark. Common in moist forests, on sheltered slopes and in gullies, from Otways through eastern ranges to NSW.

LEAVES: Alternate, rather stiff, margins slightly toothed, 6–16 cm × 3–8 cm, green and hairless above with slightly impressed regular vein pattern, *silvery beneath with minute silky hairs and lateral veins just raised* ('*argo-phylla*' means 'silvery-leaved').

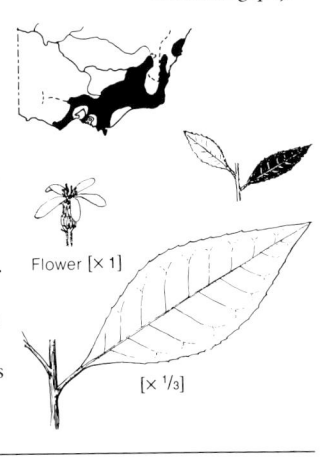

Flower [× 1]

[× ⅓]

FLOWERS (Oct–Dec): In yellow and white *daisy-type* heads about 1 cm across, which are clustered terminally (in corymbs).

FRUIT: Single-seed achenes with numerous bristles at top, released from heads.

Family ASTERACEAE (the 'composites')

Austral Mulberry

Hedycarya angustifolia

Shrub to slender-trunked small tree, 3–7 m. Common in forest understoreys on damp sheltered slopes and in gullies, near-coast to about 1200 m in eastern ranges.

LEAVES: *Opposite, completely hairless when adult*, not stiff, 6–12 cm × 2–5 cm, smooth glossy dark green above with distinctive yellowish vein pattern (net-veined between main veins), paler *green* beneath (lateral veins just raised), margins usually with forward-pointing teeth.

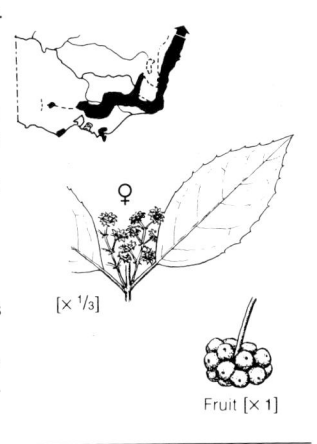

♀

[× ⅓]

Fruit [× 1]

FLOWERS (mostly spring): In greenish small disc-shaped bodies grouped on stalks in axils, male and female separate.

FRUIT: Small yellow drupelets packed into rounded mulberry-like bodies (not edible).

Family MONIMIACEAE

Hazel Pomaderris

Pomaderris aspera
Pomaderris apetala

A tall shrub or small slender tree (3–8 m), *P. aspera* is the most conspicuous and common member of this complex genus (mainly shrubs). Frequent in forest under-storeys on sheltered slopes and in gullies where soils are moist and deep, not only in mountains. Regenerates densely after fire.

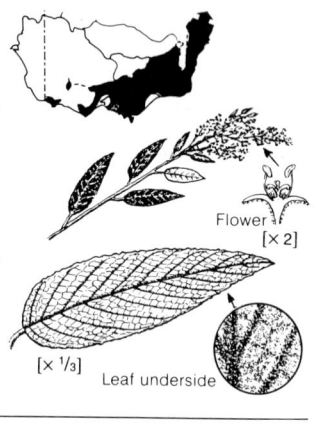

LEAVES: Large (6–16 cm × 2–6 cm), dark green and *wrinkled above with veins deeply impressed, pale greenish beneath with felty hairs* (*brown* on *strongly raised* veins), the blade surface just visible through the hairs. In similar *P. apetala* (in Grampians), the undersurface is obscured by denser hairs.

FLOWERS (Oct–Dec): Greenish, showing mainly stamens, numerous in long plumes.

Family RHAMNACEAE

Flower
[× 2]

[× 1/3]
Leaf underside

Victorian Christmas Bush

Prostanthera lasianthos

Shrub or small tree, 1–8 m, leaves some-times *minty* (as are most in *Prostanthera* 'mint-bushes'). Common in moister forests (to subalps), usually in shaded gullies, but sometimes on lower slopes in drier forests.

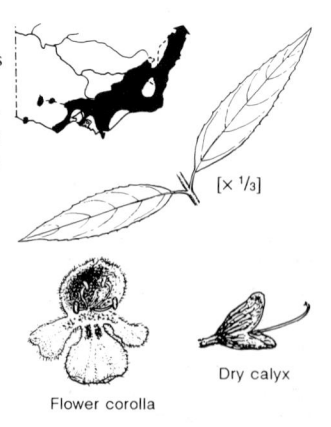

LEAVES: *Opposite, hairless, ± thin*, dull dark green above, paler green beneath, 4–11 cm × 1–3 cm, *margins with small teeth.*

FLOWERS (Nov–Jan): Soft, hairy, white (or mauve), with orange and purple spots in the throat which expands into an upper segment and a larger spreading 3-lobed lower segment; in branching elongated clusters; *conspicuous in early summer.*

FRUIT: Enclosed in the dry two-lipped calyx after the flower has died off.

Family LAMIACEAE

[× 1/3]

Flower corolla

Dry calyx

Tree Lomatia

Lomatia fraseri

Shrub or small tree, 2–7 m. Frequent (but not as common as foregoing understorey species) in forests on moist sheltered slopes and in gullies, mainly in E Vic ranges.

LEAVES: Alternate, stiff, fairly long elliptic (5–15 cm × 1.5–4.5 cm), glabrous green and faintly net-veined above, *satiny with appressed silvery hairs beneath*, margins sometimes ± wavy, *usually with sharp forward-pointing teeth* (often irregular).

FLOWERS (Dec–Feb): Creamy, externally hairy, of a type similar to *Grevillea, Hakea,* etc. in which a hooked style emerges from a splitting perianth; in elongated loose compound structures (raceme-like).

FRUIT: Dry leathery follicles, 2–3 cm long.

Family PROTEACEAE (includes *Banksia,* etc.)

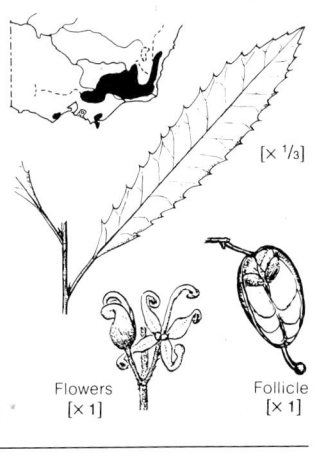

[× 1/3]

Flowers
[× 1]

Follicle
[× 1]

Privet Mock-olive

Notelaea* ligustrina

Tall shrub or small bushy tree, 2–9 m. Scattered occurrences, mostly on sheltered rocky slopes and near gullies, especially in understorey of montane forests in E Vic highlands, also Otways and Grampians.

LEAVES: *Opposite,* flat, lanceolate (4–10 cm × 1–2.5 cm), wholly glabrous, dull dark green above, slightly paler beneath, *lateral veins obscure.*

FLOWERS (Jan–Apr): Very small, yellowish, in compound structures (racemes) to 4 cm.

FRUIT: *Fleshy ovoid drupes* 6–10 mm long, white, pink, purple or black.

Family OLEACEAE (the olive family) [*Some authorities have transferred this species from *Notelaea* to a separate but closely related genus *Nestegis.*]

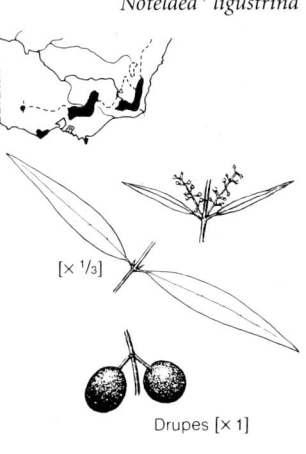

[× 1/3]

Drupes [× 1]

Banyalla

Pittosporum bicolor

Dark green bushy shrub or small tree, 3–10 m. Scattered but not uncommon in forest understoreys, in sheltered valleys and near streams, mainly in eastern ranges (below about 1300 m).

LEAVES: Alternate, 3–8 cm × 5–18 mm, glabrous dark green but not shiny above, *pale beneath with appressed silvery hairs*, margins usually just turning down.

FLOWERS (Sept–Nov): Somewhat bell-like with 5 petal-lobes curving back, yellow touched with maroon on outside (hence '*bi-color*'), on long stalks, 1 (or more) hanging from upper axils.

FRUIT: Small yellow-grey capsules, opening in two valves to expose sticky red seeds.

Family PITTOSPORACEAE [See also pp. 12, 35]

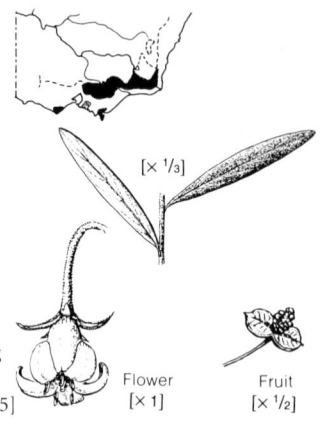

[× 1/3]

Flower [× 1]

Fruit [× 1/2]

Muttonwood

Rapanea howittiana

Tall shrub or small tree, 3–10 m, bark often whitish. Sporadic distribution in eastern forests on damp slopes or *near streams*, mostly on coastal side of Divide; along Yarra R east of Melbourne, and close to coast on south Mornington Peninsula.

LEAVES: Alternate, clustered near ends of branches, smooth, glabrous, shiny darker green above, pale green beneath, 5–10 cm × 2–4 cm, usually broadest beyond middle, rather leathery, *edges wavy*.

FLOWERS (spr–sum): Small, greenish, 5-lobed, on stalks 3–5 mm, clustered in axils or on older wood.

FRUIT: Small globular drupes (5–7 mm), becoming violet, on stalks, in clusters.

Family MYRSINACEAE

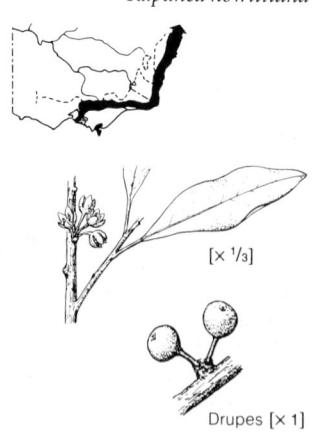

[× 1/3]

Drupes [× 1]

Mountain Pepper

Tasmannia lanceolata

Tall shrub or small tree, 2–6 m, with *smooth red branchlets.* Frequent on cool moist slopes and in gullies, chiefly in taller forests of E Vic ranges, lower montane to subalps.

LEAVES: Alternate, around ends of branchlets, smooth and hairless, glossy dark green above, slightly paler beneath, flat, 4–12 cm × 7–30 mm, hot-tasting. [*T. xerophila*, a shrub in subalps, has smaller thicker blunt-tipped leaves on rough red branchlets.]

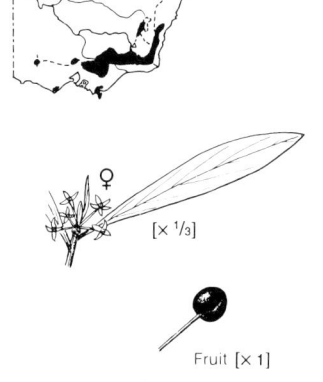

[× ⅓]

FLOWERS (Sept–Nov): Creamy, stalked, clustered in axils at ends of branchlets, male and female on different plants.

FRUIT: *Globular berries about 5 mm diam.,* becoming *lustrous black,* on straight stalks, clustered in terminal axils.

Fruit [× 1]

Family WINTERACEAE

Elderberry Panax

Polyscias sambucifolia

Very variable shrub or small tree, 1–6 m. Common mainly in mountain forests of E Vic and NSW, usually in moist gullies and on sheltered slopes, ascending to subalps. Regenerates prolifically after fire.

LEAVES: *Compound,* wholly hairless, with extreme variation in size (8–40 cm long). *Leaflets* always opposite and one terminal, dark green above, *smooth flat-whitish green beneath,* but narrow or broad, 2–20 cm long, simple or repeatedly divided (fern-like); the greatest range is in E Gippsland.

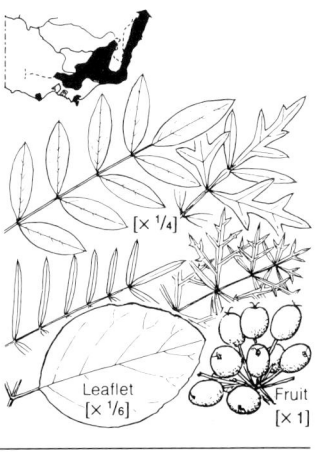

[× ¼]

FLOWERS (Nov–Jan): Small, yellow-green, in clusters at the ends of fine stalks.

FRUIT: Small, bead-like, slightly flattened laterally, becoming bluish (± translucent).

Leaflet [× ⅙]

Fruit [× 1]

Family ARALIACEAE

Geebungs

Persoonia, in family Proteaceae, has small yellow tubular flowers with the perianth splitting into 4 curling-back segments, and has firm green grape-like drupes as fruit.

[A] *Velvety Geebung* is a shrub–small tree, 2–5 m, *branchlets and foliage sub-velvety*. Rare in *montane–subalpine forests* near the highest parts of Main Divide, e.g. Bogong, Kosciusko areas. LEAVES mostly alternate, green (darker above) with *close short hairs both sides*, 3–7 cm × 8–18 mm. FLOWERS (summer) in axils, perianth to 14 mm long.

[B] *Tree Geebung* is a small tree, 5–9 m, endemic in Victoria. Uncommon, in moist gullies in the C-E highland forests (mainly Toolangi to Baw Baws). LEAVES alternate, *glabrous above*, paler green beneath with minute hairs, 5–10 cm × 8–18 mm. FLOWERS (summer) *longer* than in [A] (15–20 mm).

Persoonia subvelutina [A]
Persoonia arborea [B]

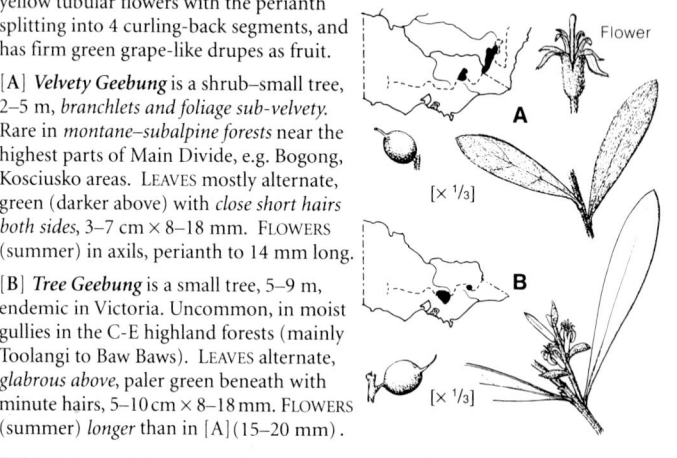

Flower

A

[× ⅓]

B

[× ⅓]

Tree Bitter-pea

Large shrub or small tree to 10 m, locally abundant in moist *montane* forests of *C-E Vic*, often with wattles under Alpine Ash.

LEAVES (PHYLLODES): Alternate, green or greyish, often with slightly wavy edges, to 15 cm × 3 cm, without distinct leaf-stalk (i.e. like some wattles); *lateral veins tending lengthwise with coarse network between*.

FLOWERS (Oct–Jan): Yellow *pea-type*, very fragrant, evenly spaced along extended axillary stalks (racemes) to 11 cm long.

FRUIT: Flat, ± triangular yellow-brown pods 7–10 mm long; valves curl when split.

Family FABACEAE [Shrubs *D. latifolia,* and *D. laevis* (Grampians) have ± similar leaves]

Daviesia laxiflora
(formerly *D. mimosoides* var. *laxiflora*)

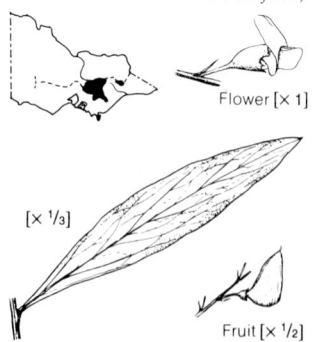

Flower [× 1]

[× ⅓]

Fruit [× ½]

Satinwood

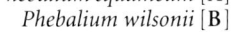

Phebalium squameum [A]
Phebalium wilsonii [B]

[A] Typical *P. squameum* is a densely-foliaged shrub or small tree, 3–12 m. In Vic, restricted to moist forests in *Otways*; more extensive in Tas, also in Sydney area.

LEAVES: Alternate, 3–9 cm × 6–20 mm, glabrous glossy green and gland dotted above, *silvery-scaly beneath*; branchlets smooth (*without tubercles*).

FLOWERS (Sept–Nov): White, starry with prominent stamens and five petals *without* scales on outside; several on axillary stalks.

[B] *P. wilsonii* was described as a new species in 1988. It is a shrub or small tree (to 10 m), known only from one locality in mountain ash forest south of Mt Grant in C Vic highlands. Leaves similar to above species, but *branchlets have tubercles*, and flowers have *tiny scales on outside of petals*.

Family RUTACEAE

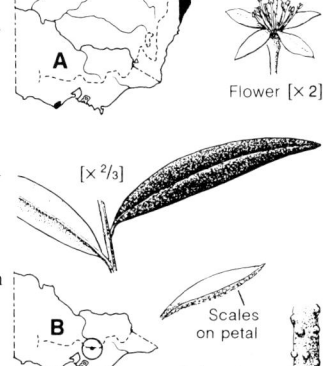

Flower [× 2]

[× 2/3]

Scales on petal

Tubercles on branchlet

Gully Grevillea

Grevillea barklyana

Large-leaved tall shrub or slender tree, 3–10 m. In Vic, restricted to moist gully slopes *north of Labertouche* (Gippsland), in messmate–silvertop forest; also a sub-species near Jervis Bay, NSW.

LEAVES: Flat, large (10–20 cm long), simple (undivided) or with *1–7 large pointed lobes* alternately arranged, glabrous green above, whitish with close hairs beneath.

FLOWERS (Oct–Dec): Numerous in large *one-sided* brush-like structures (racemes) 5–10 cm long; *long pink-red styles* unfold from grey-hairy perianths.

FRUIT: Woody follicles (styles persist).

Family PROTEACEAE (includes *Banksia* etc.)

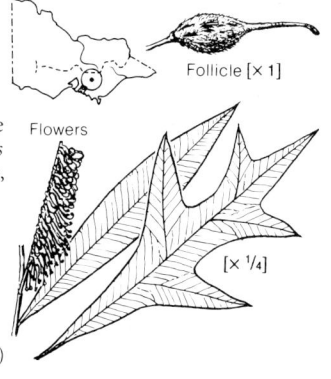

Follicle [× 1]

Flowers

[× 1/4]

EAST GIPPSLAND AND SOUTH COAST NSW

From a Victorian viewpoint, East Gippsland can be considered as that region of the state generally east of the Mitchell River and south of the Main Divide. However in physiographic and climatic terms, it is really a southern extension of near-coastal NSW. It is also the meeting ground for different plant associations from further west in Victoria, from the higher levels of the Main Divide, and from the coastal region (and even the western slopes) of NSW—indeed many East Gippsland plants occur much more extensively in NSW. It is this meeting of communities which particularly interests naturalists, and it largely explains the area's richness in species—East Gippsland is less than 8% of Victoria's area, but nearly half of the state's 3000+ native vascular plant species occur there. This is exemplified by a remarkable range of eucalypts—about 50 species.

Parts of the area have been grazed since the 1850s, and timber has been extracted for most of that time, with a marked expansion in logging activities after the Second World War. However it has only been in recent decades that the unique environmental values of the region have come to be widely recognised, and general access improved so that any interested person can explore and enjoy the area's natural features.

The summary following gives a very broad indication of the various environments, and lists some species of the major genera in Part 3 which are particularly significant in these areas. Further trees and large shrubs of the region are described on pages 26–32.

TREES OF THE NEAR-COASTAL FRINGE

Plant communities vary greatly along the coastline, according to their association with sand-dunes (often massive), heathlands, inlets and swamps, or rocky cliffs and exposed headlands. In some parts, eucalypt forests come right to the coastal edges.

More widespread coastal species 9	Giant Honey-myrtle (*Mel. armillaris*) ... 128
Tree Broom-heath (*Monotoca elliptica*) . 10	Swamp Paperbark (*M. ericifolia*) 128
Saw Banksia (*Banksia serrata*) 150	Scented Paperbark (*M. squarrosa*) 129

EUCALYPT FORESTS

The species composition of eucalypt forests in the region varies, especially as one moves from the sandy soils at lower altitudes near the coast to the higher steeper country inland. The following species have their main Victorian occurrences in eastern forests, or are particularly significant in some areas. Most of the species listed on pages 9–12 and 13–21 of the previous two sections also occur in the region.

Rough-barked Angophora (*A. floribunda*) 26	Yellow Stringybark (*E. muelleriana*) ... 107
Blue Box (*Eucalyptus baueriana*) 85	White Stringybark (*E. globoidea*) 110
Apple-topped Box (*E. angophoroides*) 78	Blue-leaved Stringybark (*E. agglomerata*) 110
Coast Grey Box (*E. bosistoana*) 87	Peppermint (*E. croajingolensis*) 93
Silver-leaved Stringybark (*E. conspicua*) 77	Gully Gum (*E. smithii*) 81
River Peppermint (*E. elata*) 96	Blue Gum (*E. pseudoglobulus/maidenii*) 63
Woollybutt (*E. longifolia*) – NSW only 114	Red Wattle (*Acacia silvestris*) 134
Southern Mahogany (*E. botryoides*) ... 113	Sallow Wattle (*A. longifolia*) 135
Red Bloodwood (*E. gummifera*) 112	White Sallow Wattle (*A. floribunda*) 136
Yertchuk (*E. consideniana*) 105	Hickory Wattle (*A. falciformis*) 139
Silvertop Ash (*E. sieberi*) 101	Bower Wattles (*A. cognata/subporosa*) 143
Red Ironbark (*E. tricarpa*) 115	Paperbark Tea-tree (*L. trinervium*) 125

WARM TEMPERATE RAINFOREST ('JUNGLE' POCKETS)

Isolated lowland pockets of closed-canopy non-eucalypt vegetation occur mainly in moist sheltered localities, dominated by (e.g.) **Lilly-pilly** (p. 16), **Blackwood** (p. 144), **Pittosporum** (p. 12) and tree-ferns. They are considered the southernmost occurrences of a rainforest type more common in coastal NSW. However in Victoria, most of the smaller tree species are those which elsewhere occur in the understoreys of moist eucalypt forests, as on pages 16–21, together with some other species on pages 26–30 (e.g. Kanooka, Blue Oliveberry, Bolwarra, Sandpaper Fig).

MONTANE EUCALYPT FORESTS / COOL TEMPERATE RAINFORESTS

At higher levels, there are several distinctive tall forest types dominated mainly by the species below. A special type of cool temperate rainforest, on the Errinundra Plateau in particular, is composed of non-eucalypts such as **Sassafras** (p. 15) and several of the species on the following pages, notably Black Oliveberry, Waratah, and Forest Geebung. **Shining Gum** (*E. denticulata*) emerges above this rainforest.

Shining Gum (*Eucalyptus denticulata*) 61	Mountain Gum (*E. dalrympleana*) 57
Brown Barrel (*E. fastigata*) 104	Alpine Ash (*E. delegatensis*) 99
Mountain Grey Gum (*E. cypellocarpa*) 60	White Ash (*E. fraxinoides*) 100

WOODLANDS OF PINE AND BOX IN THE SNOWY RIVER VALLEY

The upper parts of the Snowy River valley lie in a 'rainshadow' area in which the low rainfall and dry shallow soils provide an environment with species associations resembling those of the 'box' country inland from the Divide (see page 9).

Cypress-pines (*Callitris* species) 155-6	Suggan Buggan Mallee (*E. saxatilis*) 70
White Box (*Eucalyptus albens*) 89	Kurrajong (*Brachychiton populneus*) .. 32
Apple Box (*E. bridgesiana*) 78	Deane's Wattle (*Acacia deanei*) 134
Blakely's Red Gum (*E. blakelyi*) 53	Currawang (*Acacia doratoxylon*) 137

Angophoras or 'Apples'

Angophora floribunda [A]
Angophora costata [B]

Angophora species are closely related to the bloodwood group of eucalypts*. Only one, *A. floribunda*, occurs naturally in Vic, but *A. costata*, of coastal NSW, is commonly planted, and often mistaken for a 'gum'.

[A] *A. floribunda* (Rough-barked Angophora), of E NSW *into far E Gippsland*, is a tree of 12–30 m, with *twisting branches*, and large crown; mainly on alluvial and sandy soils of slopes and flats. BARK persistent, grey-brown, *fibrous and fissured* (like some stringybarks). ADULT LEAVES *opposite, very little odour*, dull green above, *paler beneath*, 8–12 cm long, veins spreading. BUDS bristly, on long stalks, usually in 3s in compound clusters, *sepals and petals persist on flowers*. FLOWERS (spr–sum) in *conspicuous creamy masses*, stamens prominent. FRUIT *strongly-ribbed thin-walled woody capsules*.

[B] *A. costata* (Smooth-barked Angophora) is very similar, but bark *smooth*, grey, shed (gum-like) to expose *pink-orange surface*.

Family MYRTACEAE [*See table page 42]

Flower [× 1]

[× 1/3]

Juvenile leaves

Fruit [× 1]

Buds [× 1]

Kanooka, Water Gum

Tristaniopsis laurina

Usually a spreading tree with dark green crown, 5–20 m; *bark ribbony, pale brown*. Common *along shaded lower level streams*, east from Avon River (a rainforest species).

LEAVES: Alternate, clustered at ends of branchlets, glabrous, glossy green, paler green beneath, to 12 cm × 3 cm.

FLOWERS (Dec–Feb): Compounded in 3s in axils, 5 *yellow* petals and stamen-bundles.

FRUIT: Thin-walled capsules splitting in 3.

Family MYRTACEAE

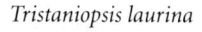
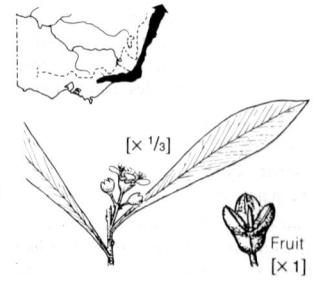

[× 1/3]

Fruit [× 1]

Tree Hakea

Hakea eriantha

Large shrub or small tree, 3–10 m; fairly large crown of *lustrous mid-green leaves.* Mostly below 1100 m in taller forests on cool sheltered sites, Walhalla area eastwards to Budawang Range (NSW).

LEAVES: Alternate, flat, slightly darker and glossier one side, 8–14 cm × 6–17 mm, single central vein with faint lateral ones.

FLOWERS (Sept–Oct): Small, white or pink, silky-hairy, of type resembling *Grevillea* etc. in which a long hooked style unfolds from the splitting perianth (about 6 mm long); in small clusters in leaf axils.

FRUIT: Distinctive *thick woody follicles* to 3 cm long, *with hooked 'beak'*, opening in 2 valves to release two flat winged seeds.

Family PROTEACEAE [Other Hakeas, p. 37]

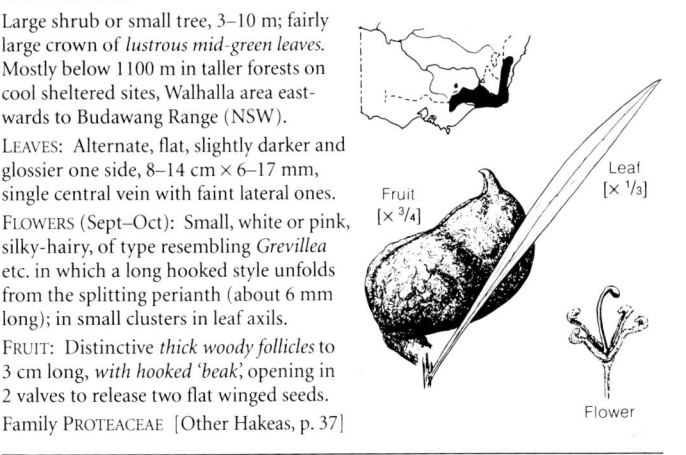

Fruit [× ³/₄]

Leaf [× ¹/₃]

Flower

Brush Kurrajong

Commersonia fraseri

Tall shrub or small tree, 3–7 m, with soft broad flat leaves on *furry* branchlets. Localised in various forests (eucalypt or rainforest) on moister lower slopes or near streams, E Gippsland–NSW.

LEAVES: Alternate, elongated heart-shape, 7–16 cm × 5–12 cm, dark green above, *pale beneath with mat of shiny star-like hairs*, margins with *coarse blunt irregular-sized teeth*; leaf-blades usually have holes.

FLOWERS (Sept–Nov): Whitish, 5–10 mm, radiating parts in 5s; in showy clusters.

FRUIT: *Soft-bristly spherical capsules,* about 2 cm across.

Family STERCULIACEAE (which also includes the Kurrajong *Brachychiton populneus*, p. 32, but these trees show no obvious similarities!)

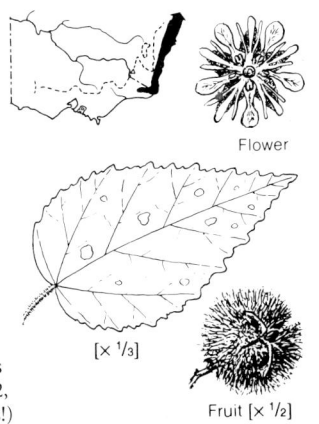

Flower

[× ¹/₃]

Fruit [× ¹/₂]

Blue Oliveberry

Elaeocarpus reticulatus

Erect shrub or small tree, 3–10 m, foliage green with odd leaves turning red before falling. Common in eucalypt forests or rainforests at lower altitudes east from Wilsons Prom., mostly in gullies or near streams. [Compare Black Oliveberry, p. 31, of cool rainforest at higher levels.]

LEAVES: Alternate, long-elliptic, 7–14 cm × 2–4 cm, glabrous both sides, bright green young becoming darker, *raised net-veins* (hence *reticulatus*), margins *finely toothed*.

FLOWERS (Nov–Jan): White-pink, *cup-like and fringed*, hanging along stalks to 8 cm long (i.e. in racemes).

FRUIT: *Ovoid blue 'berries'* (drupes) to 12 mm long, hanging along stalks.

Family ELAEOCARPACEAE

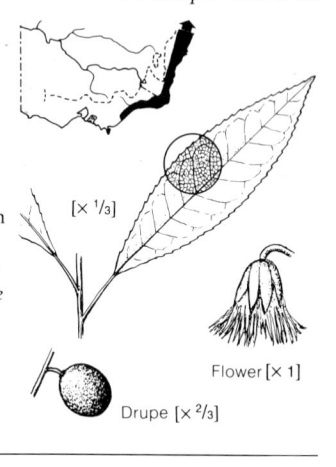

[× 1/3]

Flower [× 1]

Drupe [× 2/3]

Large Mock-olive

Notelaea venosa

Tall shrub or small tree, 2–7 m; greyish finely-fissured flaky bark. A lower level rainforest species, in 'jungle' pockets and moist eucalypt forests, especially in gullies, eastwards from Lakes Entrance area.

LEAVES: *Opposite*, firm, thickish, often broadly wavy-edged, ± ovate, 5–15 cm × 2–5 cm, glabrous (except when young), dull dark green above, paler green beneath, both sides with a *network of raised fine veins* between main veins.

FLOWERS (Nov–Jan): Very small, pale yellow, on straight pedicels, decussate in axillary clusters (racemes) to 3 cm long.

FRUIT: *Purplish-black ellipsoid drupes* (15–20 mm long), in extended clusters.

Family OLEACEAE (the olive family)

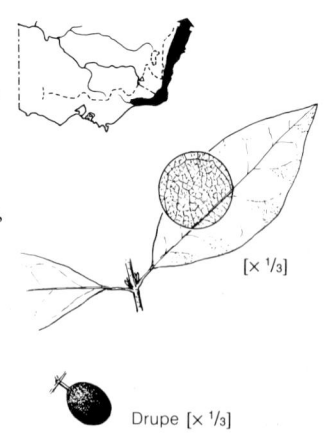

[× 1/3]

Drupe [× 1/3]

Cabbage Fan-palm

Livistona australis

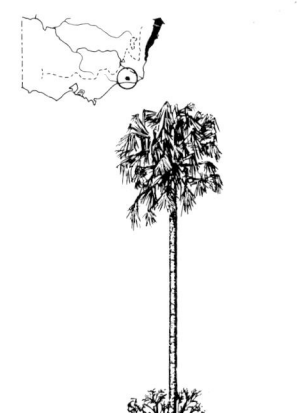

Tall palm-tree, 10–30 m; small rounded crown, and long trunk bearing the bases of old leaves (being a monocotyledon, it does not form true wood). Mostly NSW north-wards, associated with rainforest, but *rare occurrences near Orbost in East Gippsland*, (e.g. in a reserve south of Princes Hwy).

LEAVES: Large, fan-like (1–2 m across), divided into numerous narrow radiating segments. New leaf growth has been used as food, giving the name 'cabbage'.

FLOWERS (Sept–Nov): Small, yellow, fleshy, in much-branched clusters about 1 m long.

FRUIT: Globular (to 2 cm) becoming hard and blackish.

Family ARECACEAE (the palm family – exceptionally tall monocotyledons)

Sandpaper Fig

Ficus coronata

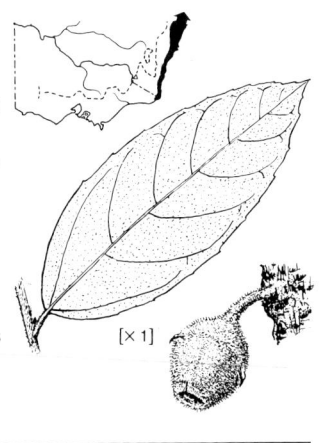

[× 1]

Dark green tree to 8 m, usually with *long sprawling branches*, and hairy branchlets. Frequent in NSW, especially in closed-forests ('jungle') and in sheltered gullies (e.g. with Lilly-pilly). *In Victoria, restricted to rare occurrences near Mallacoota Inlet.*

LEAVES: Alternate, ovate, base often slightly asymmetric, 5–14 cm × 2.5–6 cm, *dark green and roughened like sandpaper above*, paler green and less rough beneath, margins sometimes slightly toothed.

FIGS: Fleshy hollowed receptacles within which the very small flowers and fruits develop; pollination involves wasps. In this species, figs are ovoid, *hairy*, to 2 cm long on stalks of about 1 cm, *often on old wood*.

Family MORACEAE (includes all figs)

29

Yellow-wood

Acronychia oblongifolia

Erect glabrous tree, 5–12+ m, with leaves clustered near ends of branches. Associated with rainforest at low levels, including 'jungle' pockets from Mitchell R eastwards.

LEAVES: *Opposite*, the thin glabrous blade oblong, tapering back to a long petiole, 6–12 cm × 2–4 cm, dark green above, paler green beneath, oil dots visible and numerous, tip blunt (sometimes notched).

FLOWERS (Feb–Apr): Small, with four white petals about 6 mm long, few in stalked clusters 2–5 cm long in axils.

FRUIT: Firm whitish 4-lobed drupes about 1 cm across.

Family RUTACEAE [A large family including citrus trees as well as Australian genera such as *Boronia, Correa, Eriostemon*]

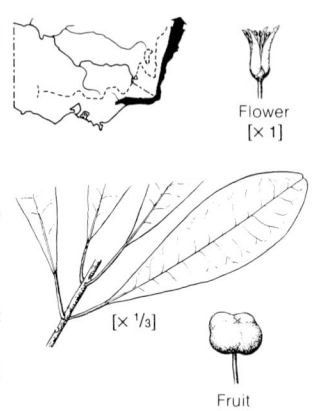

Flower
[× 1]

[× 1/3]

Fruit
[× 1]

Bolwarra

Eupomatia laurina

Waxy-leaved dense shrub or small tree, 3–8 m. Frequent in rainforests at lower altitudes, including 'jungle' pockets near shaded streams, east from Snowy River.

LEAVES: Elliptic, *regularly alternate on slightly zig-zag branchlets*, glabrous, shiny dark green above, paler green beneath, 6–12 cm × 2–5 cm, thin-textured.

FLOWER-BUDS (Nov–Feb): In axils; large, stalked, ovoid and glaucous, with a cap which falls away to expose rings of creamy, waxy, powerfully-scented petal-like stamens (some sterile, and eaten by beetles which also pollinate flower).

FRUIT: A globular or urn-shaped fleshy berry, to 2 cm across, green to brownish.

Family EUPOMATIACEAE

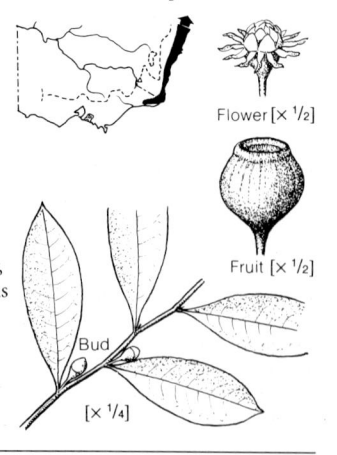

Flower [× 1/2]

Fruit [× 1/2]

Bud

[× 1/4]

Black Oliveberry
Elaeocarpus holopetalus

Densely foliaged tree, 5–16 m. In *cool rain-forests at higher levels*, notably Errinundra area of E Gippsland. LEAVES alternate on hairy branchlets, *stiff, ± elliptic*, 3–7 cm × 1–2 cm, dark green above (veins sunken), *brownish furry beneath, edges sharp-toothed and turned down*; new leaves *bright* green. FLOWERS (summer) cup-like, white-pink, petals *not* fringed, hanging on a common stalk 2–5 cm long. FRUIT ovoid *black* 'berries' (drupes) about 8 mm long.

Family ELAEOCARPACEAE [See also p. 28]

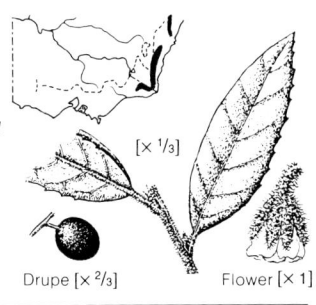

[× 1/3]

Drupe [× 2/3]   Flower [× 1]

Forest Geebung
Persoonia silvatica

Mid-green tall shrub or small tree, 2–8 m. Limited mainly to *cool montane forests*, far East Gippsland and Coast Range in NSW. LEAVES mostly alternate, on red branchlets, 4–11 cm × 8–25 mm, smooth, flat, flexible, *glabrous when mature*, bright green young becoming darker (paler green beneath), fine veins visible. FLOWERS (Dec–Feb) yellow, tubular, *to 14 mm long*, in short clusters in axils. FRUIT green ovoid drupes.

Family PROTEACEAE [Other Geebungs p. 22]

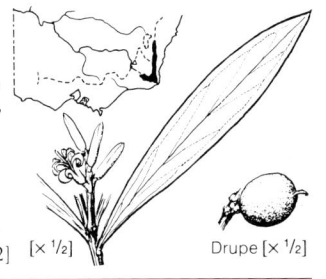

[× 1/2]   Drupe [× 1/2]

Mountain Plum-pine
Podocarpus lawrencei

Usually a dense dark-green shrub of rocky subalps to alps (with a distinctive *resinous pine smell*), but in the Goonmirk Range area (Vic) it occurs in cool montane forests as a *papery-barked small tree to 15 m*. LEAVES crowded, thick, 7–15 mm × 2 mm, dark green. MALE CONES 5–10 mm long, usually purplish; FEMALE (on different plant) developing a seed on fleshy red cup.

Family PODOCARPACEAE (of gymnosperms)

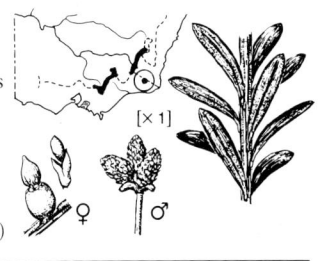

[× 1]   ♀   ♂

Gippsland Waratah

Telopea oreades

Several-stemmed large shrub or small tree, 4–12 m, locally common in E Gippsland, in cool moist gullies and montane forests, north to about Monga in NSW.

LEAVES: Alternate, *radiating around stems, long,* widening towards free end, 10–25 cm × 2–5 cm, glabrous, dull dark green above, pale green beneath, margins without teeth.

FLOWERS (Oct–Dec): *Deep crimson, many in large heads* (to 10 cm across) at ends of stems, encircled beneath by leaves; flowers are of *Grevillea* type in which long styles emerge from perianth (upper ones first).

FRUIT: *Large leathery follicles* to 8 cm long, splitting to expose rows of winged seeds.

Family PROTEACEAE [The Waratah of the Sydney region has showier *domed* heads]

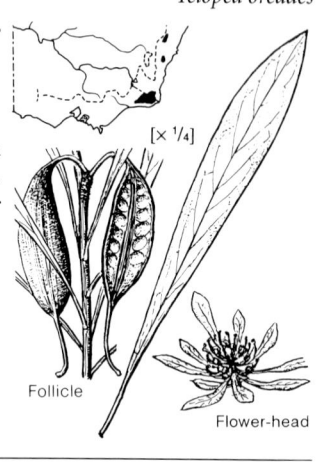

[× ¼]

Follicle

Flower-head

Kurrajong

Brachychiton populneus

Erect tree, 5–20 m, with *large dense green crown and stout tapering grey-barked trunk.* Main occurrence is in drier 'box' country of NSW W Slopes; in Victoria it occurs on *shallow soils in 'rain shadow' areas* of East Gippsland (e.g. Snowy and Mitchell River valleys), and on granite hills of north-east. Often grown for shade and fodder.

LEAVES: Alternate, on *long slender petioles,* broadest near base, *tapering to extended tip,* sometimes with 3 sharp lobes, 5–10 cm × 2–5+ cm, glabrous green, paler beneath.

FLOWERS (Sept–Dec): Bell-shaped with 5 lobes curling back, cream, flecked with red on inner surface; separate male and female.

FRUIT: *Large leathery follicles* to 7 cm long.

Family STERCULIACEAE [See also p. 27]

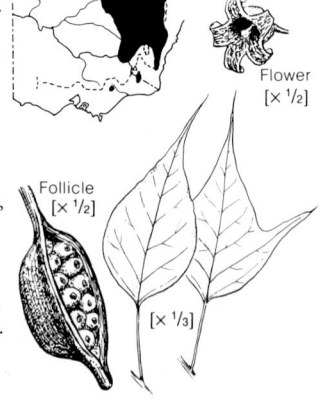

Flower
[× ½]

Follicle
[× ½]

[× ⅓]

32

WESTERN AND NORTHERN AREAS

Except for the ranges of the western Victorian Divide, the Grampians, and the Mt Lofty region of SA, the very extensive area considered in this section is of low relief and elevation—less than 200 m above sea-level. Yet across the area are numerous differing and easily recognisable vegetation types, related largely to distinctive soil types of several geological origins, but influenced also by the decrease in mean annual rainfall from about 800 mm near the coast to less than 300 mm in the north.

Most of the soils are derived from sediments of relatively recent (Pleistocene) geological origins, broadly falling into two main types— *water*-deposited or alluvial (associated with present or former rivers and floodplains, often fairly heavy with clay), or *wind*-deposited (blown from the west in drier periods, forming extensive dunes or sand-sheets). These latter sands and loams are by no means uniform in composition, being characterised by differing proportions of sand, clay, and calcium carbonate, and by varying depths, substrata, drainage and salinity.

These variations result in differences in vegetation height, density, species composition and understorey type. Most obvious is the relationship between mallee eucalypts (pages 116–123) and the wind-deposited sands. On the flatter areas of red-brown loams, remnant mallee is mostly taller with sparser understorey ('Murray Mallee'), while on the younger pale sands forming undulating dunes in the 'Deserts', the mallees are smaller, often with dense heathy understoreys ('Lowan Mallee').

The summary overleaf gives a broad overview of the main vegetation associations, but there are also numerous transitional types.

Soils formed mainly from flooding

Brownish loams formed from wind deposits

Pale wind-deposited sands (esp. 'Deserts')

Near-coast formations in south-west of area

AREAS WITH SOILS FORMED MAINLY THROUGH FLOODING
Trees along rivercourses, around lakes, and on previously flooded plains in the Wimmera, northern Victoria, and the NSW Riverina (clay-loam soils)

River Red Gum (*E. camaldulensis*) – along most watercourses and on plains 52
Black Box (*E. largiflorens*) – on occasionally flooded clayey areas 90
Willow Wattle (*Acacia salicina*) – mainly near Murray River and northward 141
Eumong (*Acacia stenophylla*) – along Murray–Lachlan–Darling R system 146
Yellow Gum (*E. leucoxylon*) – widespread in woodlands across W Vic–SA 67
Grey Box (*E. microcarpa*) – common, mainly Vic–NSW inland slopes–plains 88
Yellow Box (*E. melliodora*) – common, esp. lower slopes and Wimmera plains 86
Wimmera Mallee-box (*E. wimmerensis*) – Wimmera, esp. in and around L Desert 123
Bulloak (*Allocasuarina luehmannii*) – common on N Vic–NSW slopes–plains 152
White Cypress-pine (*Callitris glaucophylla*) – scattered on N Vic–NSW plains 155
Salt Paperbark (*Melaleuca halmaturorum*) – near salt lakes, NW Vic–SE SA 129
Weeping Myall (*Acacia pendula*) – NSW riverine plains 147

AREAS WITH SOILS FORMED FROM WIND-DEPOSITED SANDS
• Taller mallee on flatter areas of red-brown loams ('Murray Mallee')

Soils are older with more clay; understorey is sparse. The vegetation is extensively cleared, remaining mainly by roadsides. The following species tend to dominate.

White Mallee (*Eucalyptus gracilis*) 118   **Grey Mallee** (*E. socialis*) 117
Oil Mallee (*E. oleosa*) 117   **Moonah** (*Melaleuca lanceolata*) 128

• Smaller mallee on pale sandy dunes, chiefly in 'Deserts' ('Lowan Mallee')

These soils are mainly low-fertility sand, carry smaller mallees, mostly with denser heath or shrub understorey. Composition varies; the following are most common.

Yellow Mallee (*Eucalyptus costata*) ... 121   **Scrub Cypress-pine** (*Callitris verrucosa*) 155
Dumosa Mallee (*E. dumosa*) 119   **Desert Banksia** (*Banksia ornata*) 150
Narrow-leaved Red Mallee (*E. leptophylla*) 119   **Broombush** (*Melaleuca uncinata*) 129

• Pine–Belah woodlands on deeper red-brown soils, often on rises
Murray Pine (*Callitris preissii/gracilis*) 155   **Bulloak** (*Allocasuarina luehmannii*) .. 152
Belah (*Casuarina pauper/cristata*) ... 153   **Miljee** (*Acacia oswaldii*) 146

SOUTH-WEST VICTORIA to SOUTH-EAST SOUTH AUSTRALIA
Woodlands (and mallee) on and between old calcareous dunes and ridges

Coast Gum (*E. diversifolia*) – only near Portland in Vic, more common in SA 72
Stringybarks (*E. obliqua*; *E. baxteri/arenacea* esp. on poorer soils with heath) 103, 108
Shining Peppermint (*E. willisii*) – often mallee-like on poor soils with heath 95
Yellow Gum (*E. leucoxylon*) – common, often forming more open woodlands 67
Pink Gum (*E. fasciculosa*) – mainly in SA, esp. on sandy flats and depressions ... 59
Moonah (*Melaleuca lanceolata*) – can be a substantial woodland tree 128
Other widespread near-coastal species 9

Weeping Pittosporum

Pittosporum phylliraeoides

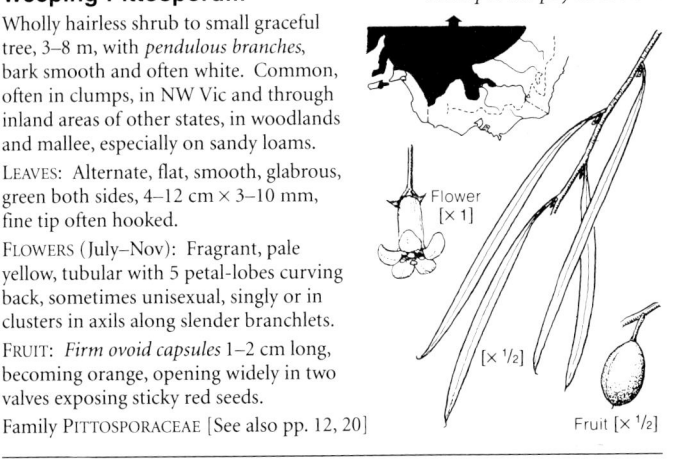

Wholly hairless shrub to small graceful tree, 3–8 m, with *pendulous branches*, bark smooth and often white. Common, often in clumps, in NW Vic and through inland areas of other states, in woodlands and mallee, especially on sandy loams.

LEAVES: Alternate, flat, smooth, glabrous, green both sides, 4–12 cm × 3–10 mm, fine tip often hooked.

FLOWERS (July–Nov): Fragrant, pale yellow, tubular with 5 petal-lobes curving back, sometimes unisexual, singly or in clusters in axils along slender branchlets.

FRUIT: *Firm ovoid capsules* 1–2 cm long, becoming orange, opening widely in two valves exposing sticky red seeds.

Family PITTOSPORACEAE [See also pp. 12, 20]

Flower [× 1]

[× ¹⁄₂]

Fruit [× ¹⁄₂]

Bell-fruit Tree, Native Poplar

Codonocarpus cotinifolius

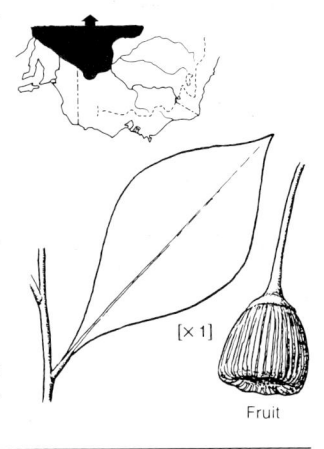

Distinctive tall leafy shrub to small *poplar-like* tree, 4–10 m, with smooth pinkish bark, and foliage throughout its height. Scattered in mallee scrub of NW Vic, and widespread in dry inland parts of other states, mainly on sandy soils. Regenerates especially after fire.

LEAVES: Alternate, ± ovate with pointed tip, 3–5 cm × 1.5–4 cm, flat, olive-green or greyish both sides, glabrous, veins faint.

FLOWERS (mainly Oct–Feb): In short clusters, male (pedicels 1–2 mm) and female (pedicels 8–20 mm) usually on different plants.

FRUITS: In long-stalked green 'bells' (about 1 cm), clustered at the tops of female trees.

Family GYROSTEMONACEAE

[× 1]

Fruit

Sugarwood

Myoporum platycarpum

Tree, often crooked, 4–12 m, with deeply fissured dark bark. Common, widespread, sometimes co-dominant in woodlands of pine–belah and others, also in tall mallee.

LEAVES: Regularly alternate on pendulous tuberculate branchlets; glabrous, dark green, smooth, firm, 3–9 cm × 4–12 mm, *margins with tiny teeth in half towards tip.*

FLOWERS (Aug–Dec): White, inside hairy with purple or orange spots; 2–12 per axil.

FRUIT: Dry, diamond-shaped, about 5 mm.

Family MYOPORACEAE [See also p. 10]

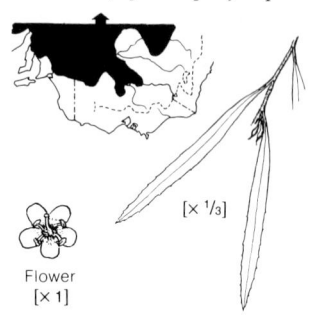

[× 1/3]

Flower
[× 1]

Quandongs

Santalum acuminatum [A]
Santalum murrayanum [B]

[A] **Sweet Quandong** (*S. acuminatum*) is a shrub or small tree, 2–6 m, with sparse *pale green* foliage. A root parasite, widespread on various drier soils, in mallee and woodland. LEAVES *opposite*, leathery, yellowish green both sides, 4–12 cm × 4–12 mm. FLOWERS creamy, 4-lobed, in loose terminal clusters. FRUIT firm globular sweet-edible drupes about 2.5 cm wide, shiny red (or yellow) when ripe, with persistent perianth; deeply pitted 'stone' with edible kernel. The best known outback fruit, used for jams etc.

[B] **Bitter Quandong** (*S. murrayanum*) is a small tree, 4–6 m; branches ± pendulous. Less common than above, mainly on dry sands. LEAVES alternate, opposite or in 3s, *greyish-green*, smaller (2–5 cm × 2–5 mm) with *hooked tips*. FLOWERS like above, but mostly in axils. FRUIT like above, but green to brownish-red, bitter and inedible, 'stone' only slightly pitted, perianth not persistent.

Family SANTALACEAE

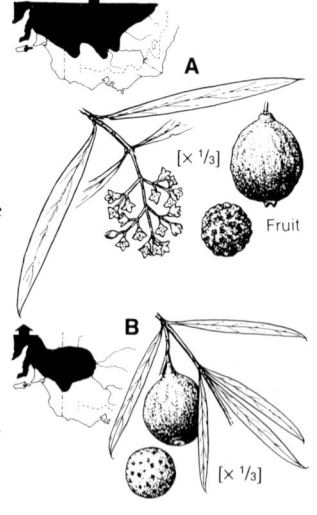

A

[× 1/3]

Fruit

B

[× 1/3]

Rosewood, Bullock-bush

Alectryon oleifolius subsp. *canescens*
(formerly *Heterodendrum oleifolium*)

Small tree, 3–6 m, with hard rough bark and (in NW Victoria) a *grey* large crown. This is the most widespread subspecies, common also across W NSW and SA, especially with Belah on reddish loams.

LEAVES: Alternate, rather stiff, 4–12 cm × 4–15 mm, *greyish both sides with fine white hairs*, venation regular.

FLOWERS (Dec–Mar): Small, cupped, without petals, in short branched clusters.

FRUIT: Hard, usually 2-lobed, hairy.

Family SAPINDACEAE

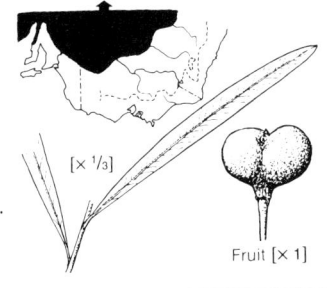

[× ⅓]

Fruit [× 1]

Needlewoods

Hakea tephrosperma [A]
Hakea leucoptera [B]

[A] **Hooked Needlewood** (*H. tephrosperma*) is a small, sometimes crooked tree, 3–12 m; branchlets often drooping, with rather sparse needle-like foliage. Quite frequent in inland Vic and NSW, just entering SA, mostly in pine–belah woodlands on reddish loams. NEEDLE-LEAVES alternate, 3–9 cm long, grey-green, *usually with curved tip.* FLOWERS (Aug–Oct) white, minutely hairy, 6–22 clustered on *short brownish-hairy common stalks.* FRUIT woody thick-walled two-valved follicles 2–3 cm long, usually wedge-pointed, seed-wing *dark.*

[B] **Silver Needlewood** (*H. leucoptera*) is usually a bushy shrub, sometimes a small tree to 6 m, extending further westward. It differs from *H. tephrosperma* in having generally straight-pointed needle-leaves; flowers ± glabrous, 18–45 on longer *white-woolly* common stalks; fruit follicles usually lacking 'horns', seed-wing yellowish.

Family PROTEACEAE [cf. *H. eriantha*, p. 27]

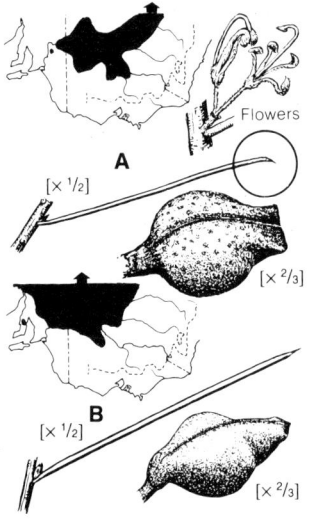

Flowers

A

[× ½]

[× ⅔]

B

[× ½]

[× ⅔]

37

Berrigan, Long-leaf Emu-bush

Dull green tall shrub or rough-barked small tree, 2–8 m, with drooping branchlets; often in clumps from root-suckering. Fairly common, and very widespread in inland, particularly on dry sandy loams.

LEAVES: Alternate, *dull grey-green* both sides with obscure central vein, 5–18 cm × 3–10 mm, usually with minute hairs.

FLOWERS (various times): 1–5 in axils; the shape typical of most emu-bushes, having a curved expanding tubular corolla with lobed upper and lower 'lips', red with tiny hairs outside; 4 long stamens projecting.

FRUIT: Fleshy ovoid drupes to 12 mm long, green becoming purplish; relished by emus (hence 'emu-bush').

Family MYOPORACEAE

Eremophila longifolia
(*Eremo-phila* means 'desert-loving')

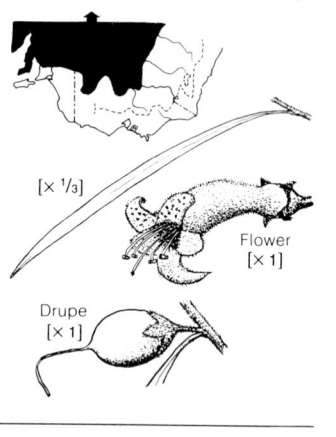

[× ⅓]

Flower
[× 1]

Drupe
[× 1]

Weeooka, Twin-leaf Emu-bush

Distinctive graceful shrub or small tree, 2–8 m, *branchlets and foliage pale grey with tiny appressed hairs.* Scattered, mostly in belah–rosewood woodland (also in tall mallee) on red-brown sandy loams of lower Murray–Darling area and inland.

LEAVES: Often (but not always) *opposite*, hoary with minute hairs, long and slender with *hooked tip*, 3–10 cm × 1–3 mm (flat or ± rounded in section).

FLOWERS (Aug–Nov): In axils; attractive curved 'bells' to 3 cm long, cream (or pinkish); persistent calyx with 5 narrow petal-like lobes to 18 mm long.

FRUIT: Dry, oblong, 2–4 angled, to 8 mm long, densely hairy.

Family MYOPORACEAE

Eremophila oppositifolia

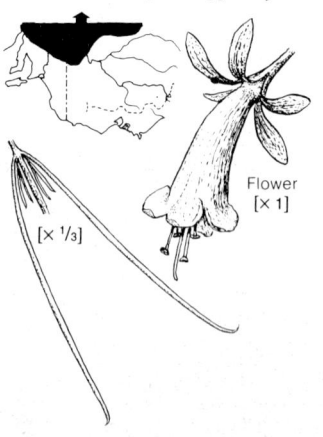

Flower
[× 1]

[× ⅓]

3 THE MAJOR TREE GENERA IN SOUTH-EASTERN AUSTRALIA

uffalo Sallee (*Eucalyptus mitchelliana*),
Victorian endemic species, known only
om the Mount Buffalo granite plateau

THE EUCALYPTS (Genus *Eucalyptus*)

Because the eucalypts (and their close relatives) dominate most of our forests, woodlands and scrubs, and in such great diversity, much of this book must inevitably be devoted to this important group.

Almost all eucalypt species were originally confined to the Australian continent (with just a few in the islands to the north), and so they were virtually unknown to European botanists until Joseph Banks and Daniel Solander collected the first specimens during James Cook's first voyage in 1770. Earlier accounts from Tasman's and Dampier's voyages had made references to trees which exuded gum or resin, and this probably contributed to the early use of the common name 'gum-tree', which was certainly on record in 1788. In that same year, the genus *Eucalyptus* was first described formally by a Frenchman, L'Héritier, from a specimen which he named *Eucalyptus obliqua* (Messmate), probably collected on Bruny Island (Tasmania) in 1777 during Cook's third voyage.

The generic name *Eucalyptus* was given in reference to what was seen as a distinctive characteristic—a 'cap' covering the stamens in bud, but falling away on flowering (*eu* = well; *kalyptos* = covered). The use of this single feature as a separating criterion is now considered unsatisfactory, and the division of *Eucalyptus* into several genera using finer criteria has been proposed. The subgroup *Corymbia* ('bloodwoods') is particularly distinctive, and considered to have closer connections with the genus *Angophora* (pages 26, 42) than with the other eucalypt sub-groups.

Evidence from fossil pollen suggests that ancestral eucalypts existed thirty million years ago, but it wasn't until mid-Miocene times (some fifteen million years ago), that they proliferated, adapting well to the extensive low-nutrient leached soils left by the previous subtropical monsoonal conditions, and progressively replacing the formerly wide-spread rainforests of southern beech (*Nothofagus*) and others.

Over 600 eucalypt species are now recognised (the exact number depending on different authorities' interpretations of a 'species'), and more are being described each year. At present, just over 100 species are recorded as occurring naturally in Victoria.

Eucalyptus is the largest genus in the myrtle family Myrtaceae; this family also includes the principally Australasian genera *Angophora*, *Leptospermum*, *Melaleuca* and *Tristaniopsis*, each of which has arboreal representatives in this book, with botanical similarities which include hard-textured leaves containing oil glands, and woody fruit capsules.

Most eucalypts are trees, though some, notably the mallees, are smaller and multi-stemmed or shrubby. Their principal continental occurrence is in the nearer-coastal areas where rainfall is higher (but not in closed-canopy rainforests). In the arid inland, where wattles (*Acacia* species) are the predominant tree type, eucalypts are confined mainly to periodic stream courses and other areas with some subsoil moisture. Nonetheless, when one thinks of a typical Australian landscape, one inevitably includes eucalypts. Of course, many visitors from overseas are already familiar with some species such as Blue Gum and Red Gum— they are now extensively planted in many countries around the world.

Numerous features contribute to the overall appearance which makes eucalypts so recognisable; it is also worth noting how some such features aid the trees' survival in the often harsh conditions of poor soil and long dry periods. Their generally tapering (lanceolate) adult leaves are usually clumped right at the ends of the branches, and hang vertically so that they do not receive the full intensity of the midday sun, yet are able to receive light to photosynthesise on both surfaces (usually equally green). They cast little shade, but allow moisture to drip freely. The leaves have a leathery (sclerophyllous) texture which resists wilting. They are rich in various oils which give most species a characteristic individual odour, and which can be very volatile in hot dry conditions. The tiny oil glands are visible in most species when the leaves are held up to the light. Although the adult leaves can be susceptible to insect attack, they are unpalatable or even toxic to most larger animals; the koala, however, is adapted to live almost exclusively on a diet of young eucalypt leaves.

To an eye that is attuned to the more regular shape and symmetry of northern hemisphere trees, eucalypts can appear 'untidy', but the form of some, such as Red Gum and Snow Gum, gives them a unique rugged beauty, sometimes enhanced by attractive bark colourings.

SIMPLIFIED SUMMARY OF MAIN BOTANICAL GROUPS FOR THIS BOOK'S AREA, AND SOME CHARACTERS USEFUL FOR FIELD RECOGNITION

Subgenus / Genus	GROUPS	TREE/BARK/WOOD	JUVENILE LEAVES	ADULT LEAVES	BUDS/FLOWERS/FRUITS
Related genus *Angophora*	Related genus *Angophora*	Trees with twisting branches. Bark fibrous (*A. floribunda*) or smooth (*A. costata*).	Opposite, sessile, pale green; widely spreading lateral veins.	Opposite, stalked, lanceolate, discolorous, widely spreading lateral veins. Lacking aroma.	Bristly buds in large compound terminal clusters. Flowers retain sepals/petals. Capsules ribbed.
Subgenus *Corymbia*	Red bloodwoods	Bark usually short-fibred and tessellated (as in *E. gummifera*).	Soon alternate; early leaves with simple hairs, and with leaf-stalks set in from base.	Discolorous. Closely spaced widely-spreading lateral veins.	Buds club-shaped and in large compound clusters at outside of crown. Fruit capsules ± urn-shaped (i.e. with a 'neck' below opening).
Subgenus *Corymbia*	Yellow bloodwoods	Bark sometimes of smooth gum type (as in *E. maculata*).	Concolorous. Widely spaced lateral veins.	Concolorous. Widely spaced widely-spreading lateral veins.	
Subgenus *Symphyomyrtus*	Mahoganies	In *E. botryoides*, trunk bark thick compact-fibrous, limbs smooth.	Alternate, stalked, discolorous, glabrous.	Thick, strongly discolorous. Close widely-spreading veins.	Simple axillary clusters of 7–11 buds. Fruit cup-shape.
Subgenus *Symphyomyrtus*	Red gums	Bark grey gum-type, shed in large flakes. Wood hard, red, durable.	Alternate, stalked, concolorous green.	Rel. narrow, straight or curved. Well spaced lateral veins.	Buds in 7s; caps pointed. Fruits with projecting valves.
Subgenus *Symphyomyrtus*	Swamp gums	Bark rough on some of trunk, but upper trunk and/or limbs smooth.	Alternate, stalked, concolorous green.	Generally broad, sub-glossy, often with wavy edges.	Simple axillary clusters of 7 buds. Fruits often conical.
Subgenus *Symphyomyrtus*	Manna gums, blue gums, etc.	Bark smooth gum-type (often ribbony), or rough on trunk.	Opposite, sessile, often glaucous, discolorous.	Relatively long; straight or curved.	Simple axillary clusters of 1, 3 or 7 buds.
Subgenus *Symphyomyrtus*	Boxes	Bark usually persistent, scaly. (box-type) on trunk; limbs smooth. Wood dense, strong, durable.	Alternate, stalked, greyish or dull.	Generally smaller, lighter-textured than in gums, often greyish.	Bud/fruit clusters usually in branching compound arrangement ('panicles').
Subgenus *Symphyomyrtus*	Ironbarks	Bark usually hard, thick, deeply fissured (smooth in *E. leucoxylon*). Wood strong, hard, very durable.	Alternate and stalked, or opposite and sessile; usually greyish.	Generally gum-like, often greyish.	Simple axillary clusters of 3–7 long-stalked buds. Fruit large, cup-shaped, stalked.
Subgenus *Symphyomyrtus*	Mallees	Multi-stemmed mallees or small trees in dry country. Connections with boxes or WA mallees. Bark usually smooth on stems.	Adult leaves often narrow, thick, gland-dotted, usually greyish.	Diverse characteristics.	Diverse characteristics.
Subgenus *Monocalyptus*	Peppermints	Most with short-fibred greyish bark, persistent to small branches; some with smooth gum-type upper trunk and limbs.	Opposite and sessile on rough glandular branchlets; peppermint smell.	Conspicuous glands, strong peppermint smell and taste; lateral veins at small angles to midrib.	Simple axillary clusters of numerous (>11) small club-shaped buds. Fruits fairly small, mostly ± pear-shaped.
Subgenus *Monocalyptus*	Ashes	Stringybarked or 'half-barked' tall trees; or smooth-barked smaller trees (including 'sallees' and 'scribbly gums').	Mostly alternate, stalked; flat, glabrous, broad and oblique, hanging; shiny green or dull bluish.	Lateral veins at small angles to midrib; veins almost parallel in 'sallees'. Usually curved (falcate), often oblique.	Buds club-shaped, in simple axillary clusters of 7–15. Fruits usually pear- or barrel-shaped.
Subgenus *Monocalyptus*	Stringybarks	Usually medium-sized to tall trees with coarse overall appearance and long-fibred ('stringy') bark on trunk and large limbs.	Alternate, short-stalked, wavy, tiny hair-tufts on the discolorous green early leaves.	Leathery, glossy green, relatively broad, curved (falcate), often asymmetrical and oblique.	7–11(+) buds per cluster. Fruits often ± globular, relatively broad, valves at rim-level or projecting.

Note (BUDS/FLOWERS/FRUITS column): the Symphyomyrtus groups (Mahoganies through Mallees) are grouped under "Buds with two caps, shed separately or together"; the Monocalyptus groups (Peppermints, Ashes, Stringybarks) are grouped under "Buds with only one cap".

A feature which eucalypts share with other indigenous plant groups is their evolutionary relationship with fire, which must have been a natural element of the Australian environment for millions of years— ever since climatic conditions have produced hot dry seasons.

Everything about eucalypts seems to contribute to a fire-favouring environment—the constant dropping of dry leaves and bark flakes, the volatile, flammable oils in the leaves, and the nature of the wood itself. Yet like other native plants, all eucalypts have mechanisms for survival, varying to some extent between species. Initially, survival will depend largely on the insulating properties of the bark, whether this is of the thin but moist live 'gum' type which is usually non-combustible, or a thicker persistent type, as in stringybarks, in which generally only the dead outer bark burns. In many species, trees whose crowns are completely burnt can quickly produce new shoots from 'emergency' epicormic buds under the bark, some of which become new branches. Another common means of survival, evident particularly in mallees, depends on an organ called a lignotuber—a swelling at the base of the trunk with food reserves and dormant growth buds which can produce new stems from ground level.

A few forest species, including Mountain Ash and Alpine Ash, do not possess either of these survival abilities, and the trees can be killed by intense bushfire. However, for these (if mature), the heat of the fire causes the opening of their abundant fruit capsules which drop great quantities of seed on to the now open ground in conditions conducive to regeneration. With the rain that often follows bushfire, seed germination occurs rapidly, ultimately producing a new forest of even age and height.

CLASSIFYING AND IDENTIFYING EUCALYPTS

All the eucalypts in this book's area of coverage fall into three major classification groups or 'subgenera', these being *Corymbia* (bloodwoods), *Symphyomyrtus* (mahoganies, gums, boxes, ironbarks, mallees) and *Monocalyptus* (peppermints, ashes, sallees, stringybarks). Characters useful for comparing the main subgroups (and related genus *Angophora*) are summarised in the table opposite. The book's sections based on bark types largely reflect these botanical groupings, but with some exceptions.

Growth habit, size and distribution

Before closely examining the smaller parts of a tree, it can be helpful to consider its position, general shape and size, as well as the hue, texture and density of its crown. While crown characteristics are often subtle and hard to describe in words, they provide, when coupled with bark type and growth situation, the sort of aggregate impression that the experienced bush observer tends to use for initial distance recognition.

The maps should be checked for distribution, and considered in conjunction with habitat conditions as described. The sketches indicate typical growth habit, but it must be remembered that environmental conditions and formation density can strongly influence the tree's size and shape, especially when the species has widespread distribution. For example, Brown Stringybark (*E. baxteri*) can be a tall tree in forests, but small and shrubby, without 'stringy' bark, in harsh exposed areas such as on Wilsons Promontory or rocky escarpments in the Grampians.

Terms describing tree size are often relative, but the following can be taken as a general guide: *small*—under 10 m; *medium-sized*—10–30 m; *tall*—30–50 m; *very tall*—over 50 m.

Bark type

The differences in eucalypt bark types were recognised from the earliest days of settlement, and so the commonly used descriptions such as 'stringybark' and 'ironbark' often feature in early Australian literature as well as in the long-established popular names.

Broadly, bark is either relatively thin and smooth on much of the trunk as well as the limbs, as in the gums, being shed annually in large flakes, strips or ribbons (described as *decorticating*), or rough, thicker and *persistent*, as in the stringybarks, ironbarks, and others. Some species (the 'half-barks' such as Alpine Ash) have persistent bark on the lower trunk, but smooth decorticating bark on the upper trunk and limbs.

Groupings based on various bark types, first proposed by Ferdinand Mueller in 1859, are still useful for quick field recognition, and have been used to some extent in this book. However, some potential difficulties with this system must be recognised. Firstly, closely related species, such as Red Ironbark (*E. tricarpa*) and White Ironbark or Yellow Gum (*E. leucoxylon*), can be very similar in most respects *except* bark type. Secondly, bark can vary a great deal within the one species. Manna Gum (*E. viminalis*) is one example; another is Red Box (*E. polyanthemos*) which, in Victoria, usually has quite typical 'box' bark (persistent-scaly), whereas in New South Wales its trunk can be smooth and gum-like. Thirdly, a few bark types, such as that of Silvertop Ash (*E. sieberi*) do not readily fit into any easily recognised group.

More explanation of bark type in relation to other characteristics is included in the introduction to each of the eucalypt sections.

Leaves

It is a particular characteristic of eucalypts that the leaf-form passes through marked stages of change with the growth of the plant, usually described as *seedling, juvenile, intermediate*, and *adult* leaves.

Juvenile leaves

Differences in seedling and juvenile leaf development are particularly important in taxonomic studies. In this book, juvenile leaves have been separated out and illustrated because of their value in field identification. These can be regarded as the leaf-form when a young plant is about 50–150 cm tall, or the similar leaves appearing on epicormic shoots from the trunk and large limbs when a tree is burnt or otherwise damaged.

In some species, such as Manna Gum (*E. viminalis*) and Candlebark (*E. rubida*), the adult leaves, buds and fruit can be very similar, but the juvenile leaves quite different. Look around for either small regrowth plants, or new shoots where the trunk or limbs have been damaged. Contrasts between species can be particularly obvious after bushfire.

Juvenile leaves are commonly *opposite* (in pairs on the branchlet) and *sessile* (stalkless or even stem-clasping). In some species (particularly in some 'gum' groups) they can be quite grey, or *glaucous* (bluish-green with a white-waxy coating which can sometimes be rubbed off). The two surfaces may be distinctly different in colour (*discolorous*). In a few cases (e.g. Silver-leaved Stringybarks), juvenile leaf-forms can persist on the

SOME CHARACTERISTICS OF LEAVES

ADULT LEAVES   Some variations in size, shape and vein pattern

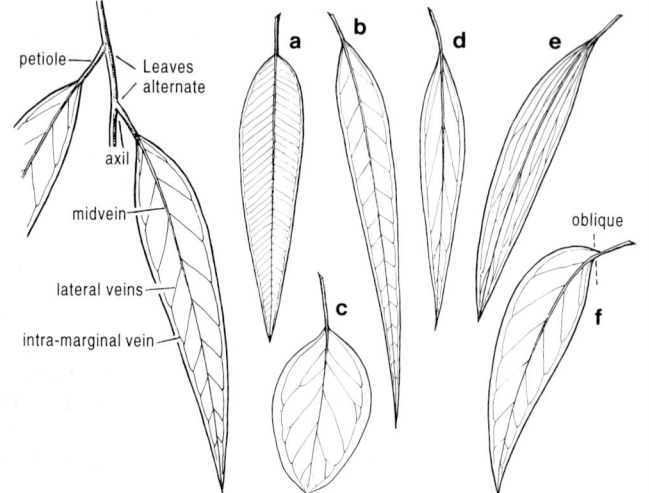

a Lateral veins at large angle to midvein (e.g. Mahogany, Bloodwood)
b Long lanceolate leaf (e.g. Manna Gum group)
c Ovate leaf, intra-marginal vein distant from margin (e.g. Red Box)
d Lateral veins at small angle to midvein (e.g. Narrow-leaved Peppermint)
e Lateral veins tend longitudinal (e.g. Snow Gum)
f Leaf broad, curved, asymmetrical, oblique (e.g. Messmate)

JUVENILE LEAVES

Manna Gum   Candlebark   Yellow Box

Opposite, sessile (stalkless)   Alternate, stalked

mature tree. Some species may develop an *intermediate* leaf form more like the adult leaves, but sometimes much larger—more than 50 cm long, for example, in Blue Gum (*E. bicostata*). However in some groups (e.g. in the 'boxes'), the juvenile leaves soon appear stalked and alternate, grading without abrupt change into the intermediate or adult form.

Adult leaves

These are the final stage in leaf-form transition, occurring on the mature plant. Adult leaves almost always appear *alternate* in their arrangement on the branchlet (they are more accurately described as *disjunct*). Most have the same colour both sides (*concolorous*), but the adult leaves of a few species are paler green on one side (*discolorous*), e.g. in the 'mahoganies', 'bloodwoods', the related genus *Angophora*, and some stringybarks. This characteristic is useful for recognising these groups and species.

It should be noted that new leaf growth at the ends of older branches is *young adult* foliage, *not* juvenile; this can be seasonally distinctive in colour—commonly bright green, but sometimes grey, mauve or red.

Even though the adult leaves of many eucalypts may be superficially similar, close examination of the vein patterns can reveal consistent differences which are useful for identification. The illustrations opposite show some variations which can be found in

- the angle of lateral veins to the midvein
- spacing and branching of the lateral veins
- distance of the intramarginal vein from the leaf margin.

The adult leaves can also show variation from the basic lanceolate shape, in terms of their relative width to length, amount of curvature, asymmetry, or 'obliqueness' at the base.

The relationships between these patterns and the various groups is explained in the introduction to each of the sections.

Buds, flowers and fruits

While all the previous features can often give a good initial indication of a tree's identity, buds and/or fruits should be sought to provide a more positive identification.

BUDS, FLOWERS AND FRUITS

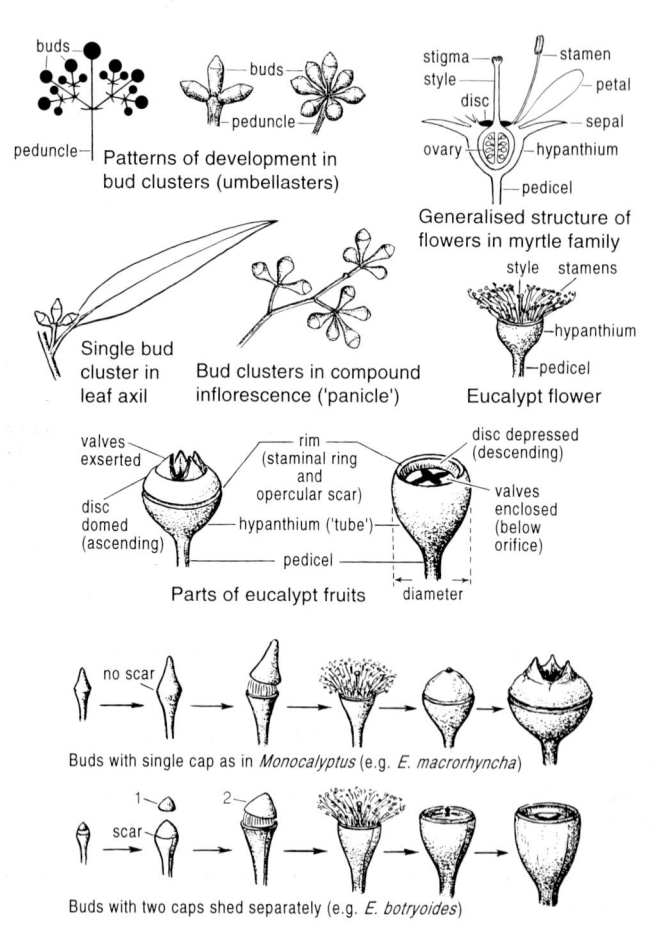

Patterns of development in bud clusters (umbellasters)

Generalised structure of flowers in myrtle family

Single bud cluster in leaf axil

Bud clusters in compound inflorescence ('panicle')

Eucalypt flower

Parts of eucalypt fruits

Buds with single cap as in *Monocalyptus* (e.g. *E. macrorhyncha*)

Buds with two caps shed separately (e.g. *E. botryoides*)

Buds

Buds develop seasonally (and in some species not every year), hence their size—if they are present at all—will depend on degree of maturity. However, regardless of their stage of development, some key diagnostic features will soon become apparent, as illustrated on the opposite page.

The number of buds in a cluster (botanically termed an *umbellaster*) can vary even within one species, but there are some fairly consistent patterns. For example, *E. globulus* has solitary buds, *E. rubida* has clusters of three, *E. goniocalyx* has clusters of seven, and *E. radiata* has eleven or more buds in a cluster. The reason for the numbers 1, 3, 7, 11, etc. is explained by variation in the degree of development in the pattern shown in the diagram opposite. However, some buds may fail to develop, or be lost, often giving apparent departures from these typical numbers.

In most species, the clusters occur as solitary units at the base of the leaf stalk of younger leaves near the ends of the branchlets (i.e. in the leaf *axils*). However, in the 'box' group in particular, several clusters can develop along a leafless common stalk, giving a *compound* structure which has previously (though not strictly correctly) been termed a panicle. Because the bark of some boxes can be very variable, this characteristic ('panicle' in the descriptions) can greatly aid recognition of a box.

Each bud always has what is simply termed in this book a 'cap' (*operculum* or *calyptra*). In subgenus *Monocalyptus*, there is only one cap to be shed before flowering. In the other subgenera, two closely fitting caps develop, the outer one equivalent to a 'fused' calyx, the inner one a 'fused' corolla. These are shed together in some species, separately in others. Thus the open flowers of all our species lack sepals and petals.

When examining buds, note the shape of the visible cap, and its size compared with the basal outer body of the bud (strictly termed the *hypanthium*, but called the floral 'tube' in this book). In buds in which two caps are shed separately, a distinct 'ring-scar' will remain where the inner cap joins the 'tube', indicating the earlier shedding of the outer cap.

After shedding of the cap(s), the numerous stamens (male) encircling the stigma (female) open out, giving the eucalypt blossom its colour—usually cream, but occasionally pink or red (as in some ironbarks).

Flowering time is partly dependent on seasonal climatic variations, and many trees do not flower every year. The time range given for each species is that most commonly observed for the species in Victoria, and is particularly important for apiarists. Birds and insects are attracted to the flowers especially for their nectar, but of course insects in particular also perform a vital role in carrying pollen from tree to tree for fertilisation.

Fruits

After the flower is fertilised, the hypanthium expands to become a woody *capsule*, and the enclosed ovules develop into the seeds. Once the capsule is mature and woody, drying conditions (especially fire) cause the valves to open and the seeds can fall. Unless germination occurs rapidly, most of these seeds will be harvested by insects, mainly ants.

For identification purposes, the fruit capsule is extremely useful, as its shape is slightly different in almost every species. These variations are best shown with illustrations. Just a few words of caution, however –

- the numbers of capsules in a cluster can vary because not all buds develop to fruits, or some capsules may fall early;
- there can be some variation in size and shape with degree of maturity, and even variation within a species;
- while the number of valves (or cells) can sometimes be helpful (e.g. for *E. bosistoana*), in most species the number varies within a range of 3–5, the actual number being of no particular significance.

Hybridisation

Finally, the field observer should be alert to the possibility of finding hybrid trees, which are recognisable by the presence of characters intermediate between those of the parent species, and which are often associated with areas of some ecological disturbance (e.g. clearing or fire). For hybridisation to occur, several conditions are necessary –

- both parent species would be (or have been) in the vicinity;
- they are in the same subgenus, and often in close groups within the subgenus (e.g. *E. pryoriana* and *E. cephalocarpa* in *Symphyomyrtus*);
- their flowering times would have coincided.

Candlebark (*E. rubida*), with adult leaves (top) and juvenile leaves (bottom)

Mountain Swamp Gum (*E. camphora*), rough-barked at base, ribbony above

The Gums (smooth-barked eucalypts)

Although 'gum tree' was the original popular name for most eucalypts, and remains so to some extent, the description 'gum' has been generally narrowed to refer to the tree species which have **mainly smooth, pale bark shed annually in ribbons, strips or large flakes** (i.e. said to **decorticate**). In some gums (e.g. Candlebark), the whole trunk is smooth; in others (e.g. Manna Gum and Swamp Gum), darker rough bark can persist on the base of the trunk to varying heights.

While most of the eucalypts in this section are closely related (i.e. are 'true' gums falling within sub-genus *Symphyomyrtus*), there are a few bearing the name 'gum' which more strictly belong with non-gum groups, e.g. Pink Gum (p. 59) with the boxes, Snow Gum (p. 64) with the ashes, and Yellow Gum (p. 67) with the ironbarks. Their gum-type barks, however, immediately point to this section for field identification.

The adult leaves of most 'true' gums are relatively long, often weeping, and have similar vein patterns. The juvenile leaves can be distinctive, most being opposite and sessile. Bud clusters occur singly in leaf axils, not in a compound form as in the boxes.

51

River Red Gum

Eucalyptus camaldulensis

Medium-sized to tall impressive tree (to 45 m), with thick trunk, heavy twisting branches and spreading open crown. Common and widespread, often the main (or only) eucalypt *along lowland rivers and dry watercourses* (especially along the Murray R and tributaries; fine stands of tall trees in the Barmah forest). It also forms open woodlands on plains (e.g. SE of Melbourne, Gippsland, Wimmera). Prefers deep moist subsoils with some clay. In NW Vic, Black Box adjoins it at slightly higher occasionally flooded levels.

BARK: Smooth, dull grey, sometimes with cream or reddish patches, peeling in large irregular flakes over most of the trunk.

LEAVES: Adult—Rather variable in length (10–22 cm); dull, often pale- or greyish-green; new growth bright green.

　　　　Juvenile—Greyish-green, alternate and stalked after a few pairs; can be narrower or broader than adult leaves.

BUDS: Usually 7 per cluster; *distinctively contracting pointed caps*; pedicels *slender* (3–10 mm long). Flowers mainly Oct–Jan.

FRUIT: *On slender stalks; disc domed; 3–5 strongly projecting and incurved valves.*

WOOD: Red, hard, resistant to decay and termites. Used for stumps, posts, walls, sleepers, etc. Burns well on a hot fire.

COMMENTS: Occurs in all mainland states. A favourite subject for photographers and painters. Risky to camp under as limbs can fall unexpectedly. Popular for honey. Intergrading occurs between various red gum species; this and the species opposite have similar wood and honey properties.

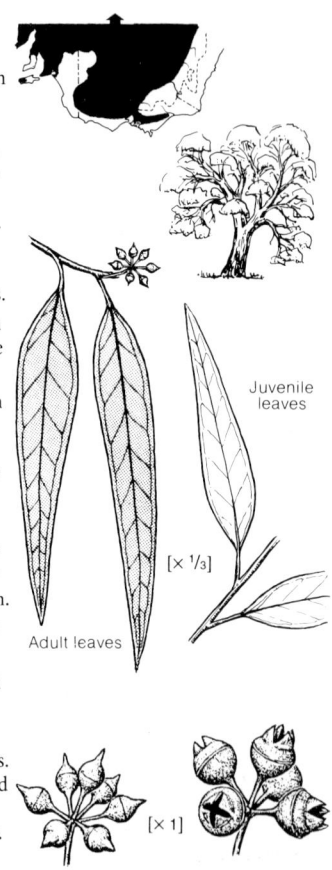

Juvenile leaves

[× ⅓]

Adult leaves

[× 1]

Buds

Fruit

Blakely's Red Gum
Forest Red Gum

Eucalyptus blakelyi [A]
Eucalyptus tereticornis [B]

[A] **Blakely's Red Gum** (*E. blakelyi*) is a small to medium-sized tree, usually low-branching. In Vic, *mainly in the NE* (also U Snowy R, and scattered elsewhere, west to Kooyoora S Park); *chiefly on drier well-drained soils*, e.g. on granite hills, with other species such as boxes and Black Cypress-pine. More common in NSW tableland area (including ACT). [Some populations, e.g. in Warby and Strathbogie Ras of NE Vic, may be an undescribed related species.]

BARK: Similar to River Red Gum.

LEAVES: Adult—Green, to 16 cm long.
Juvenile—Broad, greyish-green.

BUDS: To 7(11) per cluster, pedicels usually shorter than in River Red Gum, *caps longer and conical*. Flowers August–January.

FRUIT: Fairly small; 4(5) exserted valves.

[B] **Forest Red Gum** (*E. tereticornis*) is medium-sized to *tall* (20–45 m), usually with *long straight trunk and ascending branches*. On *coastal* side of Divide; in Vic, only in E Gippsland plains area; more common in NSW (e.g. on alluvial soils or granitic hillslopes, often with *Angophora floribunda*). In fairly open formations (the name 'forest' is rather inappropriate).

BARK: Similar to the other red gums.

LEAVES: Adult—Long (to 20 cm), green.
Juvenile—Broad, ± bluish-green.

BUDS: To 7(11) per cluster, *caps long, conical, horn-shaped* (hence *'tereti-cornis'*). Flowers mainly August–December.

FRUIT: Similar to River Red Gum but usually slightly larger; 4(5) exserted valves.

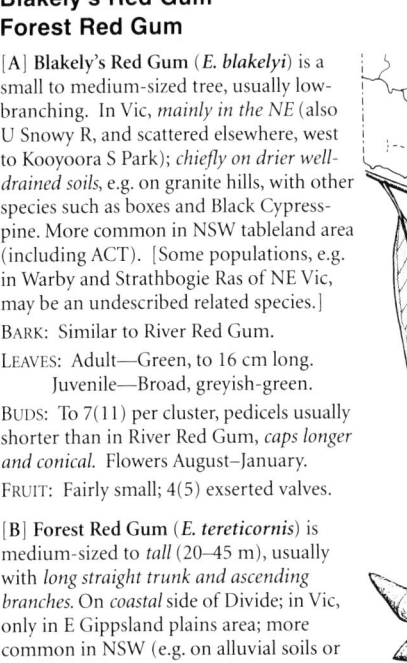

Juvenile leaves [× 1/3]

Adult leaves [× 1/3]

A

Fruit [× 1]

Buds [× 1]

A

Buds [× 1]

B

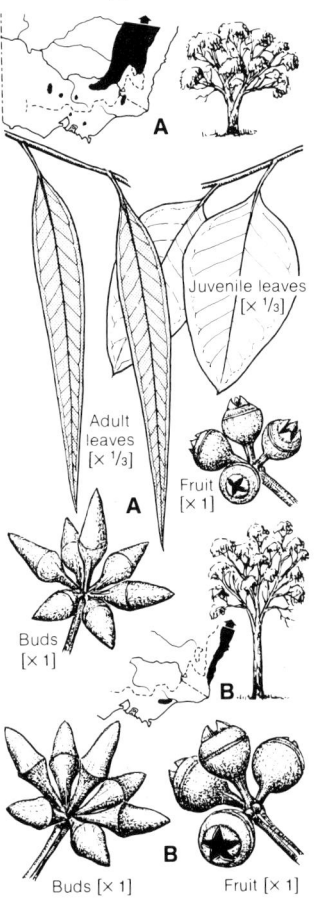

B

Buds [× 1] Fruit [× 1]

Swamp Gum
Mountain Swamp Gum

Eucalyptus ovata [A]
Eucalyptus camphora
subsp. *humeana* [B]

[A] **Swamp Gum** (*E. ovata*) is the most common and widespread member of the swamp gum group. A small to medium-sized tree, usually with an open crown of sparse foliage at the ends of long smooth branches. On *poorly drained sites*, mostly on flats and dips in hills *south* of Main Divide, usually associated with stringy-bark–peppermint–gum formations.

BARK: Dark and rough at base of trunk; shed in ribbons from upper trunk and branches leaving a cream-grey surface.

LEAVES: Adult—Thick, dark green, sub-glossy, *usually broad (ovate) with wavy edges*, but sometimes longer and narrower (lanceolate). New growth brighter green.

Juvenile—Dull green, ± rounded, stalked and alternate.

BUDS: About 7 per cluster; cap usually conical giving the bud a *diamond shape.* Flowers mainly May–September.

FRUIT: *Funnel-shaped and flat-topped* (6–8 mm wide, but larger in populations near Vic–SA border); 3–4 *horizontal* valves.

[B] **Mountain Swamp Gum** is similar to *E. ovata* and the two have been confused. It may be differentiated by: Occurrence on poorly-drained sites *mainly in mountain country* east from Yarra Glen area, and especially in *NE* Vic–NSW; LEAVES ovate, often *broader* than *E. ovata*; BUDS similar to *E. ovata*, but *narrower*; FLOWERS March–April; FRUIT smaller than *E. ovata* (4–6 mm wide) and with small *projecting* valves.

See pages 55 and 75 for other species in the swamp gum group.

Juvenile leaves
[× 1/3]

Adult leaves
[× 1/3]

Buds
[× 1]

Fruit
[× 1]

B
[× 1/3]

B

[× 1]

[× 1]

Strzelecki Gum

Eucalyptus strzeleckii

Described as a distinct species in 1992, this was previously considered a form of *E. ovata*. It is a *medium-sized to tall erect tree*, in forests and hilly farm country of high-rainfall S Vic, *mainly SW Gippsland*.

BARK: Smooth almost to base in mature trees, whitish with red-brown mottling.

LEAVES: Adult—Similar to *E. ovata*, but usually narrower (more lanceolate). Spring growth tips often distinctly waxy.

Juvenile—Soon alternate, generally narrower (lanceolate or ovate) and more lustrous compared with *E. ovata*.

BUDS: Usually 7 per cluster, *more ovoid* than in *E. ovata*. Flowers spring.

FRUIT: Commonly smaller than *E. ovata*, tapering to thinner pedicels.

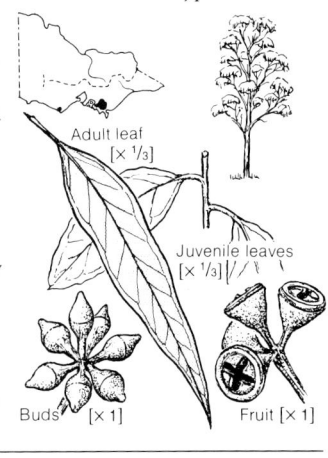

Adult leaf [× 1/3]

Juvenile leaves [× 1/3]

Buds [× 1]

Fruit [× 1]

Brooker's Gum

Eucalyptus brookeriana

Medium-sized to tall *erect forest tree*; in Vic, *restricted to Otway Ras and Woodend–Daylesford area*. Prefers moist but well-drained hilly sites. More common in Tas.

BARK: *Fibrous grey-brown* and persistent for several metres on lower part of trunk, but *conspicuously smooth above* (with grey, creamy, green, or bronzy patches).

LEAVES: Adult—Usually more lanceolate than in *E. ovata*, edges often wavy.

Juvenile—*Rounded, lustrous green above, paler and duller beneath, margins distinctly crenulate* (see illustration).

BUDS: Similar to *E. ovata*, but usually more ovoid. Flowers summer–autumn.

FRUIT: Slightly more cup-shaped than *E. ovata*, pedicel distinct, 3–4 *exserted* valves.

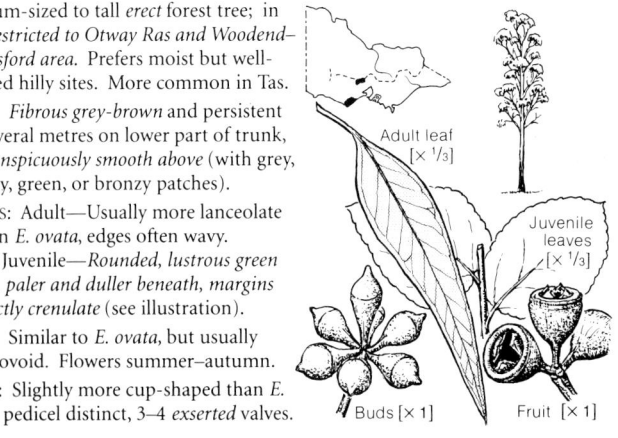

Adult leaf [× 1/3]

Juvenile leaves [× 1/3]

Buds [× 1]

Fruit [× 1]

Manna Gum, Ribbon Gum

Eucalyptus viminalis
subsp. *viminalis*

This species is common and widespread, but varies considerably in form, bark and habitat. In its best form, subsp. *viminalis* is a handsome tall ribbony-barked forest tree (to 45 m) near mountain streams, preferring moist well-drained soils, but it can also be smaller and more spreading in woodland situations, sometimes even on ridges. Its crown is fairly open with narrow weeping leaves. Often occurs with Messmate, Peppermint, and other gums (e.g. Swamp Gum, Mountain Grey Gum).

BARK: Rough, persistent at base to varying heights on trunk; smooth and white above, *with ribbons hanging from limbs.*

LEAVES: Adult—Fairly narrow, mid-green, 10–20 cm long. Young growth (brighter green) is a favoured food of koalas, but they also feed on several other species.

Juvenile—*Narrow-lanceolate, green* (never glaucous), *opposite, stalkless.*

BUDS: *Usually in 3s* in the form of a cross (sometimes to 7). Flowers mainly in summer (–autumn).

FRUIT: On very short pedicels, usually to 3 per cluster (sometimes to 7); somewhat rounded (6–9 mm diam.) with broad ascending disc, 3–4 projecting valves.

WOOD: Pale, not strong or durable, burns quickly.

COMMENTS: Hybridises with other related 'gum' species (including *E. cephalocarpa*). This, and its variability over a wide geographic range, has led to difficulties in its definition and taxonomy. See p. 76 for *rough-barked* subspecies *cygnetensis,* and *E. pryoriana* (formerly a subspecies).

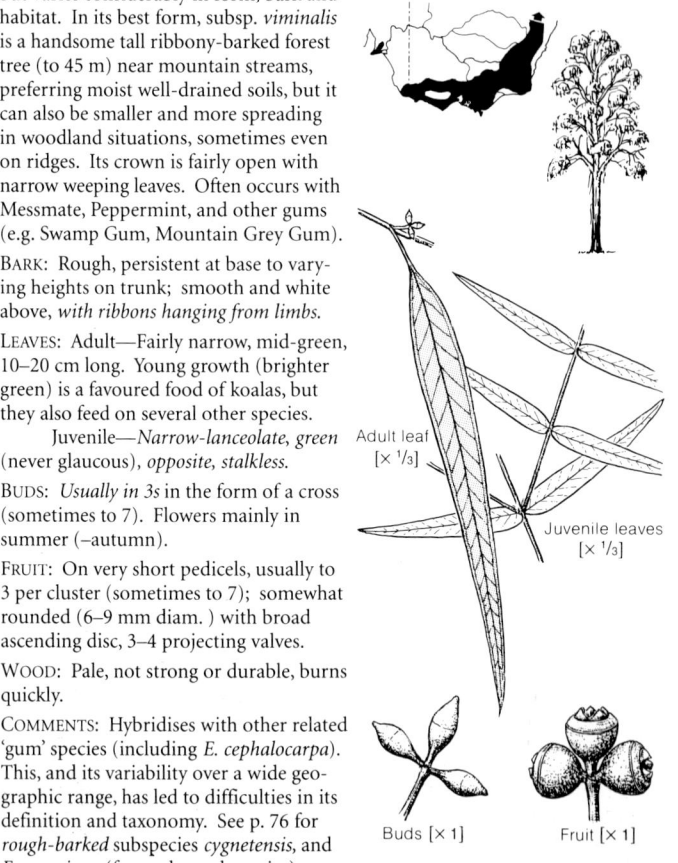

Adult leaf [× ⅓]

Juvenile leaves [× ⅓]

Buds [× 1]

Fruit [× 1]

Candlebark
Mountain Gum

Eucalyptus rubida [A]
Eucalyptus dalrympleana [B]

[A] **Candlebark** (*E. rubida*) varies from small (e.g. near Yarra R in hills east of Melbourne) to taller and straighter (to 35 m) in forests of ranges. Compared to Manna Gum, it usually has smooth bark on most of the trunk, lacks ribbons, occurs on generally drier shallower soils, and has rounded grey juvenile leaves.

BARK: *Smooth, white almost to ground*, but tends to develop reddish patches before peeling in summer (hence '*rubida*').

LEAVES: Adult—Narrow, green or grey-green, 10–20 cm long.

Juvenile— Generally ± *rounded, grey* (glaucous), opposite and stalkless.

BUDS: *In 3s* in widespread subsp. *rubida*, green (sometimes glaucous), caps conical. In 7s in subsp. *septemflora* of mountains in NE Vic. Flowers summer.

FRUIT: Mostly in 3s, like Manna Gum but often slightly smaller (5–7 mm diam.); disc broad, domed; 3–4 projecting valves.

WOOD: Tough but not durable, of little economic value. Superior in [B] below.

[B] **Mountain Gum** (*E. dalrympleana*) is a medium-sized to tall tree (to 40 m), often hard to distinguish from Candlebark. Bark can turn reddish in summer. Common in forests above about 700 m in mountains, *sometimes as the dominant species*, often with peppermints and various other montane to subalpine species (see p. 8). Distinguishable from Candlebark by:
ADULT LEAVES shinier green and often wavy; JUVENILE LEAVES greener; BUDS and FRUITS slightly larger; FLOWERS March–May.

Juvenile leaves [× 1/3]

Adult leaves [× 1/3]

Buds [× 1]

A Fruit [× 1]

B Juvenile leaves

Buds [× 1]

Fruit [× 1]

Brittle Gum, Red-spotted Gum

Eucalyptus mannifera

A small to medium-sized tree (to 20 m), occurring in drier hill country of eastern Vic (east from Eildon and Mitchell R areas) and tablelands area of NSW, chiefly on poorer shallow and stony soils, commonly with peppermints, boxes, Red Stringybark, Candlebark, Inland Scribbly Gum (NSW). Previously two intergrading subspecies [ssp. *mannifera* and ssp. *maculosa*] were recognised for this book's area; these are now not maintained, but as indicated in the descriptions below, there is marked variability in several characters.

BARK: Smooth to ground level, *powdery white* (or cream or grey), developing reddish patches in summer before being shed in flakes (hence former *'maculosa'*).

LEAVES: Adult—Dull, grey-green, veins faint; 10–18 cm long; 10–25 mm wide.

Juvenile—*Soon becoming alternate and short-stalked*, dull greyish-green. Variable in width from curved narrow-linear to broad-lanceolate.

BUDS: Ovoid, *to 7 per cluster*, with short rounded or conical caps. Flowers mainly November–April.

FRUIT: Size variable (4–6 mm diameter), with short pedicels, rounded base, variably raised disc; 3(4) protruding valves.

WOOD: Pinkish-brown, straight-grained, brittle, not durable and of little use.

COMMENTS: Can superficially resemble Candlebark—distinguish by combination of more buds and fruits per cluster, stalked alternate juvenile leaves. The form with narrow grey leaves is popular as a street tree, having seasonally coloured bark.

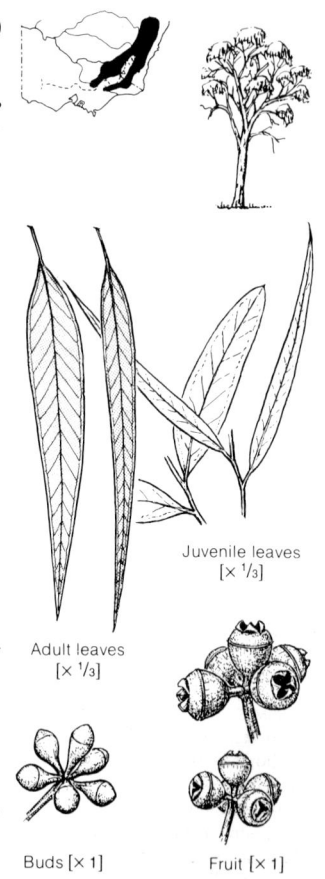

Juvenile leaves
[× 1/3]

Adult leaves
[× 1/3]

Buds [× 1]

Fruit [× 1]

Pink Gum

Eucalyptus fasciculosa

Generally a small and rather crooked tree, but sometimes taller (to 18 m), with fairly open crown. Common from near Dergholm (just east of Vic–SA border), through flatter country of south-east SA, also in south Mt Lofty Ranges; usually in woodlands or open scrub on poorer and often sandy soils (sometimes in poorly drained depressions). Commonly occurs with Yellow Gum, stringybarks or others.

BARK: Smooth on most of the trunk, white with streaks or patches of pale colours; sometimes scaly with irregularly peeling flakes.

LEAVES: Adult—To 14 cm long, green, dull or slightly glossy, thick and firm, sometimes oblique; veins faint.

    Juvenile—Soon alternate, stalked, ovate, dull green both sides.

BUDS: Clusters of 4–7, *in compound branching structures ('panicles') at the ends of branchlets*; club-shaped with short conical caps narrower than top of 'tube'. Flowers mostly December–May.

FRUIT: Fairly long; rim thin and often split; 3–4 small valves below rim level. *Clusters in compound arrangement.*

WOOD: Pinkish brown, hard, tough, fairly durable, useful for posts and fuel.

COMMENT: Although appearing to be a 'gum', this species is placed botanically in the box group (note, for example, the stalked alternate juvenile leaves, the better quality wood, and particularly the compound arrangement of the bud/fruit clusters—*'fasciculosa'* (meaning 'bundled') refers to this characteristic.

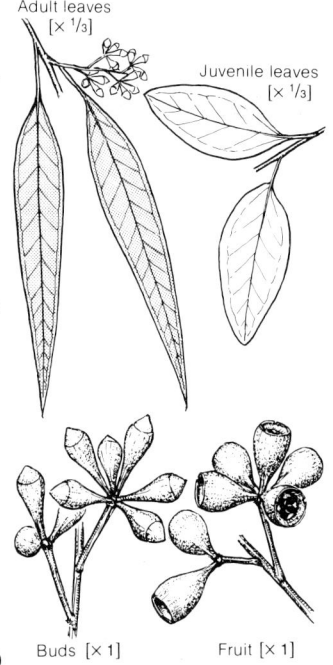

Adult leaves [× ⅓]

Juvenile leaves [× ⅓]

Buds [× 1]   Fruit [× 1]

Mountain Grey Gum

Eucalyptus cypellocarpa

Medium-sized to tall straight tree (can be more than 50 m). Most common and best developed in moist forests of eastern ranges, but also occurs in the Grampians and on some lowland sites. Always in mixture with other species, particularly stringybarks (e.g. Messmate), peppermint, and other gums (e.g. Manna Gum).

BARK: Smooth, grey, often with yellowish patches, shed in strips or plates; may be rougher, darker and persistent at base. Commonly with horizontal 'cuts' (scars left by insect larvae).

LEAVES: Adult—*Long* (to 25 cm, or more in intermediate stage), *dark green* both sides, veins regular and distinct, intra-marginal veins *close* to margins.

Juvenile—Opposite, stalkless, broad-lanceolate (–ovate), glossy dark green above (sometimes glaucous), paler beneath.

BUDS: *Distinctively elongated,* with two fine ribs or angles continuing up the cylindrical 'tube' from the short bud-stalk (pedicel); cap conical. Clusters usually of 7 on a *long flattened stalk* (peduncle). Flowers mainly February–June.

FRUIT: Barrel-shaped (1–2 fine ribs) on short pedicels, 3–4 valves at or below rim level. *Long peduncles broadly flattened.*

WOOD: Hard, heavy, fairly strong and durable, used for general construction.

RELATED SPECIES: Smaller trees with similar buds, fruit and adult leaves (but differing juvenile leaves), and rough bark to varying heights (appearing intermediate between this and Long-leaved Box) are described as a new species *E. alaticaulis* (see page 79).

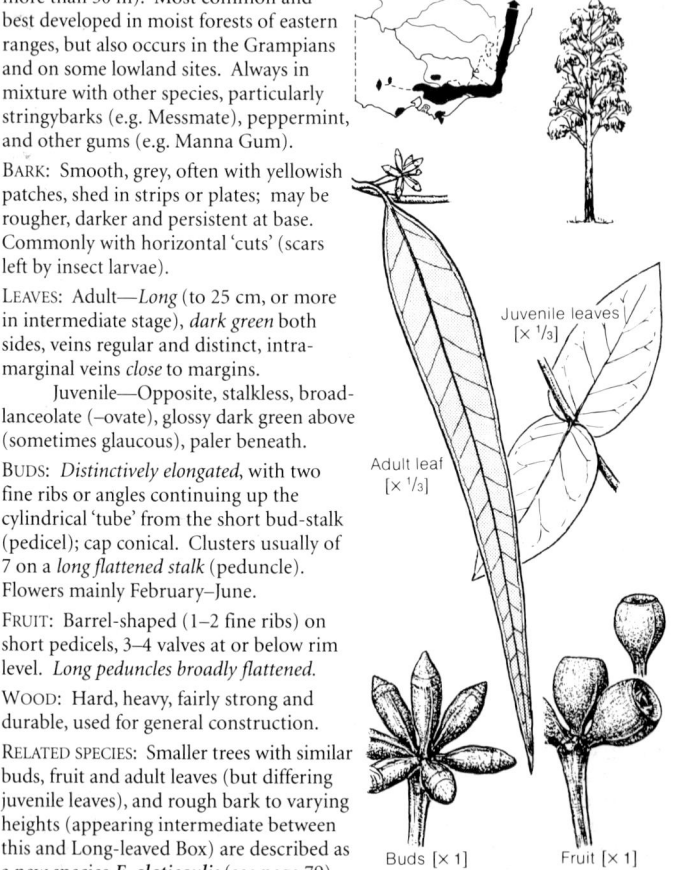

Juvenile leaves [× 1/3]

Adult leaf [× 1/3]

Buds [× 1]

Fruit [× 1]

Shining Gums

Former '*E. nitens*' showed some distinct variation within its range through E Vic and SE NSW. In 1991, the mainly East Gippsland form was described as a new species, *E. denticulata* (see below).

Shining Gum (*E. nitens* [A] as now defined) is a tall smooth-barked forest tree with separated occurrences (at about 650–1300 m altitude, often with Alpine Ash) in mountains of east-central Victoria (e.g. Mts St Leonard, Selma, Wellington, Erica); also on coastal ranges of SE NSW.

BARK: Smooth, white or greenish-grey over most of trunk, peeling in long strips.

LEAVES: Adult—*Long* (to 30 cm), thick, dark green, the intramarginal veins *well spaced* from the smooth (entire) margins.
    Juvenile—Opposite, *glaucous* (bluish), distinctly stem-clasping, on square-sectioned branchlets.

BUDS: Usually in 7s in *compact* clusters; shiny, small, sessile, 'tube' ± angular, cap conical. Flowers mainly summer.

FRUIT: *Small, barrel-shaped, closely packed in clusters; distinctly shiny* ('*nitens*' means 'shiny'); 3(4) valves at or below rim level.

[B] *E. denticulata* occurs mainly in the Errinundra Plateau area where it forms an overstorey to cool-temperate rainforest species (e.g. Sassafras, Black Oliveberry); also in some E-C Vic localities, e.g. Mt Baw Baw. Differences from *E. nitens* are: ADULT LEAVES with shallowly 'toothed' (denticulate) margins; JUVENILE LEAVES narrower, less stem-clasping; BUDS longer, less angular; FRUIT more cup-shaped, often with slightly protruding valves.

Eucalyptus nitens [A]
Eucalyptus denticulata [B]

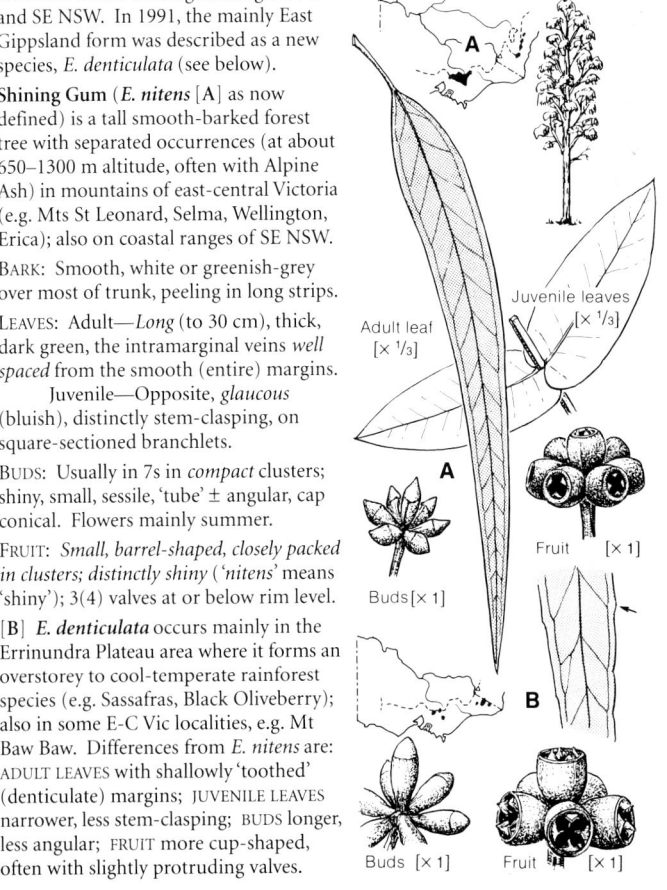

Adult leaf [× 1/3]

Juvenile leaves [× 1/3]

A

Buds [× 1]

Fruit [× 1]

B

Buds [× 1]

Fruit [× 1]

Blue Gums

Four closely related 'blue gums' occur
in Vic (–NSW). Originally described as
separate species, they were grouped as
subspecies of *E. globulus* in 1974. Some
botanists now return them to species
status (as below) although intergradation
occurs. They are fast-growing trees, and
appear similar – the often-present large
bluish juvenile leaves and strong eucalyptus
aroma suggest a blue gum; the buds, fruits
and distribution differentiate the species.

BARK: Rough, dark, persistent at base,
smooth higher, peeling in strips giving
pale shades of grey, blue, cream, brown.

LEAVES: Adult—Long (12–30 cm) and
hanging; *thick and leathery*, glossy dark
green, veins fine but distinct and regular.

Juvenile—*Large* (to 20 cm × 10 cm),
glaucous (bluish-white) with waxy bloom;
opposite, stalkless on square-sectioned
branchlets. Some intermediate leaves may
be very long (more than 50 cm).

WOOD: Pale, hard, heavy, moderately
strong and durable. Used for heavy and
light construction, poles, tool handles.

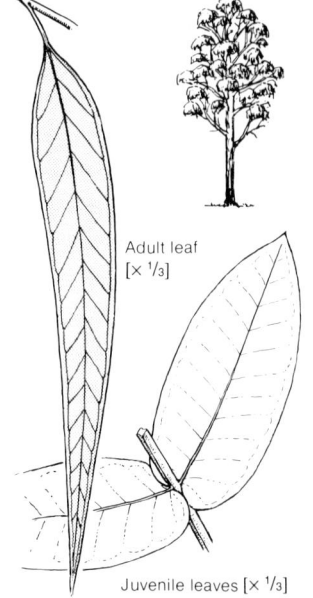

Adult leaf
[× ⅓]

Juvenile leaves [× ⅓]

Southern Blue Gum

Usually a tall tree (25–60 m), trunk often
stout, crown large. A mainly Tasmanian
species, limited on mainland to remnants
in South Gippsland and Otways, mostly
in moist hilly dairy country. BUDS usually
solitary, large, sessile, 4-angled, warty and
glaucous, cap with central point. Flowers
June–Nov. FRUIT sessile, *large* (more than
18 mm diam.) with 4 strong ribs, broad
thickened disc.

Eucalyptus globulus

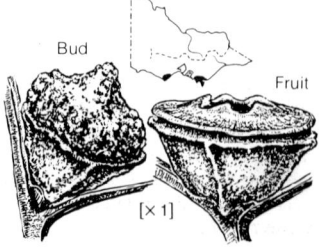

Bud

Fruit

[× 1]

Victorian Blue Gum

Eucalyptus bicostata

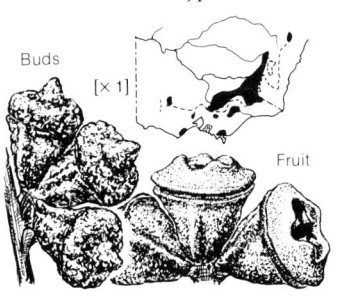

Tall tree (to 45 m). Numerous separated occurrences in Victoria, locally abundant especially in the north-east, often on granite-type outcrops; less frequent in NSW. With other forest species (e.g. stringybarks, peppermints, Mountain Grey Gum) in moist or dry hill country. BUDS sessile, glaucous, smaller than in *E. globulus*, 2-ribbed; *in 3s with peduncle scarcely developed.* Flowers Sept–Jan. FRUIT *in 3s but peduncle virtually absent*; more than 12 mm diam., 2-ribbed.

Victorian Eurabbie

Eucalyptus pseudoglobulus

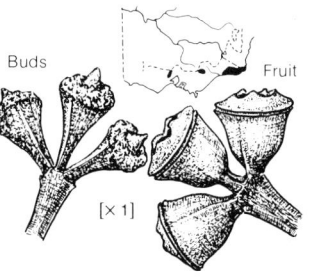

Tall tree (20–45 m), in forests mostly in near-coastal East Gippsland (e.g. along Princes Hwy) to Disaster Bay (NSW), usually on moist lower slopes of valleys; also in Lerderderg Gorge west of Melbourne. BUDS *in 3s on broad flat peduncle*; smaller than in *E. bicostata*, tapering into a pedicel, 2-ribbed. Flowers Sept–Jan. FRUIT less than 15 mm diam., smooth with 1–2 ribs, short pedicels; *in 3s on flattened peduncle.*

Maiden's Gum

Eucalyptus maidenii

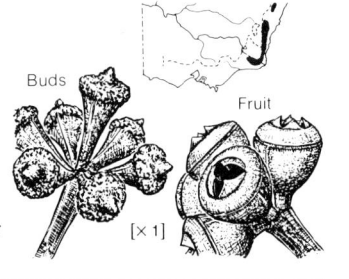

Tall tree (30–70 m). Confined to a fairly narrow band below about 1000 m along coastal escarpment of NSW Tablelands, extending to U Snowy R area in Vic. Commonly with Mountain Grey Gum, stringybarks, Silvertop. BUDS rather like *E. pseudoglobulus*, but in *clusters of 7 on flattened peduncle*. Flowers Mar–Sept. FRUIT *in clusters of 4–7*; fairly smooth, pedicels short; disc convex, 3–4 triangular valves protruding.

Snow Gums, White Sallee

Eucalyptus pauciflora

Trees with 'snow gum' characters (notably leaves with *distinctive longitudinal veins*) occur over a wide area, sea-level to *subalps* (where dominant), but with variations (e.g. in leaf, bud and fruit size, and degree of waxiness/glaucousness). This has led to questions about the evolution of the group, and problems with its taxonomy. Subspecies as presently described are given below.

BARK: Smooth, white or with grey strips, but may turn shades of red or olive-green. Subalpine trees often have 'scribbles'.

LEAVES: Adult—Leathery, lanceolate or ovate, *conspicuous veins running lengthwise.* Juvenile—Opposite, ovate, grey-green, soon becoming larger and alternate.

BUDS: Ovoid to club-shaped, 7–11+ per cluster; cap short. Flowers mainly Oct–Feb.

FRUIT: Pear-shaped to cup-shaped, waxy-glaucous in some subalpine subspecies.

[a] Ssp. *pauciflora*: 'mallee' or open tree to 20 m; widespread (incl. lowlands, e.g. SW Vic, Mornington Pen.); adult leaves long, glossy; fruit ± pear-shaped, non-glaucous.

[b] Ssp. *parvifructa*: small dense 'mallee'; Mt William Ra (Grampians); leaves shiny; buds/fruit small; only young parts waxy.

[c] Ssp. *acerina*: large 'mallee'; mainly Baw Baw plateau; leaves small and shiny green; buds/fruit small, subsessile, non-waxy.

[d] Ssp. *hedraia*: Falls Creek; larger bluish grey leaves; buds/fruit large, sessile, waxy.

[e] Ssp. *niphophila*: highest parts of ranges; all parts glaucous, but smaller than in [d].

[f] Ssp. *debeuzevillei*: Kosciusko area–ACT; buds and fruit large, glaucous, ± angular.

Juvenile leaves

Adult leaves

[× 1/3]

[× 1]

a

b

c

d

e

f

Buds

Fruit

Black Sallee

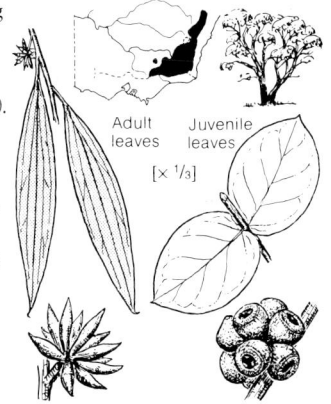

Eucalyptus stellulata

Small tree, 5–14 m; trunk usually dividing near ground; fairly dense crown of small leaves. In subalps, high plains and table-lands (800–1700 m), *localised on poorly drained flats and depressions (frost pockets)*. Distinguish from Snow Gum (usually nearby on better-drained sites) by darker trunk and smaller leaves.

BARK: Base rough and dark; *upper trunk smooth, gunmetal-grey to olive-green.*

LEAVES: Adult—5–10 cm long, green and *non-shiny, veins almost longitudinal.*

Juvenile—Opposite, sessile, ovate.

BUDS: *Many (8–20) in star-like clusters* (hence '*stellulata*'); *caps sharply conical.*

FRUIT: *Small, almost globular, crowded,* disc ± flat; valves tiny (usually 3).

Adult leaves Juvenile leaves
[× ⅓]
Buds [× 1]   Fruit [× 1]

Buffalo Sallee

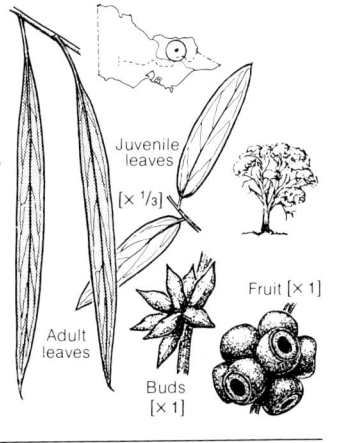

Eucalyptus mitchelliana

Small attractive tree, 4–14 m, branching low to produce an umbrella-like crown of narrow leaves. *Confined to Mt Buffalo plateau* (photo p. 39) scattered amongst granite tors mostly with Snow Gum.

BARK: Shed in ribbons from upper trunk and branches leaving smooth pale surface, sometimes streaked with colours.

LEAVES: Adult—*Relatively narrow* and almost straight, to 14 cm long, *shiny green, lateral veins few and very acute.*

Juvenile—Opposite, oblong, soon becoming alternate, lanceolate.

BUDS: Sessile, *7–11 in star-like clusters*, caps sharply conical. Flowers Nov–Jan.

FRUIT: Shiny, sub-globular with flat horizontal disc; *tightly clustered.*

Juvenile leaves
[× ⅓]
Adult leaves
Fruit [× 1]
Buds [× 1]

Inland Scribbly Gum

Eucalyptus rossii

Small to medium-sized tree, 8–25 m, in *NSW tablelands area* (incl. ACT), e.g. along Hume Hwy. Usually on shallow dry soils, with e.g. Red Stringybark. Not a 'true' gum – closely related to peppermints, ashes.

BARK: Smooth, cream-white-grey, turning reddish before shedding in flakes. *Often with 'scribbles' left by insect larvae.*

LEAVES: Adult—Lanceolate, commonly narrow; dull grey-green, veins rather faint. New growth bright green.

Juvenile—Soon alternate, greyish.

BUDS: 7–15 per cluster, club-shaped with short rounded cap. Flowers summer.

FRUIT: Rather small; disc reddish, flat or convex, fairly wide; valves (usually 4) tiny, at rim level.

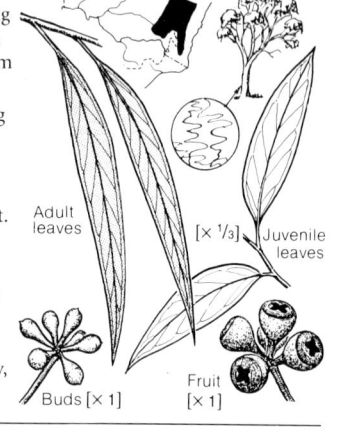

Adult leaves [× ⅓]

Juvenile leaves

Buds [× 1]

Fruit [× 1]

Sugar Gum

Eucalyptus cladocalyx

Extensively planted, especially along roadsides and fencelines in west Vic; its natural occurrence is restricted to a few localities in SA (S Flinders Ras, Kangaroo Is, Eyre Pen.). A small to large tree (8–35 m) with glossy leaves at the ends of long ascending branches. Drops fruit capsules abundantly.

BARK: Smooth, shed to give irregular white, yellow and grey patches.

LEAVES: Adult—*Dark oily-green lustre* one side, *paler* on the other. *Little odour.*

Juvenile—Pale green, thin.

BUDS: In clusters of 7–11, *elongated 'tube' with small cap*, becoming ribbed when dry. Flowers January–February.

FRUIT: *Barrel-shaped with constricted opening*, ribbed especially when dry.

Widely planted

Adult leaves [× ⅓]

Fruit [× 1]

Buds [× 1]

Yellow Gum, White Ironbark

Eucalyptus leucoxylon

A small to medium-sized tree, 5–30 m, with yellowish or mottled gum-type bark on most of trunk. Somewhat variable— five subspecies are presently described: [a] subsp. *leucoxylon* (SW Vic; S Lofty Ra and Kangaroo Is, SA); [b] subsp. *pruinosa* (most extensive, e.g. box–ironbark areas of C–W Vic; SE SA and Mt Lofty Ras); [c] subsp. *connata* (Studley Park, Sunbury, Brisbane Ras and Anglesea area in Vic); [d] subsp. *stephaniae* (often mallee-like, mainly in Vic–SA 'Deserts'); [e] subsp. *megalocarpa* (mostly near coast in SE SA).

BARK: Dark and scaly at base, smooth above, pale shades of yellow, blue, grey.

LEAVES: Adult—Variable in length and width (7–18 cm × 15–35 mm), olive- or greyish-green, veins distinct.

Juvenile—*Persisting opposite; grey-green;* broad or narrow heart-shaped to lanceolate-ovate, pairs sometimes joined at base in [b] and [c]; waxy in [b].

BUDS: *In 3s* (rarely 7s), ovoid or globular *on distinct slender stalks.* Flowers creamy, pink or red (May–November).

FRUIT: Very variable, but *usually fairly large,* cup- or barrel-shaped on *distinct pedicels sometimes longer than capsule;* largest in [e], smallest in [c] and [d]; disc depressed, 4–6 enclosed valves.

WOOD: Pale, hard, strong, very durable.

COMMENT: Although its bark makes it appear to be a 'gum', all other characters place this species with the 'ironbarks' (see Red Ironbark, p. 115, for similarities). Var. *rosea* is a popular cultivated form commonly grown in streets and gardens.

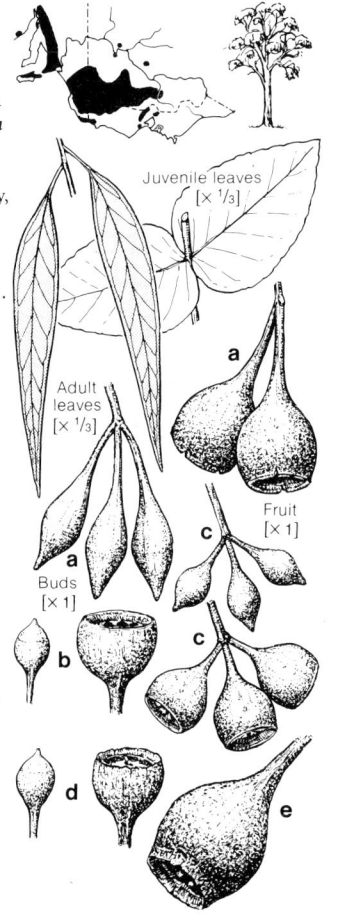

Juvenile leaves [× 1/3]

Adult leaves [× 1/3]

Fruit [× 1]

Buds [× 1]

67

Spotted Gum

Eucalyptus maculata

[A] This tall straight tree (20–45+ m), with distinctive bark, occurs intermittently throughout much of the east coast, south of Bundaberg, Qld – conspicuous along the Princes Hwy in South Coast of NSW. *The only occurrence in Victoria is south of Buchan.* Best growth is where soil is well-drained but not too dry, often over shale.

BARK: Smooth, *often with dimples,* grey or pinkish, shed in patches in summer giving yellow and grey *mottled or spotted surface* (hence *'maculata'*), then yellowish.

LEAVES: Adult—Dark green both sides, 10–25 cm long, 15–30 mm wide.

Juvenile—Alternate and stalked, *broad-ovate,* green, slightly paler one side.

BUDS: Ovoid, *in 3s in compound structures terminal to branchlets.* Flowers July–Aug.

FRUIT: Thick, woody, 10–14 mm diam., small opening and sometimes short neck; valves deeply enclosed; stalks coarse.

WOOD: Pale, tough, strong, used for general construction, poles, tool handles.

COMMENTS: A fire-resistant species. Commonly planted as a quick-growing fairly densely-foliaged tree. This species and *E. citriodora* (below) are not true gums, but smooth-barked 'bloodwoods' in subgenus *Corymbia* (see page 42).

[B] **Lemon-scented Gum** (*E. citriodora*), a Qld species, is closely related, and has very similar buds and fruits. Often planted as a particularly attractive tree. Distinguish by *narrower, paler green leaves with lemon scent* when crushed, smooth pale grey or pinkish bark, and more open crown.

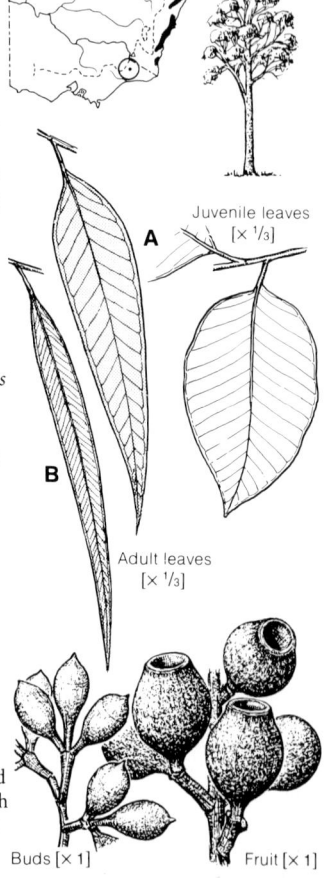

Juvenile leaves
[× 1/3]

A

B

Adult leaves
[× 1/3]

Buds [× 1]

Fruit [× 1]

Bog Gum, Gippsland Mallee

Eucalyptus kitsoniana

Small tree, often mallee-like, *endemic to southern Vic*, localised in near-coastal sites (Wilsons Prom. area, near Apollo Bay, L Glenelg–Portland area), usually on poorly-drained sandy or alluvial flats.

BARK: Smooth, pale, shed in strips.

LEAVES: Adult—Lanceolate (to 16 cm long), often relatively broad; thick.

Juvenile—*Opposite, sessile, broad-ovate, paler green one side.*

BUDS: Ovoid, *rather squat, clusters of 7 on broad flattened peduncle*, surrounded by conspicuous bracts when immature. Flowers summer.

FRUIT: Cup-shaped, *sessile, in fairly tight clusters on stout flattened peduncles.* Disc about horizontal, 3–4 valves at rim level.

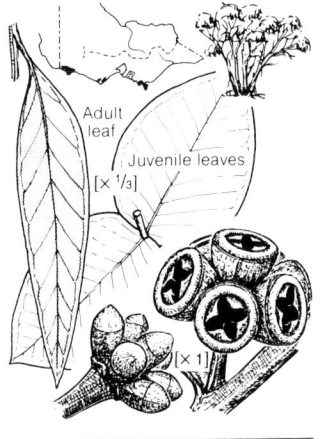

Adult leaf [× 1/3]

Juvenile leaves

[× 1]

Spinning Gum

Eucalyptus perriniana

Small tree, 3–6+ m, often straggly or mallee-like. *Juvenile leaves tend to persist with adult leaves.* Sporadic occurrences in *high plains and subalps* (e.g. Dargo, Nunniong Plateaus), chiefly with Snow Gum, from which it can be distinguished at a distance by its greyer mauvish hue.

BARK: Smooth, ribbony, white or shades of brown and green.

LEAVES: Adult—Lanceolate, thick, dull grey-green.

Juvenile—*Glaucous (grey-mauve), opposite and often joined at bases, encircling branchlet, sometimes spinning free.*

BUDS: Glaucous, *in 3s.* Flowers Jan–March.

FRUIT: *In 3s*, sessile, cup-shaped, glaucous; 3–5 valves at or below rim level.

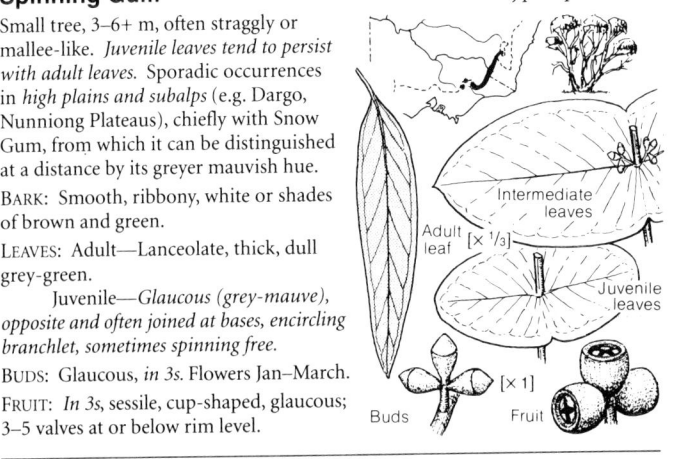

Intermediate leaves

Adult leaf [× 1/3]

Juvenile leaves

[× 1]

Buds   Fruit

69

Tingaringy Gum

Eucalyptus glaucescens

Varies considerably in growth habit – mallee-like in several isolated *subalpine* localities (e.g. Mt Tingaringy, Nunniong Plateau), taller tree in montane forests on Mt Erica–Baw Baw granite.

BARK: Rough and subfibrous at base of trunk, peeling in ribbons above, leaving smooth surface of various pale shades.

LEAVES: Adult—Curved-lanceolate, to 13 cm long, green or greyish-green, firm-textured.

Juvenile—*Conspicuously glaucous, broad, opposite, sessile, 'notched'.*

BUDS: Glaucous, *in 3s,* 'tube' cylindrical, cap short. Flowers mainly autumn.

FRUIT: *Cup-shaped, sessile,* glaucous or shiny, 3(4) valves at or below rim level.

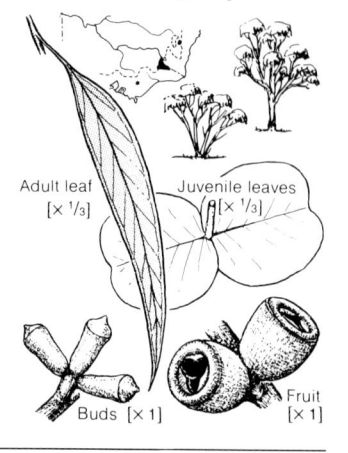

Adult leaf [× 1/3]

Juvenile leaves [× 1/3]

Buds [× 1]

Fruit [× 1]

Suggan Buggan Mallee

Eucalyptus saxatilis

Mallee or small tree (to 10 m), mainly on high *rocky* sites (hence *'saxatilis'*) in Upper Snowy River area (e.g. Little River Gorge, Mt Wheeler and Stradbroke Chasm in Vic, also in NSW just north of the border). Closely related to *E. glaucescens*.

BARK: Peeling in ribbons to base of stems leaving smooth surface (yellow-orange when first exposed).

LEAVES: Adult—Curved-lanceolate, to 15 cm long, bluish-grey, dull.

Juvenile—*Glaucous, opposite and sessile, ± rounded and often 'notched'.*

BUDS: *Glaucous, in 3s,* 'tube' cylindrical, *expanded at junction with the short cap.*

FRUIT: Almost *sessile,* bell-shaped with *flared rim,* disc level to raised, 3–5 valves.

Adult leaf [× 1/3]

Juvenile leaves

Buds [× 1]

Fruit [× 1]

Mt Imlay Mallee

Eucalyptus imlayensis

Mallee (to 7 m) known only from near the summit (east side) of *Mt Imlay* (near Eden, just north of the Vic border).

BARK: Smooth, shed from stems in strips or ribbons, greenish, becoming shades of brown or grey.

LEAVES: Adult—Curved-lanceolate, to 15 cm long, thick, green, held somewhat erect, forming dense canopy.

    Juvenile—Opposite, sessile on square-sectioned branchlets, *glossy dark green* (never glaucous), elliptic–ovate, margins slightly crenulate.

BUDS: *Non-glaucous, in 3s*, with *short* pedicels; cap slightly 'beaked'.

FRUIT: 6–8 mm diam., disc ascending, 3–4 valves *strongly* exserted.

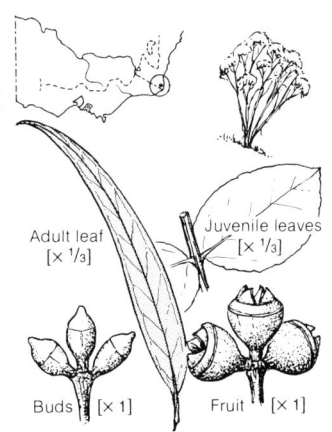

Adult leaf [× ⅓]

Juvenile leaves [× ⅓]

Buds [× 1]

Fruit [× 1]

Nunniong Mallee

Eucalyptus elaeophloia

Mallee or small tree to 12 m, known only from two localities *near Brumby Point on the Nunniong Plateau* (between Omeo and Snowy R). Closely related to *E. imlayensis*.

BARK: Smooth, initially pale grey, but becoming darker and olive-green with age ('*elaeo-phloia*' means 'olive-bark').

LEAVES: Adult—Green, curved-lanceolate, 8–11 cm long.

    Juvenile—Initially opposite, sessile, becoming alternate, short-stalked, elliptic to rounded, *bluish-green*, margins slightly crenulate; branchlets square-sectioned.

BUDS: *In 3s, sessile* on short flattened peduncle, ellipsoid shape, not glaucous.

FRUIT: *Sessile*, 6–9 mm diameter, disc ascending, valves exserted.

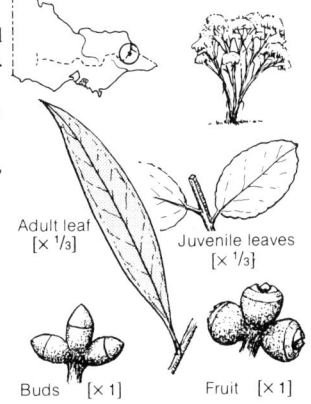

Adult leaf [× ⅓]

Juvenile leaves [× ⅓]

Buds [× 1]

Fruit [× 1]

Cup Gum

Bushy shrub, mallee or small tree, with fairly dense crown. *Confined to southern Mt Lofty Range and Kangaroo Is (SA)*, often as an understorey to stringybarks or Pink Gum, on rather infertile and often waterlogged soils. Closely related to *E. longifolia* (p. 114).

BARK: Matt white or grey surface after shedding of irregular brownish flakes.

LEAVES: Adult—Lanceolate, often fairly broad, thick and leathery, dull green.

    Juvenile—Ovate, greyish-green.

BUDS: *In 3s, large,* ovoid; caps rounded with short point. Flowers about winter.

FRUIT: In 3s, *large* (12–18 mm diam.), *cup-shaped with thick walls,* usually with 2 fine ribs; 4–5 valves just below rim level.

Eucalyptus cosmophylla

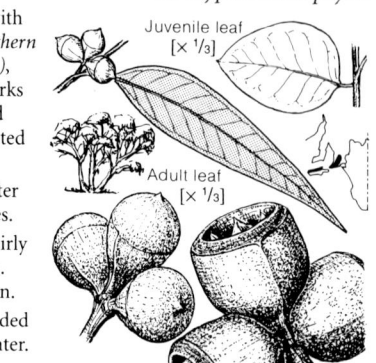

Juvenile leaf [× 1/3]

Adult leaf [× 1/3]

Buds [× 1]

Fruit [× 1]

Coast Gum, Soap Mallee

Mallee or small tree, 3–8 m. In Vic, *an isolated occurrence on Cape Nelson*, but *common near coast in SA*, chiefly on limy (calcareous) soils, with other mallees. *New adult foliage sub-glaucous, but becoming dark green with age (hence 'diversi-folia').*

BARK: Smooth throughout, pale shades (but not a 'true' gum).

LEAVES: Adult—Thick, smooth, initially greyish but becoming sub-glossy green.

    Juvenile—Opposite, sessile, ovate–elliptical, dull to waxy.

BUDS: Clusters of 7–11 along smallest branchlets. Flowers mainly Aug–Dec.

FRUIT: To 14 mm diameter on very short pedicels; disc flat or slightly domed or depressed; 3–4 valves at disc level.

Eucalyptus diversifolia

Juvenile leaves

Adult leaf [× 1/3]

Buds [× 1]

Fruit [× 1]

Kybean Mallee-ash

Eucalyptus kybeanensis

Usually a mallee, 2–5 m, rarely a small erect-stemmed tree. Small isolated *sub-alpine* occurrences, e.g. Nunniong Plateau, U Thomson–U Macalister R areas in Vic, Kosciusko area in NSW.

BARK: Smooth, white, grey, greenish or coppery, shed in ribbons (but not a 'true' gum – belongs in 'ash' group – see p. 97).

LEAVES: Adult—Lanceolate, to 9 cm long, rather thick, shiny green both sides, veins obscure; often held erect.

Juvenile—Sessile, elliptical, but soon becoming like adult leaves.

BUDS: *Sessile*, 3–11 per cluster, *minutely pimply or warty.* Flowers Nov–Dec.

FRUIT: *Sessile and crowded*, disc broad, horizontal to ascending; 4–5 valves.

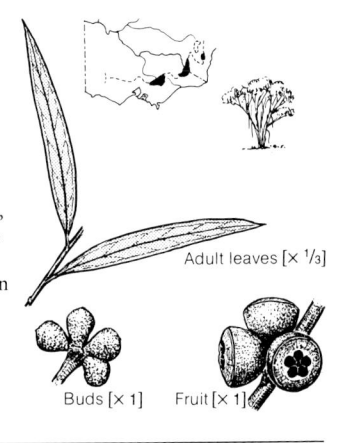

Adult leaves [× ⅓]

Buds [× 1]   Fruit [× 1]

The following trees commonly have smooth bark on much of their trunks and may appear to be gums, but are included in other sections:

Apple Box (*E. bridgesiana*) – scaly box-like bark, but leaves, buds and fruit of a gum

Scent-bark (*E. aromaphloia*) – bark coarse and fibrous, but other characters gum-like

The 'Rough-barked Gums'

'Rough-barked Gum' may appear to be a contradiction in terms, but this highlights the practical difficulties associated with grouping eucalypts.

All the species in this section have **rough persistent bark on all or most of the trunk,** and some of them (as on pages 77–79) bear the common names 'stringybark' or 'box' because of their particular bark types.

However, **on the basis of most *other* botanical characters, they look like gums,** and are in fact classified in two 'true' gum groups in subgenus *Symphyomyrtus*—the 'swamp gum' group and the very large group which includes Manna Gum (*E. viminalis*). Most fall within this latter group, and their relatively long and weeping adult leaves with the 'Manna Gum' vein pattern are a good clue to this; the distinctive and often persistent juvenile leaves which are opposite, sessile, and commonly glaucous, are another useful field indicator.

For comparison, 'true' stringy-barks (pages 102–110) usually have glossier, broader, asymmetrical adult leaves. The bud clusters in the 'true' boxes (pages 83–91) mostly occur in compound structures, whereas in the 'gums' they are solitary in leaf axils.

Yarra Gum

Eucalyptus yarraensis

Small to medium-sized tree, with short trunk and large spreading crown. A member of swamp gum group (see pages 54–55); endemic to Vic, mainly south of Divide on scattered poorly-drained sites.

BARK: Dark, rough, subfibrous or scaly on trunk and larger limbs, smooth on small branches.

LEAVES: Adult—*Elliptic, ovate or broad-lanceolate* (to 10 cm long, *smaller* than in swamp gums on pp. 54–55), *glossy* green both sides, edges broadly wavy.

Juvenile—Green, stalked, ovate.

BUDS: Fairly small, on distinct pedicels, to 7 per cluster. Flowers Dec–March.

FRUIT: *Small, more hemispheric than in other swamp gums, on distinct pedicels.*

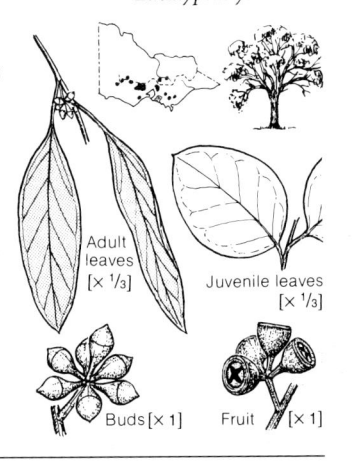

Adult leaves [× 1/3]

Juvenile leaves [× 1/3]

Buds [× 1]

Fruit [× 1]

Black Gum

Eucalyptus aggregata

Small to medium-sized tree, mainly in depressions on NSW tablelands; *an isolated Victorian occurrence near Woodend.*

BARK: Rough, firm, fissured, grey (sometimes dark), persistent to small branches.

LEAVES: Adult—Lanceolate, to 12 cm long, generally narrower than in all previous swamp gums, green both sides.

Juvenile—Green, stalked, elliptic, narrower than in other swamp gums.

BUDS: Usually 7 per cluster (sometimes more); rather small. Flowers summer.

FRUIT: *Small, shallowly hemispherical, almost sessile, fairly tightly clustered.*

Related *E. cadens* (rare, on boggy sites in NE Vic, e.g. Warby Ra) has ribbony bark on upper parts, *glaucous new growth*, conical fruit.

Adult leaves [× 1/3]

Juvenile leaves [× 1/3]

Buds [× 1]

Fruit [× 1]

E. cadens

Adult leaf

Rough-barked Manna Gums

Manna Gum (*E. viminalis* in the original broad sense) has wide distribution in SE Australia, in various habitats. It varies considerably in size, form, and height of 'rough' (persistent) bark. Buds may be 3 or 7 per cluster. The typical *E. viminalis* subsp. *viminalis* (p. 56) has smooth bark on much of trunk, grows mainly on more moist and fertile soils, and has buds in 3s. The following 'rough-barked' forms have been given distinct status.

[A] *E. pryoriana,* previously considered a form of *E. viminalis*, is a small to medium sized tree, usually heavily branched and with a large crown. It occurs *only in Vic, mainly on near-coastal grey sands, from east of Pt Phillip Bay to West Gippsland.* Hybridizes particularly with Silver-leaved Stringybark (*E. cephalocarpa*, p. 77).

BARK: Brown, rough, coarse, subfibrous and persistent on the whole trunk and often on larger branches.

LEAVES: Adult—Narrow-lanceolate, green.
      Juvenile—*Green, opposite, stalkless, lanceolate* (as in other Manna Gums).

BUDS: Usually in 3s, sometimes in 7s.

FRUIT: 3–7s, very similar to *E. viminalis*.

[B] *E. viminalis* subsp. *cygnetensis* is a small to medium-sized tree, branching low to produce a broad crown; bark rough and persistent on trunk and larger branches. It occurs *mainly in woodlands of SW Vic to Mt Lofty Ra and Kangaroo Is area of SA,* on flat or undulating country. BUDS in *clusters of 7.* Other characters as for typical *E. viminalis*.

Eucalyptus pryoriana [A]
Eucalyptus viminalis
      subsp. *cygnetensis* [B]

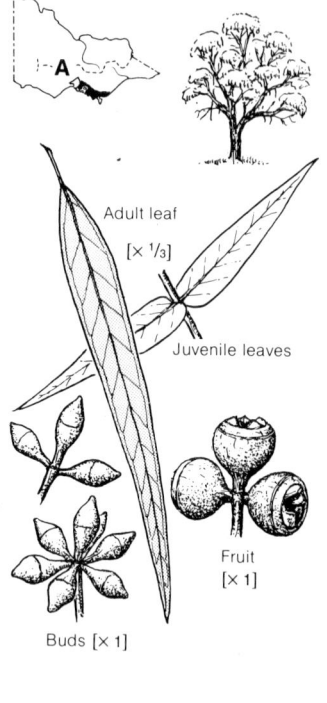

Adult leaf
[× 1/3]

Juvenile leaves

Fruit
[× 1]

Buds [× 1]

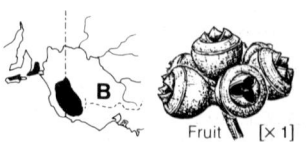

Fruit [× 1]

Silver-leaved Stringybarks

Eucalyptus cephalocarpa [A]
Eucalyptus conspicua [B]
Eucalyptus alligatrix [C]
Eucalyptus cinerea [D]

A complex group recognisable by rough bark, glaucous ('silvery') juvenile leaves, *transitional leaf forms occurring to various degrees*, variable greyness of adult leaves, and buds which are often glaucous (white-coated). Although called 'stringybarks', they are closely related to the 'gums' of the Manna Gum group. Small to medium-sized and irregularly shaped trees, they occur *mostly on poorly-drained low-nutrient sandy soils*, but sometimes on shallow clay soils. Species differences are given below, but separation is not always clear-cut.

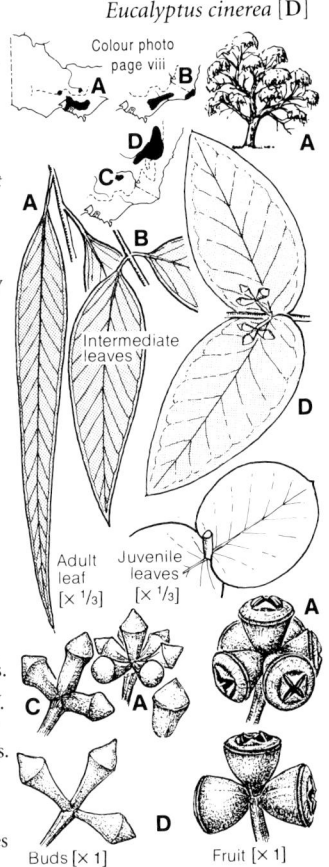

Colour photo page viii

Intermediate leaves

Adult leaf [× 1/3]   Juvenile leaves [× 1/3]

Buds [× 1]   Fruit [× 1]

BARK: Grey-brown, fibrous, thick, coarsely fissured, persistent to small branches.

LEAVES: Adult—Alternate, lanceolate, dull greyish-green especially as new growth.
Juvenile—*Opposite, sessile, ovate or almost round, becoming broad-lanceolate; grey-green or glaucous*; often persisting.

BUDS: In 3s, 7s, or more, often glaucous, usually more diamond-shape than ovoid.

FRUIT: Sessile; disc slightly ascending; 3–4 valves just projecting.

[A] *E. cephalocarpa* (sometimes called Mealy Stringybark): Around Melbourne, C Vic, W Gippsland. Adult leaves mostly lanceolate, dull green – new leaves similar but grey (not vividly glaucous); buds in 7s.

[B] *E. conspicua*: Gippsland–S Coast NSW. New adult leaves (sum–aut) conspicuously glaucous, ovate, opposite, sessile; buds in 7s.

[C] *E. alligatrix*: In NE Vic. Adult leaves lanceolate and glaucous; buds in 3s.

[D] *E. cinerea* (Argyle Apple): NSW. Leaves mostly opposite, glaucous; buds in 3s.

77

Apple Box, But-but
Apple-topped Box

Eucalyptus bridgesiana [A]
Eucalyptus angophoroides [B]

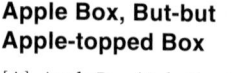

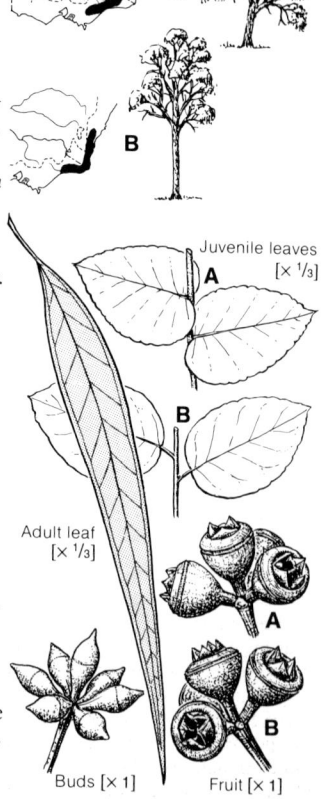

[A] **Apple Box** (*E. bridgesiana*) is a medium-sized tree (to 20 m) with box-type bark; often low-branching with a large spreading crown and rather pendulous branchlets. It is common in eastern areas, mostly in box woodlands on gentle slopes with better soils, at moderate altitudes.

BARK: *Box-like*–greyish, fairly coarse, scaly and short-fibred on trunk and large limbs.

LEAVES: Adult—Long, tapering to a fine point; *equally green (or greyish-green) both sides*, lateral veins fine and widely spaced. New growth bright green.

    Juvenile—*Stalkless and opposite to alternate, glaucous (grey); margins crenulate*.

BUDS: To 7 per cluster; ovoid, cap with short point. Flowers February–April; a favoured tree for honey.

FRUIT: Hemispheric (5–7 mm diam.) on distinct pedicels; disc slightly domed; 3–4 projecting valves.

WOOD: Pale brown, soft, light, of little practical use.

[B] **Apple-topped Box** (*E. angophoroides*) is closely related, but is taller, straighter (to 40 m), and occurs in forests of East Gippsland and SE NSW, mostly near watercourses. It differs from *E. bridgesiana* in the following additional respects:

ADULT LEAVES: Slightly paler on one side.

JUVENILE LEAVES: Darker green above, more rounded and soon becoming short-stalked.

FRUIT: Slightly larger with flatter disc. Flowers October–December.

Juvenile leaves [× ⅓]

Adult leaf [× ⅓]

Buds [× 1]

Fruit [× 1]

Long-leaved Box, Bundy

[A] *E. goniocalyx* is the most common and widespread of these related species. It is a box-barked small to medium-sized tree (to 16 m), generally of poor form with short crooked trunk and large crown of long dark leaves. It occurs mainly on drier shallow soils of foothills (especially with Red Stringybark, Red Box, Peppermint).

BARK: *Greyish, rough, coarse and scaly, persistent to small branches.*

LEAVES: Adult—Long (12–22 cm) and tapering; usually dark green, firm texture.
Juvenile—*Opposite, stalkless, broad, rounded, grey-green (slightly discolorous).*

BUDS: *Sessile, ± cylindroid,* usually with 2 ridges; cap conical. Mostly in 7s on *broad flattened peduncles.* Flowers March–August.

FRUIT: Cup- or barrel-shaped (rather variable); *sessile* and packed in clusters on *broad flattened peduncles*; 3–4 valves at about rim level.

WOOD: Of little value, even as fuel.

[B] *E. nortonii* is similar in the size and shape of most of its parts, but its leaves, buds, fruit and branchlets are *glaucous* (i.e. have a whitish coating). It occurs mainly on dry sites in NSW and E Vic.

[C] *E. alaticaulis* (described in 1987), is a 'mallee' or tree (to 30 m) in the Grampians, showing links with *E. cypellocarpa* (p. 60); it has rough persistent bark to a variable height, juvenile leaves *ovate and shiny green above,* fruit almost sessile, flowers summer. The populations in the *Anglesea* area, with mostly smooth bark, but buds and fruits like *E. goniocalyx*, may be different again.

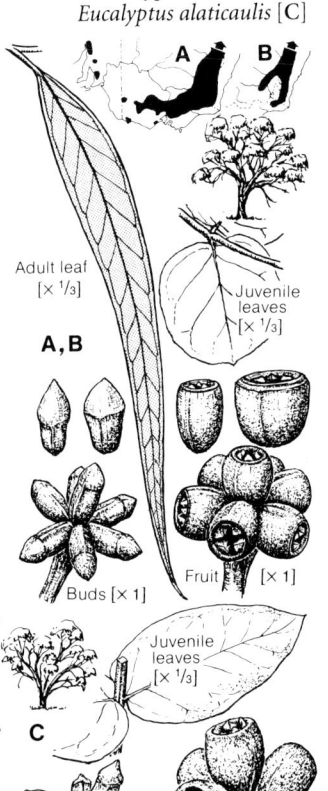

Eucalyptus goniocalyx [A]
Eucalyptus nortonii [B]
Eucalyptus alaticaulis [C]

Adult leaf [× ⅓]

Juvenile leaves [× ⅓]

A, B

Buds [× 1]

Fruit [× 1]

Juvenile leaves [× ⅓]

C

Buds [× 1]

Fruit [× 1]

Scent-bark

Eucalyptus aromaphloia [A]
Eucalyptus ignorabilis [B]

[A] *E. aromaphloia* (in the most recent sense of this species) is confined to *W Vic*, mainly from the Brisbane Ranges to the Grampians. Medium-sized tree, in forests or woodlands, mostly on lower slopes and flats. '*Aroma-phloia*' means 'scented bark', which refers to the distinct aroma when the bark is crushed and handled, but the barks of other members of the 'rough-barked gum' group (e.g. Apple Box) also contain the oil glands which give this effect.

BARK: Brown, coarse, fissured, short-fibred, persistent to small branches.

LEAVES: Adult—Lanceolate, to 17 cm long, green both sides, veins fairly distinct.

Juvenile—Opposite, *ovate, glaucous, tending to persist stalkless.*

BUDS: *Mostly 7 per cluster,* caps conical with short point. Flowers January–April.

FRUIT: *Rather small* (4–6 mm diam.), almost sessile, base hemispherical, disc domed, 3(4) short exserted valves.

WOOD: Fairly hard but not durable; of little practical value.

[B] *E. ignorabilis* was described in 1991 to separate out populations of *East Vic* (–far South Coast of NSW) which differ from *E. aromaphloia* in having juvenile leaves which are *broad-lanceolate, dull grey-green but not glaucous, and develop leaf-stalks sooner.* Otherwise, the trees themselves look similar (can also resemble forms of Silver-leaved Stringybark).

Another form (unnamed) occurring in the west Grampians–Little Desert area has very narrow non-glaucous juvenile leaves.

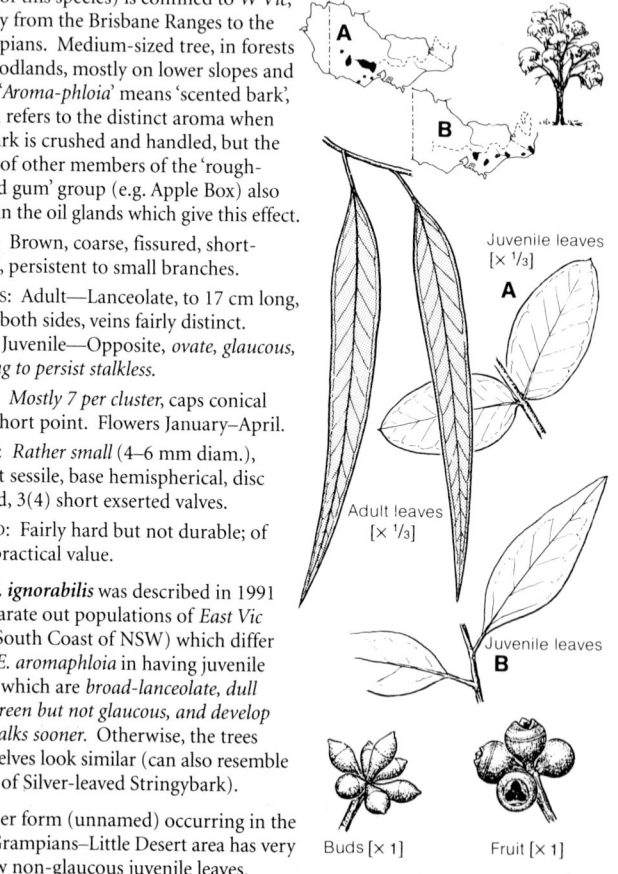

Juvenile leaves [× 1/3]

A

Adult leaves [× 1/3]

Juvenile leaves B

Buds [× 1]

Fruit [× 1]

Gully Gum

A variable-sized tree, small to tall, with an open crown of narrow leaves. Mainly in NSW near-coast areas, but scattered small occurrences in East Gippsland, usually in forests on valley slopes in hill country or on moist flats near small streams.

BARK: *Dark, compact, narrowly fissured and persistent to varying heights on trunk; smooth white above, peeling in ribbons.*

LEAVES: Adult—*Narrow-lanceolate,* to 15 cm long, dark green both sides.

Juvenile—Lanceolate, opposite, sessile, usually green, paler beneath.

BUDS: Usually *7 per cluster;* club-shaped with distinct pedicels. Flowers Jan–March.

FRUIT: Rounded with *distinctly domed disc;* on distinct pedicels; 3–4 valves.

Eucalyptus smithii

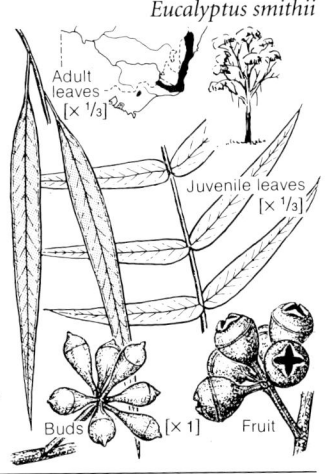

Adult leaves [× 1/3]

Juvenile leaves [× 1/3]

Buds [× 1]   Fruit

Bogong Gum

Medium-sized 'half-barked' tree, often with short trunk and long branches. *Localised and rarely conspicuous,* with other species (e.g. Alpine Ash, Peppermint) in mountain forests on higher slopes near Vic–NSW Main Divide (e.g. Mts Bogong, Buffalo).

BARK: Greyish, subfibrous, shallowly fissured on much of trunk; smooth and whitish above, peeling in ribbons.

LEAVES: Adult—*Dull green or grey-green,* lanceolate, *long* (18–30 cm).

Juvenile—*Opposite, sessile, broad and often rounded, glaucous.*

BUDS: *In 3s; glaucous;* 'tube' relatively long; cap conical. Flowers Feb–March.

FRUIT: In 3s, sessile, fairly large (to 12 mm long), disc steeply raised; 3–4 exsert valves.

Eucalyptus chapmaniana

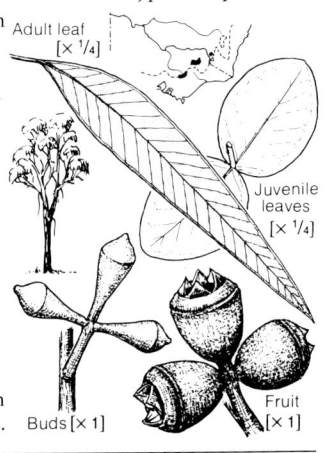

Adult leaf [× 1/4]

Juvenile leaves [× 1/4]

Buds [× 1]   Fruit [× 1]

Omeo Gum

Eucalyptus neglecta

Small bushy tree, with *conspicuously glaucous intermediate foliage and square-sectioned branchlets. Rare, near E Vic Divide only*, in headwater creek gullies, e.g. Omeo area, U Buckland R, U Big R; an understorey tree in taller forests.

BARK: Greyish, persistent, subfibrous and fissured on trunk; smooth grey or greenish on branches.

LEAVES: Adult—Broad-lanceolate, green, non-glaucous, veins very faint.

Juvenile—*Opposite, stalkless, broad-ovate, glaucous, tending to persist.*

BUDS: Small, sessile, glaucous; 7–15 in *compact* clusters. Flowers summer.

FRUIT: Sessile, in *tight* rounded clusters; ± flat-topped, narrow disc; 3–5 valves.

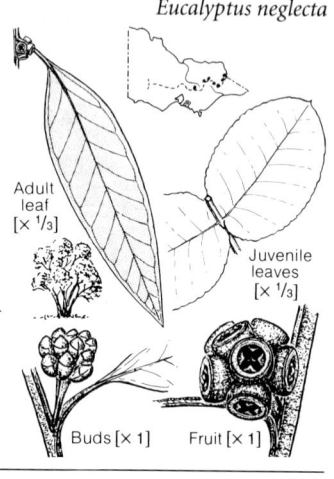

Adult leaf [× 1/3]

Juvenile leaves [× 1/3]

Buds [× 1] Fruit [× 1]

Buxton Gum

Eucalyptus crenulata

Small tree, *with markedly glaucous buds, twigs and leaf undersides.* Endemic to Vic, occurring naturally on periodically wet flats *only near Buxton and Yering*, but commonly planted as a distinctive bushy tree for cool poorly-drained sites.

BARK: Greyish, rough and persistent on much of mature trunk; smooth above.

LEAVES: Adult—*Very distinctive, persisting opposite, stalkless, generally heart-shaped, with crenulate margins;* to 7 cm long; green above, glaucous beneath.

Juvenile—Smaller than adult.

BUDS: Ovoid, cap pointed, 7–11 per cluster, *very glaucous* (white), paired in axils of opposite leaves. Flowers spring.

FRUIT: Cup-shaped, on short pedicels.

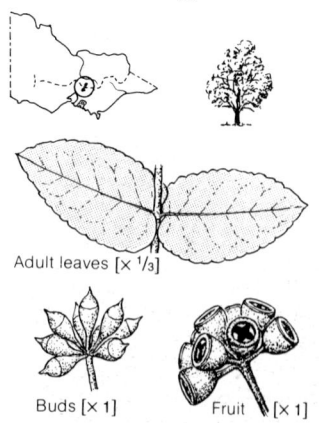

Adult leaves [× 1/3]

Buds [× 1] Fruit [× 1]

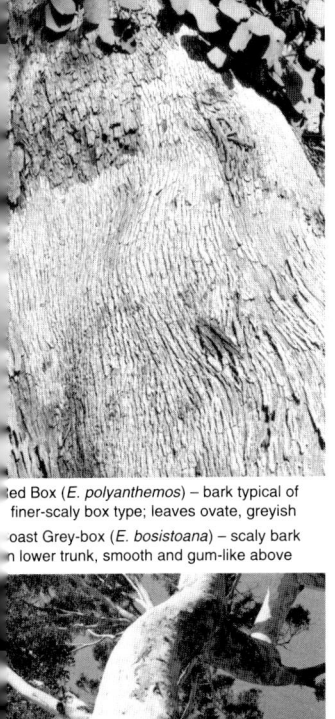

...ed Box (*E. polyanthemos*) – bark typical of finer-scaly box type; leaves ovate, greyish

...oast Grey-box (*E. bosistoana*) – scaly bark ...n lower trunk, smooth and gum-like above

The Boxes

The typical 'box' bark is persistent and subfibrous on some or all of the trunk and often larger branches, the **outer bark being finely fissured and breaking into small flakes or scales**. The remainder of the upper trunk or limbs is pale, smooth and gum-like.

Because of the variability of this type of bark (sometimes resembling that of either gums or peppermints), it is important that other characters as well as bark be examined. The adult leaves of boxes are generally smaller and lighter in texture than in the gums, and are often pale green or greyish. **The juvenile leaves become stalked and alternate early**, and are commonly pale or greyish also.

The best indicator is the presence **of bud or fruit clusters compounded into branching structures ('panicles')**, often at the ends of branchlets.

Boxes occur principally in lower rainfall inland areas, sometimes with ironbarks (which are closely related). The wood of 'true' boxes is strong and durable, and makes excellent fuel ('box' came from a resemblance of the wood to the European Box). Most boxes yield good quality honey.

Apple Box and Long-leaved Box are not true boxes, but 'rough-barked gums' (see pages 78–79).

83

Red Box

Eucalyptus polyanthemos

Small to medium-sized tree, 8–25 m, often of somewhat crooked form. Subspecies *polyanthemos* [a] has bark which is mainly smooth or with large scaly flakes on the trunk (appearing gum-like) and occurs in NSW Western Slopes area. The Victorian form is subspecies *vestita* [b] which has more typical box-type bark, and which is common *mostly on drier shallow soils in foothill country*, both north and south of the Divide, in woodlands usually with other box species, Red Stringybark, etc.

BARK: In Victoria, of grey fine-scaly box-type on trunk and large branches.

LEAVES: Adult—*Grey-green ovate* intermediate leaves tend to persist on mature tree (adult leaves are broad-lanceolate), leaf-stalks long and slender, main veins few but fairly conspicuous.

Juvenile to intermediate—Stalked, alternate, grey-green, rounded, sometimes broader than long on young plants.

BUDS: To 7 per cluster, in compound branching 'panicles'; club-shaped with slender pedicels, and *short cap narrower than the top of the 'tube'*; often glaucous. Flowers mainly September–November.

FRUIT: Pear-shaped, with *thin rim* often split, disc depressed, 3–5 enclosed valves.

WOOD: Red (hence the common name), fine-textured, hard, strong and durable. Good for posts, and excellent fuel.

COMMENTS: Easily recognised from a distance by its rather dense crown of ovate greyish leaves. '*Poly-anthemos*' means 'many flowers', referring to the numerous flowers per 'panicle'.

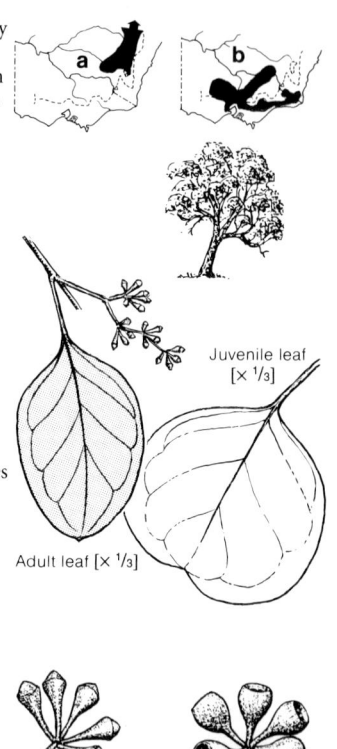

Juvenile leaf [× 1/3]

Adult leaf [× 1/3]

Buds [× 1]

Fruit [× 1]

Blue Box

Eucalyptus baueriana

Small to medium-sized tree to 20+ m, with fairly large crown; rather similar to Red Box, but ovate leaves are *greener.* Mainly in *E Gippsland–NSW near-coastal forests* (east from Heyfield area); occurrences also west of Melbourne, e.g. Bacchus Marsh area. *On loamy river flats, terraces and lower hillslopes with fairly deep moist soils.* (Red Box is usually on drier shallower soils.)

BARK: Fibrous-flaky, grey or brownish, often with whitish patches, persistent on trunk and main branches, smooth above.

LEAVES: Adult—Ovate to broad-lanceolate, somewhat similar to Red Box, but *greener* (sometimes sub-glossy), thinner, and often with broadly wavy edges.

Juvenile to intermediate—Stalked and alternate, thin, rounded (sometimes broader than wide), green both sides.

BUDS: To 7 per cluster, in compound branching 'panicles'; club-shaped with short cap narrower than the top of the 'tube'. Flowers November to January.

FRUIT: Similar to Red Box, but *more funnel-shaped* (straighter-sided) with indistinct pedicels; rim thin and often split; 3–4 valves below rim level.

WOOD: Yellow-brown, hard, strong, durable, but inferior to Red Box as fuel.

COMMENTS: In woodlands on flats north of Wagga Wagga (NSW) is a closely related species, **Fuzzy Box** (*E. conica*), which has much narrower lanceolate leaves, similar but smaller fruits and buds, and looks more like a grey box. Also closely related is Pink Gum (*E. fasciculosa*) but this has smooth gum-type bark (see page 59).

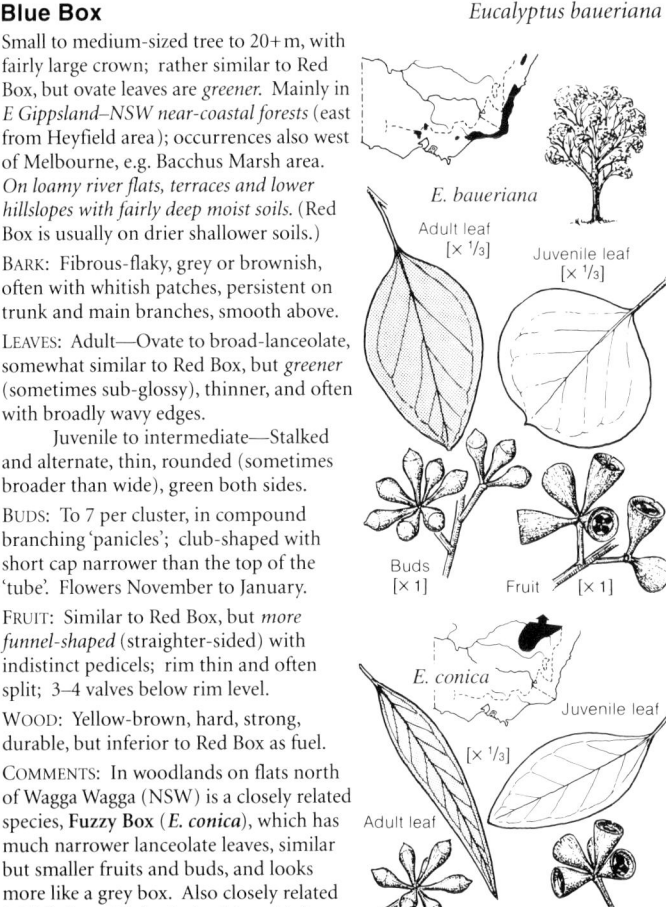

E. baueriana

Adult leaf [× 1/3]

Juvenile leaf [× 1/3]

Buds [× 1]

Fruit [× 1]

E. conica

Juvenile leaf

Adult leaf [× 1/3]

Buds [× 1]

Fruit [× 1]

Yellow Box

Eucalyptus melliodora

Medium-sized tree, 12–30 m, generally attractively shaped, with *variably scaly bark*, and *large, rounded, fine-textured* (often greyish) *crown*. Widespread and common, especially on foothills inland from the Divide in Vic–NSW, but also on hills around Melbourne, in Gippsland, and W Vic. Prefers better quality loams on lower slopes to plains, but at a higher level than River Red Gum on alluvial soils. Occurs in woodlands with various species, e.g. Apple Box, Candlebark, Yellow Gum, Scent-bark, and other boxes.

BARK: Initially yellow-brown or greyish, becoming darker with age, rough and scaly or box-like to varying degrees and heights on the trunk; upper trunk and limbs smooth, pale and gum-like.

LEAVES: Adult—Dull pale- or grey-green, thinner and smaller than in gums (7–14 cm long), veins faint, marginal veins distant from edges. New growth bright green.

Juvenile leaves [× ⅓]

     Juvenile—Alternate and stalked, elliptic, grey-green both sides.

BUDS: To 7 per cluster, in leaf axils or towards the ends of leafless branchlets giving a compound panicle-like arrangement; club-shaped with short conical cap but no scar. Flowers mainly Oct–Feb.

Adult leaves [× ⅓]

FRUIT: Ovoid, on distinct pedicels; disc flat, often with black remains of staminal ring; 4–5 enclosed valves.

WOOD: Pale yellow-brown, fine-textured, hard, strong, durable; excellent fuel.

COMMENT: Produces one of the most popular honeys; *'melli-odora'*, meaning 'sweet smell', refers to the nectar.

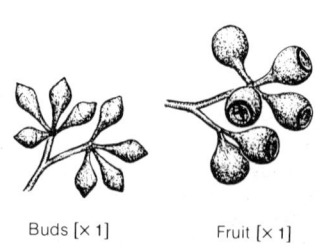

Buds [× 1]   Fruit [× 1]

Coast Grey Box

Eucalyptus bosistoana

Tall (30–50 m) with long straight trunk and relatively small crown when growing on richer alluvial flats; often smaller on shallow soils of hillslopes. Greyish box-type bark on lower part of trunk, but *distinctly gum-like above*. Limited occurrences mainly along near-coastal valleys east of Bairnsdale—some tall impressive trees remain on the Cann R flats; extends further inland in NSW. In forests it is generally intermixed with other species such as stringybarks, Mountain Grey Gum, Silvertop and River Peppermint.

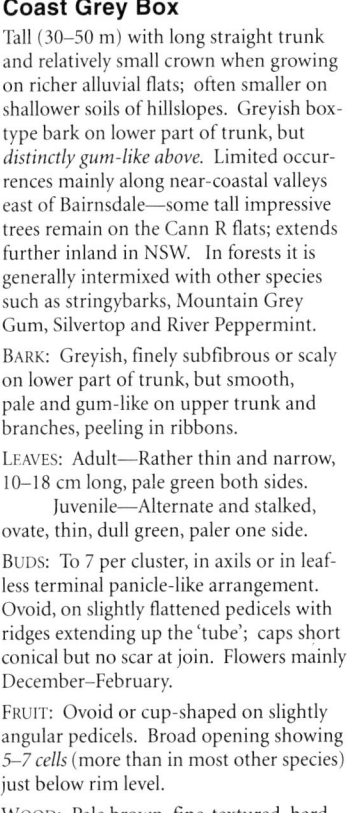

Juvenile leaves
[× 1/3]

BARK: Greyish, finely subfibrous or scaly on lower part of trunk, but smooth, pale and gum-like on upper trunk and branches, peeling in ribbons.

LEAVES: Adult—Rather thin and narrow, 10–18 cm long, pale green both sides.

Juvenile—Alternate and stalked, ovate, thin, dull green, paler one side.

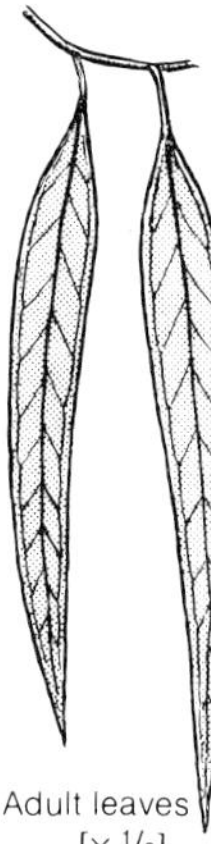

BUDS: To 7 per cluster, in axils or in leaf-less terminal panicle-like arrangement. Ovoid, on slightly flattened pedicels with ridges extending up the 'tube'; caps short conical but no scar at join. Flowers mainly December–February.

Adult leaves
[× 1/3]

FRUIT: Ovoid or cup-shaped on slightly angular pedicels. Broad opening showing *5–7 cells* (more than in most other species) just below rim level.

WOOD: Pale brown, fine-textured, hard, very strong and durable; has been used for heavy construction, poles etc. Forests containing this species have largely been cleared in East Gippsland, and being a poor regenerator, availability is limited.

Buds [× 1]

Fruit [× 1]

Grey Box

Eucalyptus microcarpa

An erect tree to about 25 m high, *usually of Y-shape with trunk about half the tree's height, and ascending branches; typical box-type grey bark on the trunk, smooth pale upper limbs.* Grey Box is dominant in woodlands on much of the drier hill to plain country inland from the Divide; reaches Tullamarine just north-west of Melbourne; isolated occurrences in SA. Associated species include mainly other boxes, also Red Ironbark, Bulloak, and cypress-pines. Occasionally mallee-like.

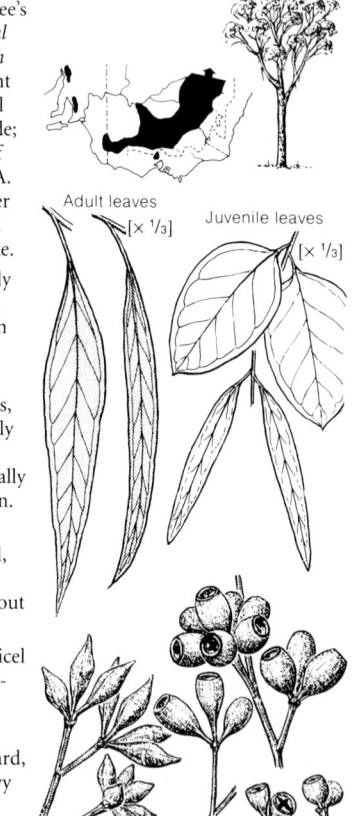

Adult leaves [× 1/3]

Juvenile leaves [× 1/3]

BARK: Grey, subfibrous-scaly and finely fissured on the trunk and larger limbs, smooth, pale and peeling in ribbons on upper branches.

LEAVES: Adult—Variably narrow- or broad-lanceolate, tapering at both ends, to 15 cm long, moderately thick, usually dull dark *green*.

Juvenile—Stalked, alternate, usually ovate (sometimes narrower), dull green.

BUDS: To 7 or 9 per cluster, forming 'panicles'; never glaucous; cap conical, often with bent tip, almost as long as 'tube', with no scar at join. Flowers about February–May.

FRUIT: Rather variable in size and pedicel length; somewhat cylindrical to barrel-shaped, about 4 valves just below rim level; not glaucous.

WOOD: Light brown, fine-textured, hard, strong and very durable; used for heavy construction; excellent fuel.

COMMENTS: Leaves, buds and fruits show variation over the species' extensive range. Yields excellent flavoured honey.

Buds [× 1]   Fruit [× 1]

White Box

Eucalyptus albens

A small to medium-sized erect tree (to 25 m), with *whitish-grey* box-type bark, and large, strongly-branched crown of distinctly *greyish* leaves. In Victoria, less common and extensive than Grey Box, having its principal occurrence in the north-east (e.g. along the Hume Hwy), where it occurs mainly with Grey Box; particularly significant in the rainshadow area along the Upper Snowy River in East Gippsland, with cypress-pines. Common, sometimes dominant, in the western slopes region of NSW; a rare occurrence in the southern Flinders Ras in SA.

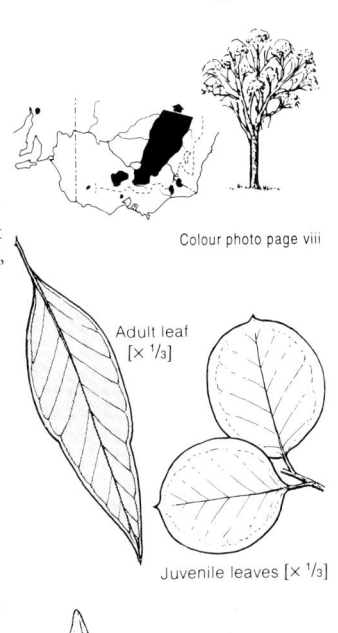

Colour photo page viii

BARK: Fine-scaly box bark on trunk and large limbs (grey with whitish patches, *paler than in Grey Box*); smooth, pale and ribbony on upper limbs.

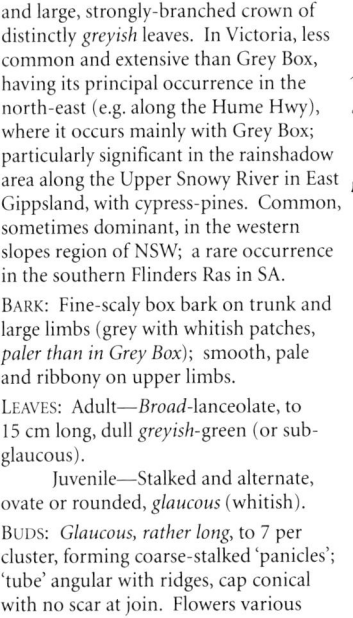

Adult leaf [× ¹⁄₃]

LEAVES: Adult—*Broad*-lanceolate, to 15 cm long, dull *greyish*-green (or sub-glaucous).

Juvenile—Stalked and alternate, ovate or rounded, *glaucous* (whitish).

Juvenile leaves [× ¹⁄₃]

BUDS: *Glaucous, rather long*, to 7 per cluster, forming coarse-stalked 'panicles'; 'tube' angular with ridges, cap conical with no scar at join. Flowers various times, usually autumn–spring.

FRUIT: Long and *somewhat cylindrical*, sometimes with 1–2 ribs, almost sessile, often glaucous; valves deeply enclosed.

WOOD: Pale brown, heavy, hard, strong and durable. Excellent fuel.

COMMENTS: Yields a first class honey. Distinguish from Grey Box by overall greyer colour, broader leaves, and larger, coarser, glaucous buds and fruits.

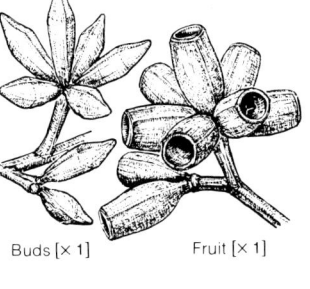

Buds [× 1]   Fruit [× 1]

Black Box
Bimble Box

Eucalyptus largiflorens [A]
Eucalyptus populnea
subsp. *bimbil* [B]

[A] **Black Box** is a small to medium-sized tree to 20 m, with *dark rough bark,* usually short trunk and spreading crown of *narrow* dull green or greyish leaves. In Vic, mainly in the NW area west of Echuca; in NSW, extensive along Murray–Darling R system. In woodlands along present or prior water courses and around lakes, on fairly heavy grey clay soils associated with occasional flooding (between Red Gum and mallees where these are present – see photo p. vii).

BARK: *Ash-grey to black,* hard, closely fissured or coarsely scaly on older trees, persistent to small branches.

LEAVES: Adult—Usually *narrow*-lanceolate, to 15 cm long, often with curved tip, dull green (often greyish), veins faint.

Juvenile—Alternate, short-stalked, very narrow, dull bluish-green.

BUDS: To 7 (or more) per cluster, forming 'panicles'; small, ovoid, with very short conical or rounded cap, scar present at join. Flowers (mainly Dec–Feb) usually cream, sometimes also pink on the same tree.

FRUIT: *Small,* pear- or cup-shaped; about 4 tiny valves just below rim level.

COMMENTS: Wood is pink to red-brown, hard, heavy, durable; good for posts, very good fuel. '*Largi-florens*' means 'abundant flowers'; yields good quality honey.

[B] **Bimble Box** is closely related to Black Box. Common on NSW plains (mainly north of Narrandera, often with cypress-pine). BARK grey-brown box-type. ADULT LEAVES glossy green, ±ovate, broadly wavy. BUDS/FRUIT rather similar to Black Box.

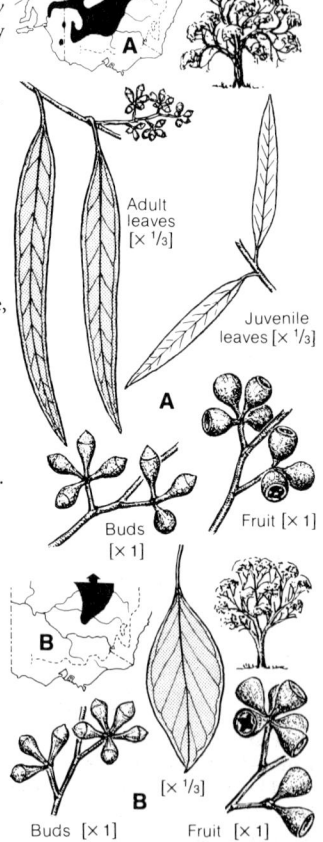

Adult leaves [× 1/3]

Juvenile leaves [× 1/3]

A

Buds [× 1]

Fruit [× 1]

B

[× 1/3]

Buds [× 1]

Fruit [× 1]

Black Mallee-box

Mallee or small tree to 10 m. Chiefly in SA, often on shallow calcareous soils; in Vic, scattered in the north-western mallee.

BARK: *Dark grey-brown scaly box-type on trunk and large branches,* smooth and greyish-white on small branches.

LEAVES: Adult—Narrow to broad lanceolate, to 12 cm long, typically *fresh green and glossy, with prominent intramarginal veins quite distant from margins.*
　　　　Juvenile—Stalked, alternate, dull dark green, elliptic–ovate.

BUDS: To 7 per cluster, mostly in leaf-axils.

FRUIT: Broadly pear-shaped, dark staminal ring often persisting; *4–6 tiny valves.*

Eucalyptus porosa

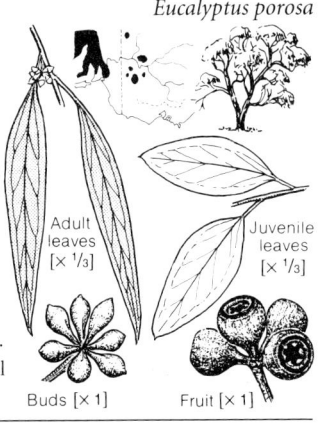

Adult leaves [× ⅓]

Juvenile leaves [× ⅓]

Buds [× 1]　　　Fruit [× 1]

Peppermint Box

[A] *E. odorata* is a small to medium-sized tree (rarely a large mallee). In *SA only* (west from Tailem Bend area); similar trees in Vic are now regarded as other species, including *E. wimmerensis* (p. 123) and [B] below.

BARK: *Dark grey, scaly-fibrous on trunk and large branches*; smooth above.

LEAVES: Adult—*Dull olive-green,* intramarginal veins well spaced from margins.
　　　　Juvenile—Stalked, alternate, dull.

BUDS: To 7 or more per cluster, mostly in leaf-axils, slightly angular with 1–3 ribs.

FRUIT: Cylindrical to ovoid, to 8 mm long, pedicels with ridges; valves enclosed.

[B] *E. silvestris* (descr. 1994), occurs in the Kaniva–Bordertown area, resembling [A], but differing in having distinctly lustrous leaves, smaller buds and fruit, and flowers in autumn (cf. winter for [A]).

Eucalyptus odorata [A]
Eucalyptus silvestris [B]

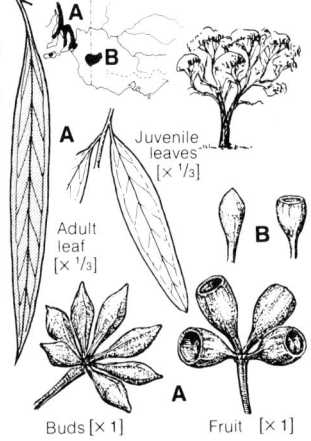

Juvenile leaves [× ⅓]

Adult leaf [× ⅓]

B

B

Buds [× 1]　　　Fruit　[× 1]

Narrow-leaved Peppermint (*E. radiata*), with the typical finely-fissured subfibrous bark

River Peppermint (*E. elata*) – bark on upper trunk is smooth, pale and ribbony like a gum

The Peppermints

The commonest peppermint species in the area—Narrow- and Broad-leaved Peppermints—have a *short*-fibred grey-brown bark which is persistent to the small branches, and which can develop a fine trellis-like pattern as it splits; these trees commonly have a dull greyish overall appearance.

However, River Peppermint and Shining Peppermint have persistent bark only at the base of the trunk, the upper trunk and limbs being smooth and gum-like; to identify these, it is necessary to examine other features, including those mentioned below.

The leaves of peppermints are distinctive in that **their prominent oil glands have a component which gives them a strong peppermint smell and taste when crushed.** The lateral veins are at small angles to the midrib.

Peppermints, together with the stringybarks and ashes, are included in the large subgenus *Monocalyptus*, which, as the name suggests, groups species with single-layered bud-caps. Unlike the stringybarks and ashes, **juvenile leaves of peppermints are opposite and sessile.** Buds are small, club-shaped, and **numerous** (usually 11 or more) in a cluster—more than in other groups. Fruits are also fairly small and often pear-shaped.

Narrow-leaved Peppermints

The narrow-leaved peppermints are very commonly distributed throughout the ranges and foothills of Victoria and NSW, with other forest species, especially stringy-barks, gums. They are small to tall trees (12–45 m), with persistent bark throughout, and *dull green fine-textured crowns.* Because of variation and hybridisation in the peppermint group, taxonomy has been difficult – the species below are those presently described, but intergrades occur.

BARK: Persistent to small branches, grey-brown, subfibrous but never stringy, finely fissured (± interlaced or trellis-like) or flaky.

LEAVES: Adult—Thin-textured, narrow-lanceolate, to 15 cm long, lateral veins at small angle to midrib, *strong peppermint smell if crushed.* New growth bright green.

Juvenile—*Opposite, sessile, narrower* (and commonly greener) than in *E. dives.*

BUDS: Small, club-shaped, *numerous in a cluster* (usually >11), in leaf-axils.

FRUIT: Small, pear-shaped, ± flat-topped.

[A] *E. radiata:* mainly around C Vic (and in E NSW); *no parts glaucous;* adult leaves dull or sub-glossy darkish-green, narrow (mostly < 20 mm wide); juvenile leaves narrow, *green;* buds with short caps.

[B] *E. robertsonii:* mainly on the inland side of the Main Divide in E Vic and NSW; adult and juvenile leaves narrow, *dull grey-green or glaucous;* buds *glaucous* with *longer conical caps.*

[C] *E. croajingolensis:* mainly south of Vic Divide, east of Mt Baw Baw; adult and juvenile leaves *broader,* dull grey green or glaucous; buds *glaucous* with *short caps.*

Eucalyptus radiata [A]
Eucalyptus robertsonii [B]
Eucalyptus croajingolensis [C]

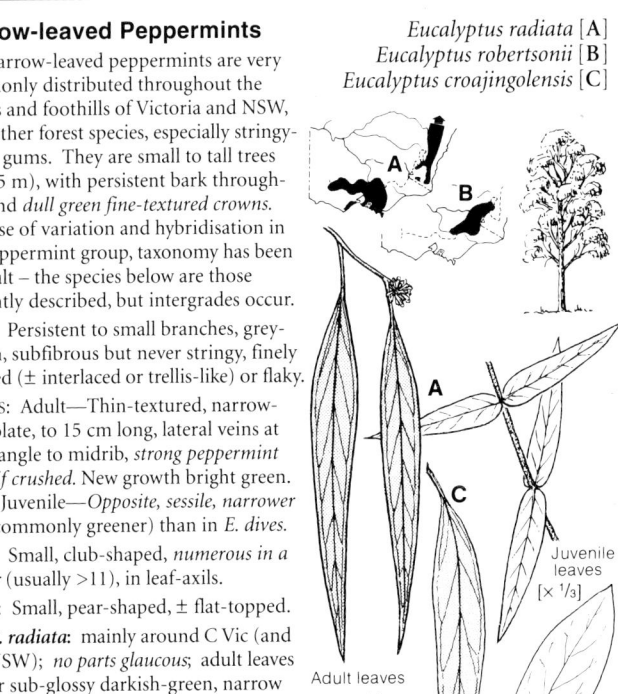

Juvenile leaves [× ¹/₃]

Adult leaves [× ¹/₃]

Buds [× 1]

Fruit [× 1]

Broad-leaved Peppermint

Eucalyptus dives

Small to medium-sized tree (8–30 m), commonly low-branching with rather large dull crown. Widespread and common *particularly in lower-rainfall hill country*. It tends to occur on drier shallower soils than Narrow-leaved Peppermint, with species such as Long-leaved Box, Red Box, Red Stringybark and Candlebark, and is more frequent on the inland side of the Divide.

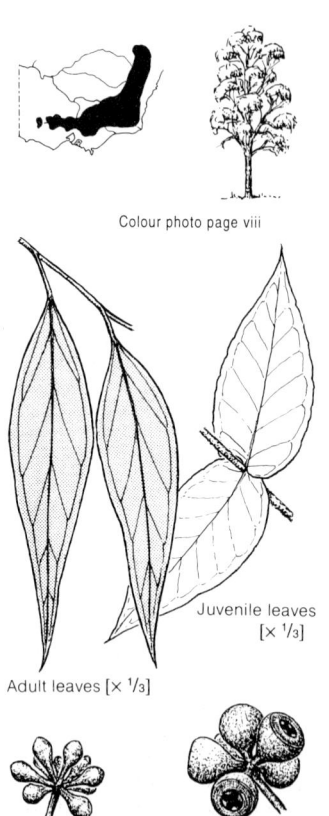

Colour photo page viii

BARK: Typical peppermint-type like Narrow-leaved Peppermint – grey-brown, subfibrous, often appearing finely inter-laced, persistent to small branches.

LEAVES: Adult—*Broad*-lanceolate, to 15 cm long, *usually more than 2 cm wide*, tapering to a fine point, dark greyish-green (but new adult leaves are bright green); *strong peppermint smell when crushed*.

　　Juvenile—Opposite, sessile, *broad-ovate to heart-shaped, greyish to glaucous* (compare Narrow-leaved Peppermints).

BUDS: Numerous (often > 11) in axillary clusters, club-shaped, with ± rounded caps, no scar at join. Flowers Sept–Oct.

FRUIT: Pear-shaped (generally slightly larger than in Narrow-leaved Peppermint) with flat or slightly raised broad disc; 3–4 valves at about rim level.

WOOD: As in Narrow-leaved Peppermint, the wood is light brown, hard, usually straight-grained, has gum veins, and tends to shrink. Not favoured as a construction timber; fair fuel (burns quickly).

COMMENTS: *'Dives'* means 'rich', probably referring to the abundance of oil in the leaves. Hybrids occur between the various peppermints, and also with some 'ashes'.

Juvenile leaves [× 1/3]

Adult leaves [× 1/3]

Buds [× 1]

Fruit [× 1]

Shining Peppermints

Eucalyptus willisii

Mainland 'shining peppermints' have had a confused taxonomic history. The currently accepted names are given here, but these may be revised to accommodate several populations with variations as below.

The group includes small trees (to 15 m), sometimes mallee-like; *upper trunk and branches smooth and pale*, persistent sub-fibrous bark only at base. Occurrences are on low-nutrient sandy soils, with other species such as Brown Stringybark, usually with heathy understorey. Presently subsp. *willisii* covers four near-coastal areas, and ssp. *falciformis* the Grampians population.

LEAVES: Adult—Lanceolate (size variable), *moderately thick, smooth and firm-textured*, green, lateral veins at small angle to midrib, strong peppermint smell when crushed.

Juvenile—Opposite, sessile, but varying as below.

BUDS: Clusters in axils with 11 or more club-shaped buds, cap rounded or conical.

FRUIT: Pear-shaped, like *E. dives*, with ± flat broad disc, 3–4 valves about rim level.

Differences in populations include–

[**a**] Wilsons Prom.: buds more numerous (>21); smaller fruit; heart-shaped juvenile leaves; affinities with *E. nitida* of Tasmania.

[**b**] Gippsland Lakes area: adult leaves shorter (to 12 cm) and narrower; juvenile leaves lanceolate, falcate, stem-clasping.

[**c**] W Vic–SA near-coastal areas: juvenile leaves opposite, sessile, broad-lanceolate, not curved or twisting.

[**d**] Grampians: juvenile leaves initially sessile, becoming falcate and twisting early.

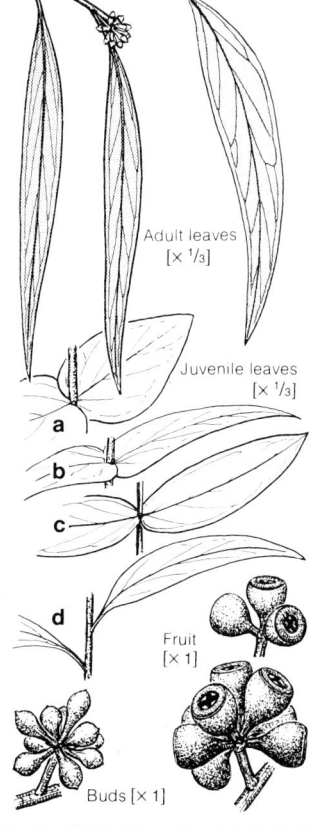

Adult leaves
[× 1/3]

Juvenile leaves
[× 1/3]

a

b

c

d

Fruit
[× 1]

Buds [× 1]

River Peppermint

Eucalyptus elata

Erect and often slender tree, medium-sized to tall (to 30 m or more), with *dark persistent bark on lower part of trunk, and smooth, pale and ribbony bark above*; foliage *fine*, sparse and *somewhat weeping*. Confined to gullies of smaller streams (sometimes ascending to gully heads with sheltered aspect) and margins of river flats, in East Gippsland and South Coast NSW. Prefers moist and fairly fertile alluvial loams. Associates with other species such as Manna Gum, Swamp Gum, Gully Gum.

BARK: Dark, compact and subfibrous on lower trunk; smooth, white (or grey or cream) and ribbony (gum-like) above.

LEAVES: Adult—*Narrow*-lanceolate, tapering at *both* ends, to 16 cm long and about 15 mm wide, green, lateral veins at small angle to midrib, strong peppermint smell when crushed.

Juvenile—Lanceolate, green, paler beneath, opposite, sessile on roughened glandular branchlets.

BUDS: *Very numerous* (15–30+) per cluster, slender club-shaped. Flowers Aug–Nov.

FRUIT: Somewhat *globular on slender pedicels, crowded in rounded clusters*, disc usually descending, valves enclosed.

WOOD: Light brown, fairly hard and strong, has gum veins, not durable; not favoured for construction.

COMMENTS: Can appear gum-like from a distance, and occurs with similar-looking Manna Gum, but easily distinguished by the narrow leaves with peppermint-type characters, and the very numerous buds and fruits per cluster. '*Elata*' means 'tall'.

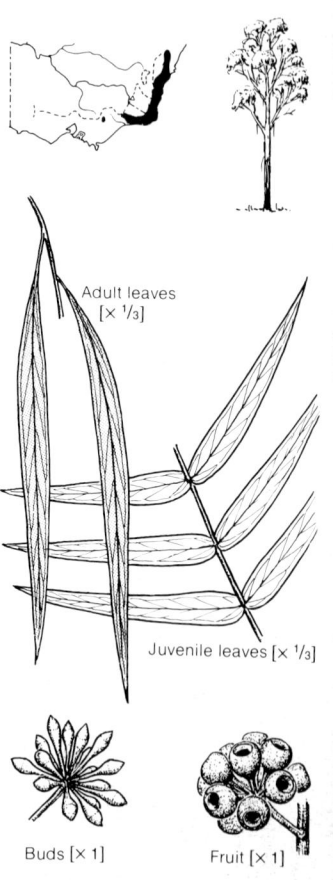

Adult leaves [× 1/3]

Juvenile leaves [× 1/3]

Buds [× 1]

Fruit [× 1]

ountain Ash (*E. regnans*) – bark subfibrous
lower trunk; smooth, pale and ribbony above

Ivertop Ash (*E. sieberi*) – grey hard fissured
ark on whole trunk; white limbs in small crown

The 'Half-barked Ashes' of tall forests

The whole 'ash' group of subgenus *Monocalyptus* is not easily defined for field recognition as it includes a wide range of bark types and growth forms—small smooth-barked trees or mallees (including 'sallees' such as Snow Gum, *E. pauciflora*), stringy-barked taller trees such as Messmate (*E. obliqua*), and **tall forest trees commonly named 'ash' which have persistent bark to various heights on the trunk, and smooth gum-like upper trunk or limbs** ('half-barks').

Only the last of these three types is covered in this section; the others have been included in the 'gum' and 'stringybark' sections respectively.

Juvenile leaves of ashes are mostly alternate, stalked, and flat with surfaces facing laterally; they are either shiny green or dull bluish. The adult leaves are usually curved and asymmetrical, often oblique, and have lateral veins at small angles to the midrib.

The name 'ash' originally came from a superficial resemblance of the wood to the unrelated European Ash. The wood of tall ashes is pale, strong, straight-grained and relatively open-textured; ashes provide most of the 'hardwood' used for building, wood-chipping and other purposes.

Mountain Ash

Eucalyptus regnans

Very tall straight tree, often over 50 m, known to have reached 100 m. The bark is *subfibrous on lower part of trunk, but smooth and ribbony above.* Occurs only in Victoria (and Tasmania), usually as tall-forest pure stands on deep moist soils in cool mountain valleys, mainly south of Divide between about 200 m and 1100 m altitude, where annual rainfall exceeds 1000 mm. Common in Dandenongs – Mt Torbreck – Walhalla area; localised in far east (e.g. Mt Elizabeth, S Goonmirk Ra), also in South Gippsland and Otways.

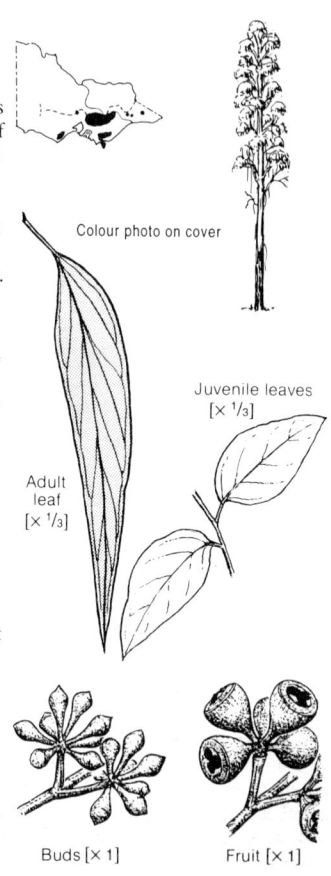

Colour photo on cover

BARK: Brown, subfibrous and persistent for lower 5–20 m; smooth, white or pale grey-green above, peeling in long ribbons.

LEAVES: Adult—Lanceolate–falcate, to 16 cm long, *slightly oblique at base*, glossy green, veins at small angle to midrib.

   Juvenile—Soon alternate and stalked, *glossy green*, broad-lanceolate, becoming particularly large and oblique at intermediate stage.

Juvenile leaves [× ⅓]

Adult leaf [× ⅓]

BUDS: Club-shaped, about 7–15 per cluster, *clusters often in pairs in axils.* Flowers January–April.

FRUIT: Conical to pear-shaped, disc about level, usually 3 valves close to rim-level. *Clusters often in pairs.*

WOOD: Pale brown, open-textured, straight-grained, fairly strong and hard. Valued for construction, veneer, packing, pulp and paper, etc., but not as poles.

COMMENTS: Notable as the tallest flowering plant and hardwood in the world ('*regnans*' means 'reigning'). Easily killed by fire, regenerating only from seed.

Buds [× 1]

Fruit [× 1]

Alpine Ash, Woollybutt (Vic)

Eucalyptus delegatensis

Usually a tall, fairly straight tree, to 50 m or more, *with lower 'half' of trunk fibrous-barked*, and fairly open crown. Common, often dominant, in montane tall forests (see page 8), especially on well-drained rocky slopes and in deep valleys of ranges, *mostly between 900 and 1450 m altitude*, from Mt Macedon east into NSW. Forms pure stands, or sometimes with others such as Mountain Gum or Shining Gum.

BARK: Grey to brown woolly-fibrous and fissured to about half the trunk height (hence sometimes called Woollybutt in Vic); smooth white or bluish-grey above, peeling in long strips, commonly showing 'scribbles' due to insect larvae.

LEAVES: Adult—Large, 12–20 cm long, *curved* (falcate) and sometimes oblique, firm-textured, green.

Juvenile—Soon becoming stalked and alternate, *broad, asymmetrical, blue-green or glaucous.*

BUDS: Club-shaped, 7–15 per cluster in axils, sometimes glaucous. Short rounded caps, no scar at join. Flowers Dec–March.

FRUIT: Barrel- or pear-shaped, shiny; disc flat or depressed, 3–5 enclosed valves.

WOOD: Pale, open-textured, straight-grained, light, easily worked. Uses are similar to Mountain Ash; poor fuel.

COMMENTS: Restricted to higher levels as seeds need the cold ground conditions produced by several weeks of snow to germinate. 'Alpine' not really appropriate as it means 'above the tree line'. Killed by severe fire, regenerating only from seed, giving conspicuously bluish new leaves.

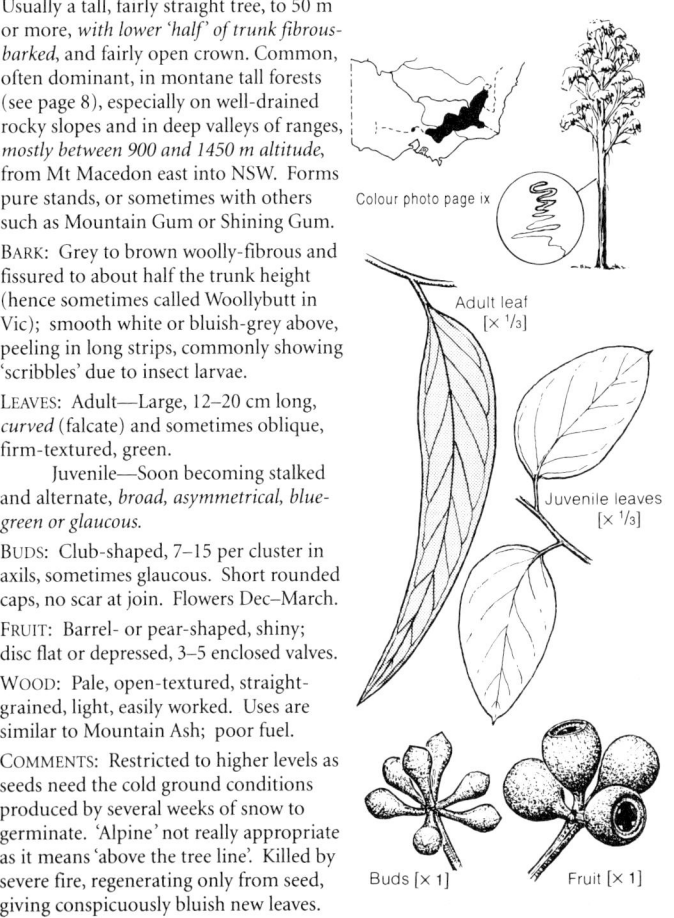

Colour photo page ix

Adult leaf
[× 1/3]

Juvenile leaves
[× 1/3]

Buds [× 1]

Fruit [× 1]

White Ash

Eucalyptus fraxinoides

Mostly medium-sized to tall (to 40 m), with *whitish bark except for a short basal stocking.* Restricted to the Coast Range of SE NSW, except for an isolated occurrence in the Howe Range in East Gippsland. Best development is on cool moist slopes from about 200 m to 800 m, associating with other tall species such as Mountain Grey Gum, Messmate and Brown Barrel; more stunted and bushy at higher exposed levels.

BARK: Dark grey or brownish, compact, subfibrous for lower few metres, only becoming fissured with age; most of the trunk is smooth, whitish, bark peeling in long strips; *'scribbles' often conspicuous.*

LEAVES: Adult—Lanceolate or falcate (curved), to 16 cm long, usually narrower than in other tall ashes, glossy green; new growth glossy red.

Juvenile—Soon stalked, alternate, ovate or lanceolate, *pale- or bluish-green.*

BUDS: 7–11 per cluster, club-shaped, sometimes finely warty; cap rounded to conical, no scar at join. Flowers Dec–Jan.

FRUIT: *Urn-shaped to almost globular with short 'neck'*; disc steeply descending, 4–5 enclosed valves.

WOOD: Similar in characteristics and uses to previous two ashes.

COMMENTS: Distinguishable from Alpine Ash (which also usually has 'scribbles') by shorter stocking of fibrous bark, different fruits. Several rare eucalypts occur in far SE NSW, including *E. spectatrix* (described 1991) which is related and similar, but of *mallee* form, occurring *only on peaks near Bega*, and having *green* juvenile leaves.

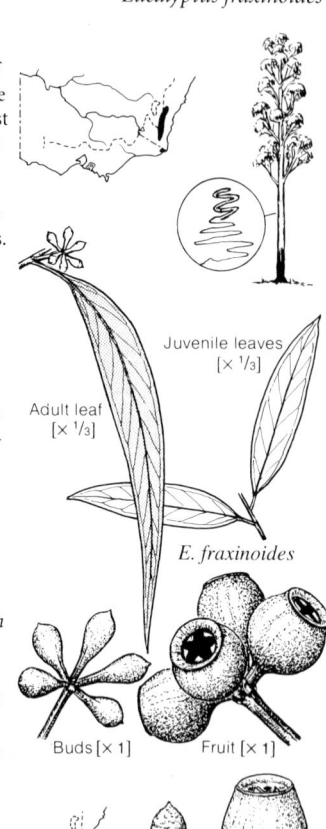

Juvenile leaves
[× 1/3]

Adult leaf
[× 1/3]

E. fraxinoides

Buds [× 1]

Fruit [× 1]

E. spectatrix

Silvertop Ash

Eucalyptus sieberi

Where best developed, as on the better soils in East Gippsland, a tall straight tree, 25–45 m, with *fissured hard dark bark on the whole trunk contrasting with smooth white branches in a relatively small crown.* On poorer sites (especially in NSW) it can be small. It occurs across eastern Victoria (from about Gembrook), chiefly south of the Divide, from coastal levels to hilltops and ridges, generally on well-drained drier soils over sedimentary rocks and granite; in pure stands, or with other species, especially stringybarks (see p. 25). An isolated occurrence in the Pyrete Range north-west of Melbourne.

BARK: Flaky grey and orange on young trees, becoming hard-fibrous, dark, thick, and deeply furrowed with age on whole trunk and base of large limbs (like iron-bark); limbs have smooth white bark.

LEAVES: Adult—Usually curved (falcate), fairly large (10–20 cm long), glossy green; prominent lateral veins at small angle to midrib. New growth crimson in summer.

Juvenile—Alternate, stalked, ovate, *grey-green*; branchlets often glaucous.

BUDS: Club-shaped, 7–15 per cluster in axils; peduncles slightly angular or flat-tened; caps rounded, no scar at join. Flowers August–December.

FRUIT: Conical or pear-shaped, tapering into pedicel; disc wide, reddish, flat or slightly raised or sunken; 3–4 valves almost to rim level.

WOOD: Characteristics and uses fairly similar to the other tall ashes. This is the main species used for woodchipping.

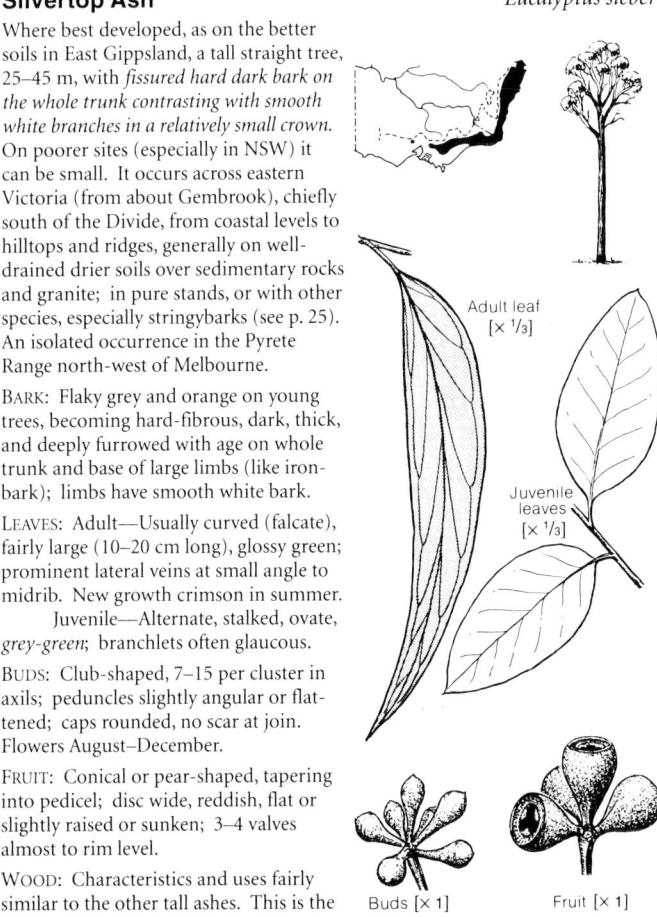

Adult leaf [× 1/3]

Juvenile leaves [× 1/3]

Buds [× 1]

Fruit [× 1]

101

Messmate (*E. obliqua*) – stringy-fibrous bark on whole tree; glossy broad curved leaves

Red Stringybark (*E. macrorhyncha*) – the commonest stringybark on drier shallow soils

The Stringybarks (and stringybarked Ashes)

The bark of most of the trees in this section is **thick and persistent over the whole trunk and large branches, tends to split in long fissures, and is long-fibred so that when torn away its distinctively 'stringy' character is apparent.** (The shorter-fibred barks, such as in the peppermints and boxes, tend to crumble when rubbed.)

The first three species (including the common Messmate) have closer botanical links with the ashes of the previous section, but they have been included here because as trees, they look like stringybarks.

The 'true' stringybarks with colour names 'red', 'yellow', 'brown', 'white' and 'blue' (for reasons which are *not* obvious!) all belong in a well-defined group. Their juvenile leaves are soon alternate and stalked; in early stages they have tiny hair tufts and are paler one side. **The adult leaves are usually rather thick and leathery, glossy dark green, relatively broad, curved, asymmetrical and often oblique.** The fruits tend to be globular in shape.

All species in this section are members of subgenus *Monocalyptus*. Stringybark timber is generally hard, strong and durable, and is valued for poles and general construction.

Messmate

Eucalyptus obliqua

In forests, a medium-sized to very tall tree, 15–60+ m. It has stringybark-type bark throughout, and usually a straight trunk and a fairly dense crown of glossy dark green leaves. *Common, widespread,* from near-coast to foothills and mountains (to about 1000 m), preferring better quality soils of moister areas, usually with other species, especially Narrow-leaved Peppermint, other stringybarks, and gums. May be stunted or mallee-like on harsher and sandy sites, especially near the coast and in western areas.

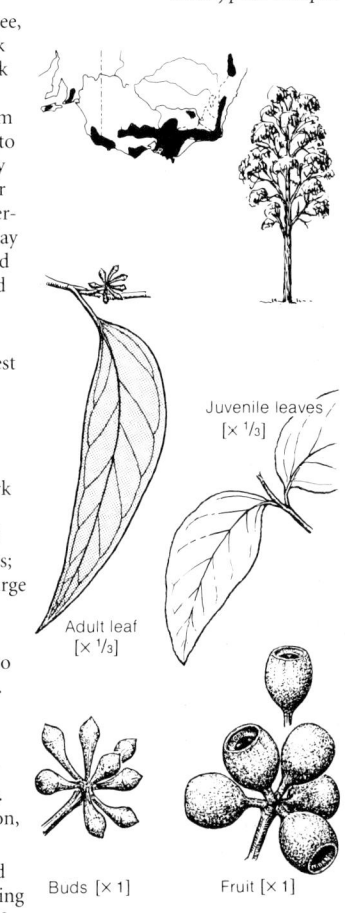

Juvenile leaves
[× ⅓]

Adult leaf
[× ⅓]

BARK: Can appear somewhat variable, but always fibrous and stringy to smallest branches; fissured to various degrees; brown, but greyish on the outside.

LEAVES: Adult—To 15 cm long, curved (falcate), asymmetrical and oblique at base (hence *'obliqua'*); thick, glossy dark green (concolorous), veins distinct.

Juvenile—Soon alternate, stalked and oblique, green, glossy, without hairs; intermediate leaves may become very large and oblique.

BUDS: 7–15 per cluster in axils; club-shaped, cap smooth with short point, no scar at join. Flowers December–March.

FRUIT: *Wine-glass shaped,* with short distinct pedicels; 3–4 valves enclosed.

WOOD: Brown, open-textured, usually straight-grained, fairly hard and strong. Used extensively for general construction, poles etc. Fair fuel.

COMMENT: The first eucalypt described (1788), collected from SE Tasmania during Cook's third voyage (1777) – see page 40.

Buds [× 1]

Fruit [× 1]

Brown Barrel, Cut-tail

Eucalyptus fastigata

Tall tree (to 50 m), fibrous-barked on trunk and large branches; often has a fairly large glossy green crown. In Victoria, confined to eastern forests near border; more common in NSW, particularly on the coastal escarpments (e.g. the Coast Range). Occurs chiefly in montane forests (at about 400–1200 m) with other species such as Alpine Ash, White Ash, Shining Gum, Messmate. Prefers loamy soils with moist but well-drained subsoil.

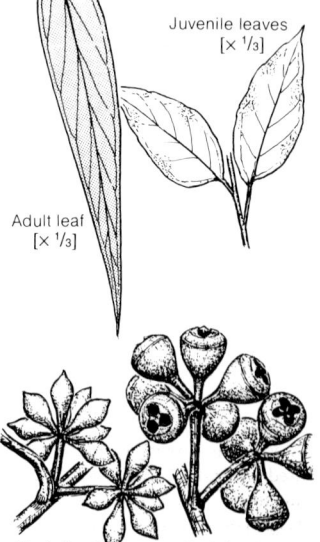

BARK: Brown, fibrous and stringy, sometimes rather coarsely furrowed, persistent to smaller branches (which are smooth with hanging ribbons).

LEAVES: Adult—Lanceolate, to 16 cm long, sometimes curved, usually oblique at base; veins at small angle to midrib.

Juvenile—Soon becoming alternate and broad-lanceolate or ovate, oblique, green, without hairs.

BUDS: Club-shaped, 7–15 per cluster, caps ± conical, no scar at join; *clusters often in pairs in leaf axils.* Flowers Dec–Feb.

FRUIT: *Rather like those of Mountain Ash* (p. 98), *but disc wider and often slightly ascending.* Valves usually 3, at about rim level. *Clusters often in pairs.*

WOOD: Pale, straight-grained, open-textured, fairly hard and strong, used for general construction, veneer, packing, etc.

COMMENT: Closely related to Mountain Ash (*E. regnans*), sharing similarities in leaves, buds, fruit, wood (note especially the pairing of bud clusters). The two are geographically separated; Brown Barrel can look like Messmate from a distance.

Juvenile leaves [× ⅓]

Adult leaf [× ⅓]

Buds [× 1]

Fruit [× 1]

Yertchuk, Prickly Stringybark

Eucalyptus consideniana

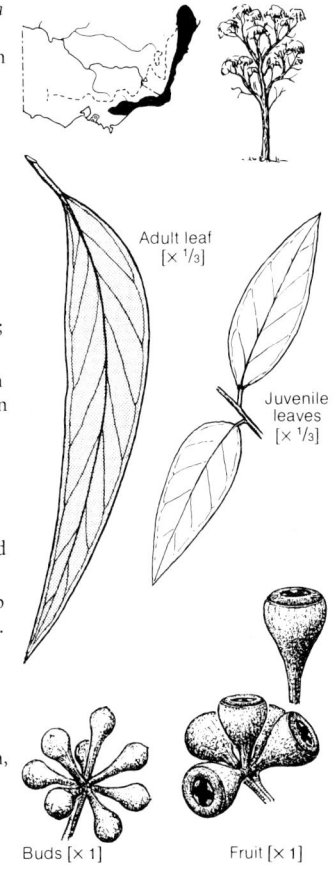

Medium-sized tree to 30 m, with fibrous bark to small branches (*can be quite like a peppermint*); erect, but usually of poor form with rather open, straggly, dull green crown. Occurs mainly on *poorer grey sandy soils of sedimentary origin*, in near-coastal lowlands of Gippsland and NSW, with various other species such as White and Brown Stringybarks, Silvertop Ash, Red Bloodwood; commonly with Saw Banksia and a heathy understorey.

BARK: Grey outside, yellowish-brown underneath, stiff-fibred but not thick, often with the trellis-like appearance of a peppermint, persistent to small branches; *prickly when lightly handled.*

LEAVES: Adult—Curved-lanceolate, often oblique, to 15 cm long, thick, glossy green or greyish-green both sides; lateral veins at small angle to midrib.

Juvenile—Soon alternate, short-stalked, often oblique, dull greyish- or bluish-green, slightly discolorous. Can become quite large (to 17 cm × 8 cm) and oblique in intermediate stage.

BUDS: Club-shaped, 9–15 per cluster, cap rounded with short point, no scar at join. Flowers November–December.

FRUIT: Pear-shaped, often tapering into the pedicel; disc reddish, wide, flat or convex; valves mostly 4, at rim level.

WOOD: Pale brown, of moderate strength, used for light construction, but not in quantity. Good fuel.

COMMENT: Closely related to Silvertop Ash with which it often occurs (note similarity in leaves buds, and fruits).

Adult leaf [× ⅓]

Juvenile leaves [× ⅓]

Buds [× 1]

Fruit [× 1]

Red Stringybark
Gippsland Stringybark

Eucalyptus macrorhyncha [A]
Eucalyptus mackintii [B]

[A] **Red Stringybark** (*E. macrorhyncha*) is small to medium-sized; straight trunk and compact crown in best form, but can be more straggly; *fibrous bark usually deeply fissured.* Common and widespread on *drier well-drained hill sites*, usually in mixture, e.g. with Red Box, Inland Scribbly Gum, Candlebark, Broad-leaved Peppermint.

Colour photo page ix

BARK: Long-fibred, red-brown inside, grey outside, persistent to small branches.

LEAVES: Adult—To 15 cm long, thick, sub-glossy, concolorous dark green, less oblique than in other stringybarks; sometimes on slender hanging branchlets.

Juvenile—Soon alternate, short-stalked, discolorous green, roughened with tiny hair tufts early, becoming glabrous.

BUDS: 7–11 per cluster, with *smooth tapering (beaked) conical caps* ('*macrorhyncha*' = 'big-beak'). Flowers Jan–March.

FRUIT: Top-shaped to sub-globular, *rim at widest part; broad domed disc*; usually *3 sharp valves strongly projecting.*

WOOD: Pale red-brown, moderately hard, strong and durable.

[B] **Gippsland Stringybark** (*E. mackintii*) was described as a new species in 1990. It is a typical stringybark, to 30 m, *known only from the foothills and plains of the Orbost–Bruthen area.* INTERMEDIATE and ADULT LEAVES larger than in above species, bluish-green. BUDS in clusters of 7–11, with conical caps. FRUIT on very short pedicels, rounded with broad flat or raised disc; valves at disc level or exserted.

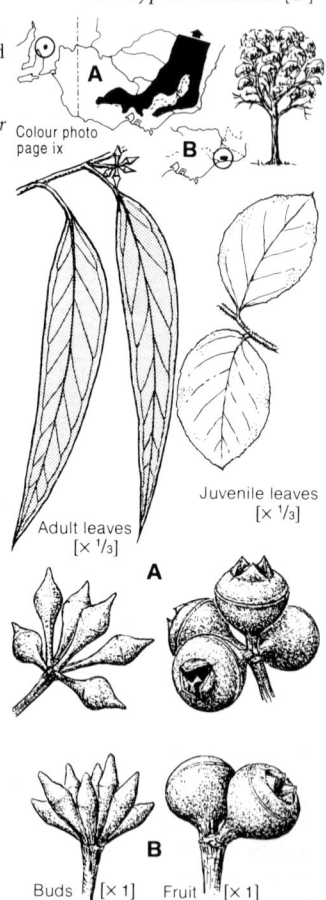

Adult leaves [× 1/3]

Juvenile leaves [× 1/3]

A

B

Buds [× 1]   Fruit [× 1]

Yellow Stringybark

Eucalyptus muelleriana

Medium-sized to tall forest tree, to 45 m, with straight trunk and well-developed crown; leaves often slightly greener than in other stringybarks, especially as new growth. Occurs particularly in sheltered positions from sea-level to about 600 m in foothill country, east from Wilsons Promontory. Best development on deeper clay loams. Rarely dominant, it associates mainly with other stringybarks, Silvertop Ash, Mountain Grey Gum.

BARK: Thick, rough, stringy, persistent to small branches, grey-brown (inner bark yellowish).

LEAVES: Adult—Asymmetrical lanceolate with oblique base, to 14 cm long; sub-glossy green, *slightly paler one side.*

Juvenile—Soon alternate, short stalked, ovate, green, strongly discolorous, roughened with tiny hair tufts in early stages, becoming glabrous.

BUDS: Clusters of 7–11, club-shaped with *smooth* rounded or conical caps. Flowers November–March.

FRUIT: Broad and almost globular, but truncated at top with flat or depressed narrow disc; usually 4 small valves at about rim level.

WOOD: Pale yellowish-brown, heavy, hard, strong and durable. Good for poles, stumps and heavy construction.

COMMENTS: Generally distinguishable from other stringybarks by greener foliage colour, slightly discolorous leaves, and fairly large truncated globular fruit. The specific name honours the pioneering botanist Ferdinand Mueller (see page 1).

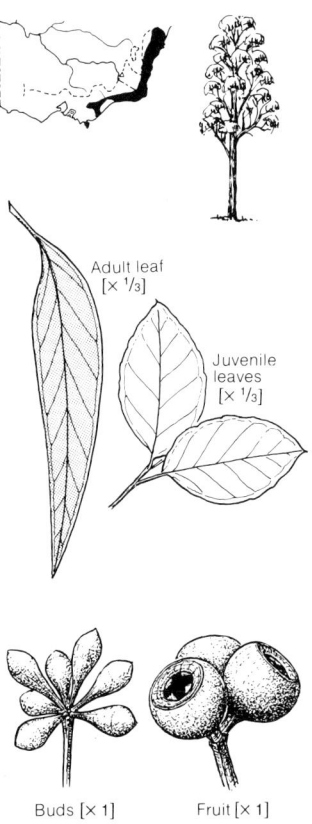

Adult leaf
[× 1/3]

Juvenile
leaves
[× 1/3]

Buds [× 1]

Fruit [× 1]

107

Brown Stringybarks

Eucalyptus baxteri [A]
Eucalyptus arenacea [B]

Variation within the 'brown stringybarks' of Vic–SA has long been recognised. In 1988, the form in the Vic 'Deserts'–SA was described as a separate species *E. arenacea*, narrowing the concept of *E. baxteri*.

[A] *E. baxteri* can be a tall tree (to 40 m) in east Vic forests, with (e.g.) Messmate, Silvertop Ash; smaller and sometimes the main species on poorer sandy soils (e.g. SW Vic), often with heathy understorey; quite stunted and shrubby, lacking fibrous bark, on harsh exposed sites such as on Grampians rocky outcrops or the coast (e.g. Wilsons Promontory). It occurs mainly in Vic, just entering the far S Coast of NSW, the far SE of SA (and also on Kangaroo Is).

BARK: Brown, thick, fibrous and stringy, furrowed, persistent to small branches.

LEAVES: Adult—Broad-lanceolate (*broad near apex*), oblique, *concolorous*, glossy green, thick on harsher exposed sites.

Juvenile—Ovate, discolorous, with hair tufts early, soon becoming glabrous.

BUDS: 7–15 per cluster, club-shaped on thick pedicels; *caps rough (warty)*, blunt.

FRUIT: Broad-rounded, smooth; *broad disc just ascending*; 4(5) slightly exserted valves.

[B] *E. arenacea* (**Mallee Stringybark**) differs from *E. baxteri* as follows: Mallee or small tree on sandy soils (hence '*arenacea*') further inland in W Vic (north Grampians, 'Desert' dunes) and the main form in SA; ADULT LEAVES narrower and more tapering to the apex; JUVENILE LEAVES narrower, becoming glabrous later in development; BUDS more slender, caps non-warty; FRUIT generally smaller and with flatter disc.

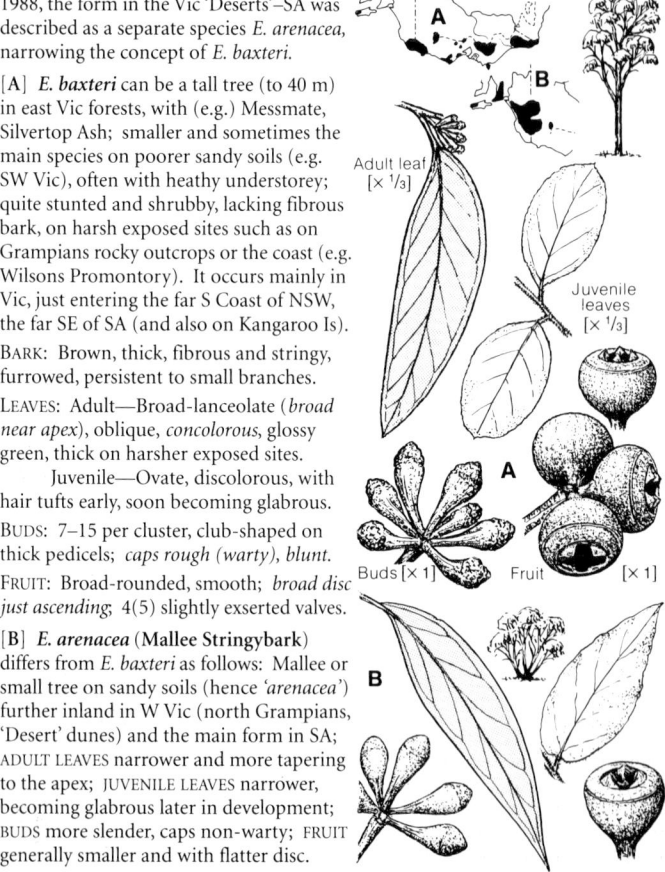

Adult leaf [× ⅓]

Juvenile leaves [× ⅓]

Buds [× 1]   Fruit   [× 1]

A

B

Grampians Gums

The small, often mallee-like trees endemic to the Grampians, and generally named Grampians Gum (previously as *E. alpina*), have long presented questions because of their variability and links with *E. baxteri*. In 1993, the following new species were described, replacing *E. alpina*. Adult leaf-bases are oblique, juvenile leaves of typical stringybark type, but *the bark of all three species is smooth on the upper trunk and limbs*. Hybridization with *E. baxteri* occurs.

[A] *E. victoriana* is a medium-sized tree (to 20 m) in the Mt Thackeray area of the Victoria Range. ADULT LEAVES thick, glossy dark green, *broad-lanceolate*, 2–3.5 cm wide. BUDS *sessile*, only the *cap* slightly warty, 7–11 per short-stalked cluster. FRUIT sessile, broad (to 13 mm across), squatter than in *E. baxteri*, disc broad, *level or only slightly ascending*, 4–5 slightly exserted valves.

[B] *E. serraensis* is a small tree or mallee of the Wonderland and north Serra Ranges. ADULT LEAVES thick, leathery, glossy green, generally *ovate* (blunt with small point), 3–5 cm wide. BUDS sessile, *warty all over*, 3–7 per cluster. FRUIT sessile, larger than [A] (to 18 mm across) with *steeply ascending broad disc*, 4–5 valves strongly exserted.

[C] *E. verrucosa* is a shrub or small tree in the south Serra Range (e.g. Mirranatwa Gap). ADULT LEAVES very thick, *ovate to almost round and often notched at apex*, to 9 cm wide. BUDS sessile, 10–14 mm long, warty all over, 1–3(–7) per cluster. FRUIT sessile, hemispherical, very warty, *large* (to 25 mm wide), disc broad, *level to slightly ascending*, often folded, 4–6 exserted valves.

Eucalyptus victoriana [A]
Eucalyptus serraensis [B]
Eucalyptus verruc[osa]* [C]

[*to be changed]

Adult leaves [× 1/3]

A

Buds [× 1]

B

C

Fruit [× 1]

White Stringybarks
Blue-leaved Stringybark

Eucalyptus globoidea and others [A]
Eucalyptus agglomerata [C]

[A] **White Stringybark** (*E. globoidea*) is a tree of moderate size, with *relatively small leaves*. Most common in eastern forests, from coast to foothills, in mixture with (e.g.) other stringybarks, Silvertop Ash; also in outer eastern Melbourne suburbs.

BARK: Thick, furrowed, long-fibred and stringy, grey outside, red-brown beneath.

LEAVES: Adult—*Smaller than in other stringybarks* (to 12 cm long), glossy green, *usually slightly paler one side*.

Juvenile—Ovate or heart-shaped, discolorous green, soon alternate, tiny hair tufts in early stages.

BUDS: 9–15 per cluster, *spindle-shaped with conical caps*, smaller than in other stringybarks. Flowers mostly March–June.

FRUIT: *Globular, often small, almost sessile*, sometimes crowded, disc ± level; 4 valves.

WOOD: Good quality for construction etc.

COMMENTS: Populations with variations (in buds, fruits and habitat, particularly in East Gippsland) suggest the likely description of new species. [B] **Thin-leaved Stringybark** (*E. eugenioides*), with longer, narrower adult leaves, and slightly larger buds and fruits, occurs north of the Towamba River in South Coast NSW.

[C] **Blue-leaved Stringybark** (*E. agglomerata*) is a forest tree of NSW near-coastal hill country, just entering far-east Gippsland. ADULT LEAVES are fairly large, *often with a bluish tinge*, especially as new growth; BUDS have conical caps; FRUIT flattened-globular, *crowded in clusters causing flattening of sides*.

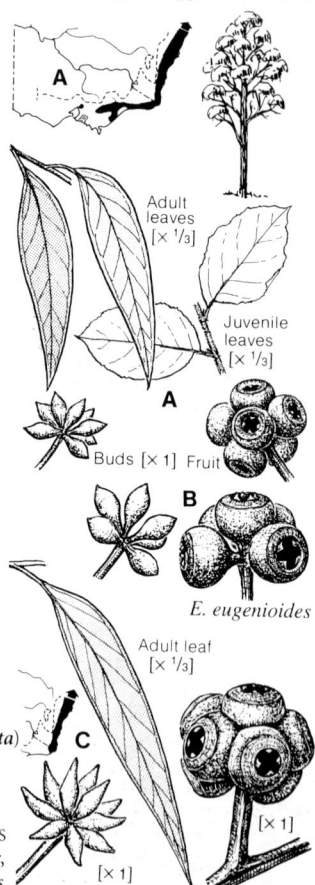

Adult leaves [× 1/3]

Juvenile leaves [× 1/3]

Buds [× 1] Fruit **A**

B

E. eugenioides

Adult leaf [× 1/3]

C

[× 1]

[× 1]

Some Rough-barked Eucalypts of Other Groups

Red Bloodwood (*E. gummifera*) – far-east area; bark tessellated; leaves paler green beneath

Mahogany (*E. botryoides*) – trunk bark spongy-fibrous, limbs smooth; leaves paler beneath

Woollybutt (*E. longifolia*) – south coast NSW; subfibrous bark flaking irregularly; long leaves

Red Ironbark (*E. tricarpa*, *E. sideroxylon*) – dry forests; bark grey-black, hard, deeply furrowed

Red Bloodwood

Usually a medium-sized tree, 15–30+ m, with irregularly twisting branches. It is common throughout near-coastal NSW, but only east of Cann River in Victoria. It occurs on flats and hills, on a range of soils, in mixture with various other species.

Colour photo page ix

BARK: *Tessellated*, as typical of the bloodwoods (most of which occur in northern Australia), grey-brown, short-fibred, persistent to small branches. A red gum substance (kino) from the wood often oozes at the surface (hence 'bloodwood', also '*gummifera*', meaning 'gum-bearing').

LEAVES: Adult—To 15 cm long; green, *paler and duller beneath*; veins fine and faint, *lateral veins close and numerous, at large angle to midrib.*

Juvenile—Similar to adult, but larger; early leaves with fine simple hairs.

BUDS: Fairly large, with rounded caps, clusters (of about 7) in *compound arrangement at ends of branchlets.* Flowers Jan–April, conspicuous at surface of crown.

FRUIT: Fairly large, urn-shape, *constricted into short neck*, valves deeply enclosed.

WOOD: Pink–red, heavy, strong, very durable for posts, sleepers etc., but gum veins make it unsuitable for sawing.

[B] Red-flowering Gum (*E. ficifolia*)— also a bloodwood (not a gum!)—is a WA species which is commonly planted in the east as a street or park tree with large densely-foliaged crown. Its leaves are similar to Red Bloodwood, its long-stalked buds produce brilliant scarlet flower-clusters, and its fruit are the very large 'gum-nuts' well known to children.

Adult leaves [× ⅓]

Juvenile leaf [× ⅓]

A

Buds [× 1]

Fruit [× 1]

B [× ⅔]

E. ficifolia

Southern Mahogany, Bangalay

Eucalyptus botryoides

A medium-sized to tall tree, 10–40 m, size and trunk length depending on site and forest density; usually well-shaped with ascending branches and a fairly large crown. The trunk has thick rough bark, but *limbs are smooth.* In Victoria, very common east of Bairnsdale, especially on alluvial or sandy soils and near gullies, at low altitudes, reaching right to the coastline. Extends northwards along NSW coast to Newcastle.

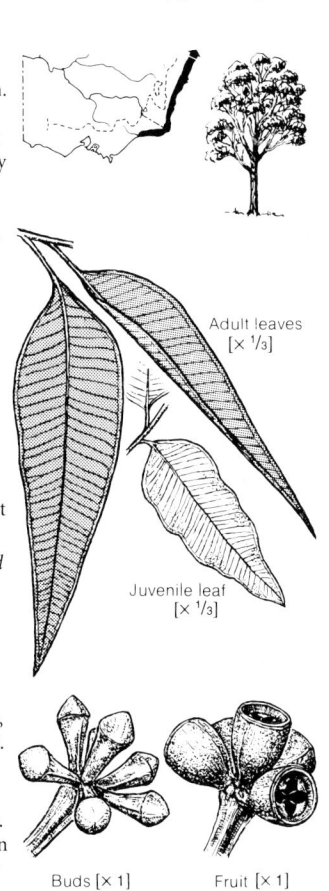

BARK: Thick, short-fibred, brown or greyish on trunk and sometimes largest branches, compact but soft, often fissured; the remainder of the branches are quite smooth and pale grey or pastel colours.

LEAVES: Adult—Broad-lanceolate, sometimes ± oblique at base, rather thick; *held with glossy darker green surface concave upwards, duller pale green beneath; many close lateral veins at large angle to midrib.*

Juvenile—Discolorous, like adult but more ovate, thinner, often wavy-edged.

Adult leaves [× 1/3]

Juvenile leaf [× 1/3]

BUDS: 7(–11) per cluster on *broad flattened peduncle;* 'tube' 2-ribbed; caps ± conical, with scar at join. Flowers January–March.

FRUIT: Cylindrical or cup-shaped, almost sessile, on *flattened peduncles;* valves (usually 4) below rim level.

WOOD: Red-brown, strong, hard, durable, suitable for general construction, poles etc.

COMMENTS: Formerly often planted in parks etc. as a fast-growing shady tree, especially near coast, but less popular now. The strongly discolorous leaf-type and vein pattern are characteristic of the mahogany group; this is the only member in Victoria, but several others occur in coastal NSW.

Buds [× 1]   Fruit [× 1]

113

Woollybutt (NSW)

Eucalyptus longifolia [A]

Medium-sized or fairly tall tree, 15–35 m, with greyish irregularly-cracked rough bark persistent to large branches; trunk straight, but branching habit irregular. *The rather distinctive vertically-hanging long curved leaves are grey-green, sometimes with mauvish hue.* Occurs in near-coastal NSW, mostly on heavier soils in shallow valleys and on low country, almost to border, but not recorded for Victoria.

BARK: Greyish, subfibrous on the whole trunk, but not thick, and tending to crack and flake irregularly.

LEAVES: Adult—To 22 cm long, dull greyish green, concolorous, veins regular and distinct, at fairly large angle to midrib.

Juvenile—Ovate, alternate, greyish-green, becoming broad-lanceolate and long in intermediate stage.

BUDS: *Hanging in threes on long stalks* in axils, fairly large with conical caps, scar present at join. Flowers Oct–Nov.

FRUIT: *Distinctively large and woody, usually in threes on long pedicels*; strong valves (usually 4) just below rim level.

WOOD: Red-brown, hard, strong and durable; used for construction, poles, etc.

COMMENT: Closely related to Cup Gum (*E. cosmophylla*) of SA (see page 72).

[B] **Blackbutt** (*E. pilularis*) is another tall tree of NSW near-coast forests, extending south to the Eden area. Related to peppermints/ stringybarks: BARK fibrous grey on trunk, smooth and pale above; ADULT LEAVES dark green; BUDS in clusters of 7–15 on flattened stalk; FRUIT broad, subglobular.

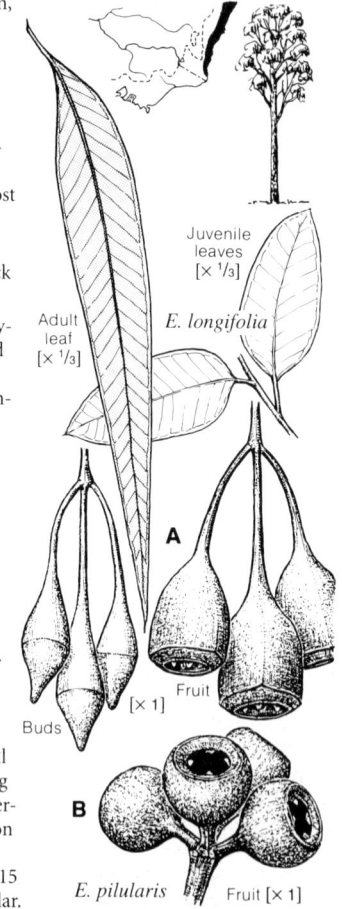

Juvenile leaves [× ⅓]

E. longifolia

Adult leaf [× ⅓]

A

Fruit [× 1]

Buds

E. pilularis   Fruit [× 1]

B

Red Ironbarks

Eucalyptus sideroxylon [A]
Eucalyptus tricarpa [B]

Previously two subspecies of *E. sideroxylon* were recognised, based on the number of buds per cluster (7 or 3). These have now been treated as distinct species, being also geographically separated. As trees they appear very similar, especially in their very distinctive deeply furrowed hard dark 'iron-bark'. Some intermediate forms occur.

[A] *E. sideroxylon* has its main distribution in NSW, chiefly in the Western Slopes areas, also in NE Vic, on dry hills or stony soils, with boxes, cypress-pines and others. Its foliage may be green or quite grey.

[B] *E. tricarpa*, with buds/fruit in 3s, is the principal species in Victoria, in several disjunct areas: the west-central quartzy 'goldfields' country, the Anglesea coastal area, the Brisbane Ras, NE of Melbourne, and east of Glenmaggie in Gippsland; also in near-coastal SE NSW. Foliage green.

BARK: *Hard, black, thick, deeply furrowed,* to small branches (which are white in [A]).

LEAVES: Adult—Lanceolate, to 15 cm long, dull green or sometimes conspicuously grey in [A]; veins fairly faint.

Juvenile—Alternate, grey or dull green, lanceolate–ovate, narrower in [A].

BUDS: Large, hanging on *long slender pedicels*; in *7s* in [A], *3s* in [B]. Caps conical, beaked, with no scar at join. Flowering time varies; high quality honey.

FRUIT: Distinctive – *barrel-shaped on long pedicels,* larger (9–15 mm diam.) in [B] compared with 5–9 mm in [A]; staminal ring often partly adheres over disc.

WOOD: Red, very hard (*'sidero-xylon'* means 'iron-wood'), strong, very durable.

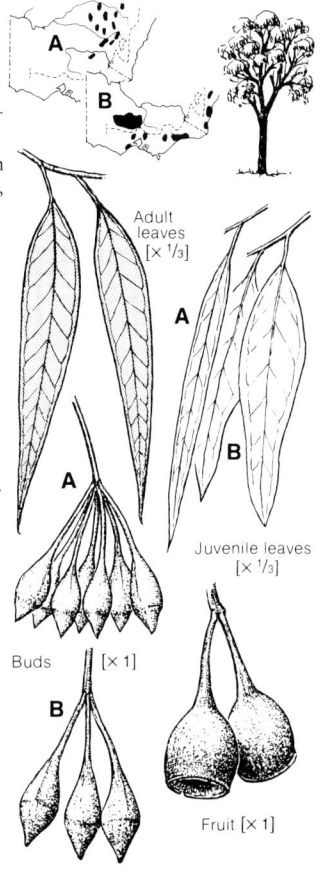

Adult leaves [× 1/3]

Juvenile leaves [× 1/3]

Buds [× 1]

Fruit [× 1]

The Dry-country Mallee Eucalypts

Although the species treated in this section are not all closely related, it is convenient to group them together for field recognition. They typically have the several stems and open umbrella-like crowns which characterise 'mallees', and their main Victorian occurrence is in the semi-arid north-west (also in a few 'outliers'), where survival requires special adaptations.

For most of the species, the Victorian Mallee area is the south-eastern limit of much wider distribution—some extend from WA through SA to west-central NSW as well as NW Victoria. Botanically, mallees fall into several groups, the last five species (pages 121–123) being related to the boxes. Variation and hybridisation are common in these groups.

Mallee scrub can appear superficially uniform, but closer observation will reveal associations of particular species and types of understorey, related largely to topography and soil type (see pages 3, 33). Substrate, as well as fire and clearing history, also influences size and form, even within one species. Thus some mallees can occur as single-trunked small trees; most have several stems arising from buds in the swollen rootstock (the lignotuber). 'Whipstick' is regrowth with particularly slender stems.

Several other 'mallee' species of mountain or near-coastal environments (e.g. *E. kybeanensis*, *E. diversifolia*, *E. kitsoniana*) are so described because of their growth habit, but these are treated in the 'gum' section.

Narrow-leaved Red Mallee (*E. leptophylla*)

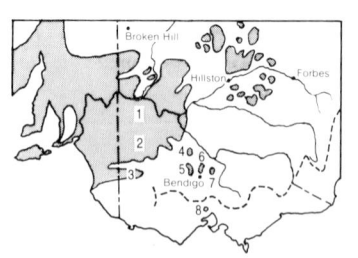

MALLEE AREAS IN SOUTH-EASTERN AUSTRALIA
Some Significant Victorian Areas

1	Sunset Country	5	Inglewood–Wedderburn areas
2	Big Desert	6	Bendigo–Kamarooka areas
3	Little Desert	7	North of Whroo
4	North of Boort	8	Djerriwarrh/Coimadai Creeks

Grey Mallee, Red Mallee

Eucalyptus socialis

Small–large mallee or small tree (to 10 m), with *dull greyish foliage.* Common in NW Vic and SA, often co-dominant (e.g. with *E. oleosa, E. gracilis*), mainly in taller mallee scrub on brown loamy sands of flatter areas (Murray Mallee); also in C NSW.

BARK: Smooth, pale ribbony, shed almost to ground level; dark and scaly at base.

LEAVES: Adult—*Dull grey-green* with faint venation; usually broader than in *E. oleosa*. Branchlets often reddish.

Juvenile—Opposite to alternate, elliptic or ovate, dull green.

BUDS: To 13 per cluster on ± flattened peduncles; caps *extended and pointed.*

FRUIT: Larger than in *E. oleosa;* 3–4 valves with *fragile needle-like extensions.*

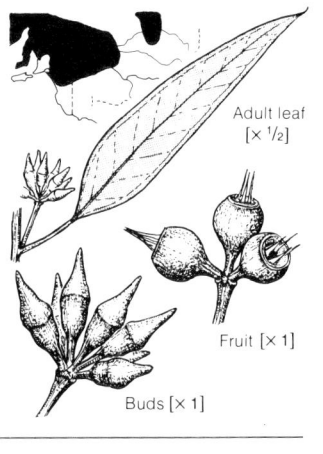

Adult leaf
[× ½]

Fruit [× 1]

Buds [× 1]

Oil Mallee, Red Mallee

Eucalyptus oleosa

Usually a taller mallee or small tree, 3–8 m, with *shiny green foliage.* Frequent in NW Vic–SA (to WA), with various other species (e.g. *E. gracilis*), chiefly on brown loamy soils of flatter areas in Murray Mallee; uncommon in SW NSW. Salt-tolerant.

BARK: Smooth, greyish on stems; rough, grey-brown, loosely persistent at base.

LEAVES: Adult—*Shiny green,* to 12 cm long, generally narrower than in closely related *E. socialis.* Branchlets often reddish.

Juvenile—*Narrow,* green.

BUDS: To 11 per cluster; caps *blunt,* giving resemblance to acorns in cups.

FRUIT: On distinct pedicels, ± globular with truncated tops, usually 3 valves with *fragile needle-like extensions.*

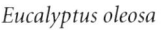

Adult
leaves
[× ½]

Buds [× 1]

Fruit [× 1]

Yorrell, White Mallee

Eucalyptus gracilis

Small–large mallee or small tree (to 10 m), with shiny green narrow leaves. Common, widespread (C NSW to WA); often co-dominant (e.g. with *E. socialis*, *E. oleosa*) especially in taller mallee on brown loamy soils (notably in flatter areas of Murray Mallee in NW Vic). Salt-tolerant.

BARK: Rough, persistent and dark at base, smooth and whitish (or coloured) above.

LEAVES: Adult—Narrow-lanceolate, shiny green, veins faint, gland-dots conspicuous.
Juvenile—Green, lanceolate.

BUDS: Club-shaped, to 7 per cluster; cap small, slightly narrower than 'tube' at join, rounded with tiny point.

FRUIT: *Thin-walled*, barrel-shaped to sub-cylindrical; valves enclosed.

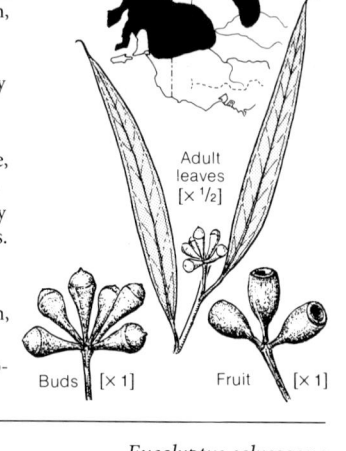

Adult leaves [× 1/2]

Buds [× 1]   Fruit [× 1]

Square-fruited Mallee

Eucalyptus calycogona

Generally a small mallee (occasionally a small tree) with glossy green (or yellowish) foliage. Frequent in NW Vic–SA (only just entering NSW), in both Murray and Lowan Mallee, but particularly on heavier reddish loams of flats or depressions, where some-times dominant, with sparse understorey.

BARK: Smooth, pale, peeling in ribbons or strips almost to ground level.

LEAVES: Adult—Narrow-lanceolate, shiny green, veins faint, gland-dots conspicuous.
Juvenile—Lanceolate, duller green.

BUDS: To 7 per cluster; *'tube' with about 4 ridges*, cap rounded to conical or beaked.

FRUIT: Somewhat urn-shaped, *with ridges giving a ± square cross-section* ('calyco-gona' means 'calyx-tube angled').

Adult leaves [× 1/2]

Buds [× 1]   Fruit [× 1]

118

Narrow-leaved Red Mallee

Eucalyptus leptophylla
(formerly as *E. foecunda*)

Small to medium-sized mallee (rarely small tree), leaves *small, narrow, and shiny green*; branchlets and buds seasonally *vivid red*. In various mallee types, but most common with *E. costata* and *E. dumosa* on deeper pale sands of 'Deserts' (Lowan Mallee).

BARK: Smooth almost to ground level, pale grey or reddish, shed in ribbons.

LEAVES: Adult—Small and narrow ('*lepto-phylla*' means 'slender leaves'), shiny green, venation obscure, gland-dots obvious.

    Juvenile—Ovate, greyish.

BUDS: In abundant clusters of 7–13 near ends of branchlets; ovoid, often reddish; cap usually about same size as 'tube'.

FRUIT: *Small*, with thick flattened rim; fragile valve-points just project.

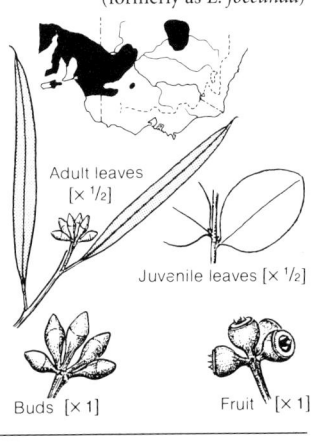

Adult leaves [× 1/2]

Juvenile leaves [× 1/2]

Buds [× 1]

Fruit [× 1]

Dumosa Mallee

Eucalyptus dumosa

Small to medium-sized mallee (rarely small tree); common and widespread in various mallee formations, most frequently with *E. socialis*, *E. calycogona*, *E. leptophylla* and *E. costata* in Murray and Lowan Mallee.

BARK: Rough and grey-brown at base, but shed in strips above leaving smooth pale-coloured stems.

LEAVES: Adult—Lanceolate, thick, dull or glossy green, venation faint.

    Juvenile—Ovate, greyish-green.

BUDS: Fairly broad, sometimes just striated or ribbed, to 7 per cluster, on stout angular peduncles; caps conical, often reddish.

FRUIT: Cup-shaped on short pedicels, often slightly ribbed; valves (usually 4) at about rim level.

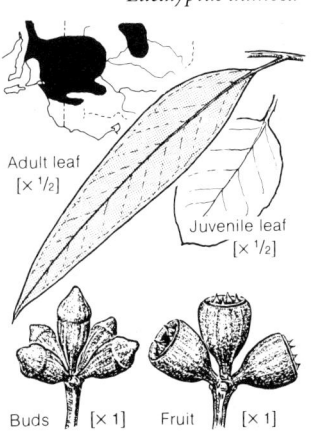

Adult leaf [× 1/2]

Juvenile leaf [× 1/2]

Buds [× 1]

Fruit [× 1]

Blue-leaved Mallee

Eucalyptus cyanophylla

Mallee, to 6 m, *with distinctly bluish foliage*; distribution apparently restricted to the Murray Mallee of far north-west Vic–SA, and an area between Wentworth and Broken Hill in NSW, on red-brown sandy loams. Closely related to *E. dumosa*.

BARK: Shed in strips from stems leaving smooth grey or brownish surface; rough, grey-brown and fibrous at base.

LEAVES: Adult—*Broad*-lanceolate, thick, *blue-grey to glaucous* (hence *'cyano-phylla'*).
　　　Juvenile—Ovate, bluish-green.

BUDS: Distinctly *ribbed*; to 7 per cluster on thick slightly flattened peduncles.

FRUIT: Somewhat cup-shaped, *coarsely wrinkled or ribbed*; thick rim; 4–5 pointed valves at about rim level.

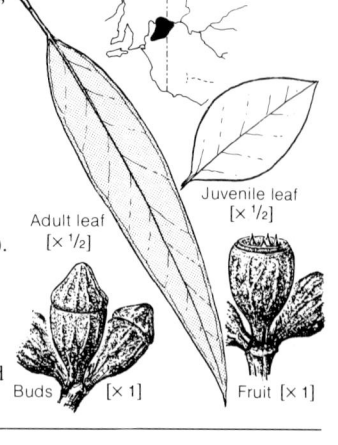

Adult leaf [× ½]

Juvenile leaf [× ½]

Buds [× 1]

Fruit [× 1]

Kangaroo Island Mallee

Eucalyptus anceps [A]

Mallee to 6 m. Mainly in 'Deserts'; chiefly in SA (to WA), scattered in W Vic (where previously referred to other species).

BARK: Smooth, grey, peeling in strips.

LEAVES: Adult—Lanceolate, glossy green.
　　　Juvenile—Elliptic-ovate, light green.

BUDS: Almost sessile, in clusters of about 7 on angular peduncles; ± slightly ribbed.

FRUIT: Sessile, fairly small, ± cup-shaped, ± ribbed, 3–4 valves at about rim level.

Note: Other mallees with *eastern limits in the Murray R area of SA* include *E. rugosa* [B] with grey-green leaves and strongly ribbed buds and fruit, and closely related *E. brachycalyx* [C] with narrower bright green leaves, small ± ribbed buds/fruit (the fragile projecting fruit-valves ± turned outwards).

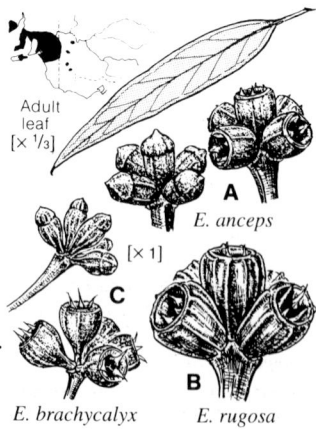

Adult leaf [× ⅓]

A

E. anceps

[× 1]

C

E. brachycalyx

B

E. rugosa

Yellow Mallee, Ridge-fruited Mallee

Eucalyptus costata [A]
(formerly as *E. incrassata*)

Usually a smaller mallee, with fairly large, leathery, shiny green leaves. Common, often co-dominant, e.g. with *E. dumosa*, *E. leptophylla*, chiefly in 'Deserts' (Lowan Mallee), on deeper pale sands of dunes; also in far SW NSW and SE SA. [Closely related **E. angulosa**, with broader leaves, and larger ribbed buds and fruit [**B**], occurs in the lower Murray area of SA.]

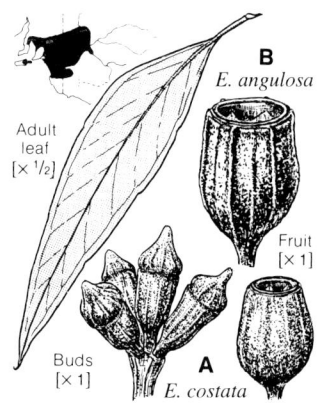

B
E. angulosa

Adult leaf
[× ½]

Fruit
[× 1]

Buds
[× 1]

A
E. costata

BARK: Smooth, greyish, peeling in strips or ribbons on whole of stems.

LEAVES: Adult—Lanceolate, glossy green, thick, venation faint.
  Juvenile—Elliptic-ovate, light green.

BUDS: In clusters of 3–7, ± ribbed, conical cap with 'beak' of varying length.

FRUIT: Thick-walled, smooth to ribbed.

Bull Mallee

Eucalyptus behriana

Mallee (often large), closely related to boxes, with *dark box-type bark* and *broad shiny green leaves*. Scattered across central–west Vic, also in C NSW and SE SA, often in localised pure stands, near Grey Box in particular; an interesting occurrence (with some understorey species normally found in inland mallee) in the dry Long Forest–Djerriwarrh Ck area west of Melbourne.

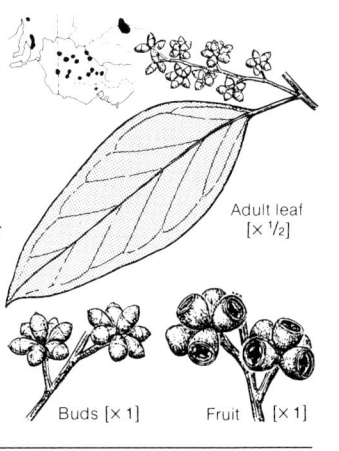

Adult leaf
[× ½]

Buds [× 1]   Fruit   [× 1]

BARK: Dark, rough, persistent on much of stems; smooth, grey-green, ribbony above.

LEAVES: Adult—*Shiny dark green, ovate.*
  Juvenile—Ovate, bluish-green.

BUDS: Small, ± sessile, 3–7 per cluster *in compound terminal 'panicles'.*

FRUIT: Small, cup-shaped, ± sessile, shiny brown; valves (usually 4) just enclosed.

Green Mallee

Mallee or small tree (to 10 m), with box-type lower bark, and *narrow dark green leaves*. Scattered occurrences, mainly in C NSW, but also in several isolated areas in NC Vic (e.g. Wedderburn area, Bendigo Whipstick), with boxes, ironbarks, mallees.

BARK: Dark, persistent and scaly sub-fibrous at base of stems; smooth greyish and ribbony above.

LEAVES: Adult—*Narrow, shiny dark green*, lateral veins not visible, but oil gland dots numerous and obvious; tips often hooked.
　　　Juvenile—Narrow, lustrous green.

BUDS: Mostly to 7(9) per cluster, usually in axils; not ribbed; caps conical, smooth.

FRUIT: Small, cup-shaped, pedicels short but distinct; tiny valves below rim level.

Eucalyptus viridis

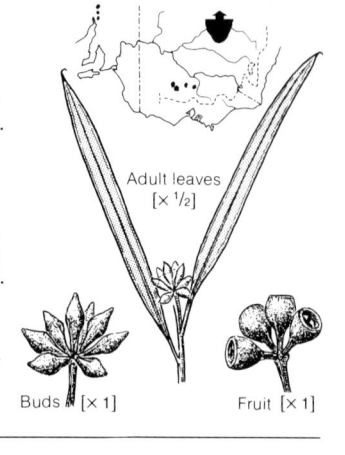

Adult leaves [× ½]

Buds [× 1]　　　Fruit [× 1]

Blue Mallee

Mallee (or small tree), with *greyish* foliage. In several disjunct occurrences in NC Vic (usually with Green Mallee), notably near Inglewood, in Bendigo Whipstick and near Wedderburn; also in Wyalong district of C NSW. Still used for oil distillation.

BARK: Rough, persistent box-type on lower parts of stems; smooth, pale greyish and ribbony above.

LEAVES: Adult—Narrow-lanceolate, *dull grey-green or bluish*; venation faint. New growth strongly bluish-grey.
　　　Juvenile—Narrow, grey or bluish.

BUDS: Small, often glaucous, in clusters of 7–11; caps rounded or conical.

FRUIT: Small, on short pedicels, valves below level of thin rim.

Eucalyptus polybractea

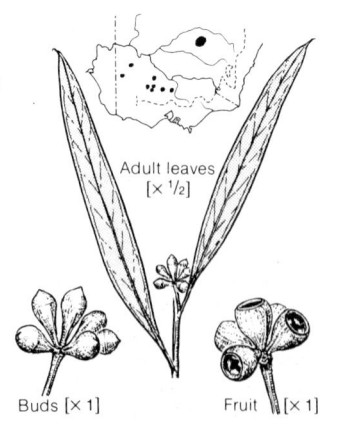

Adult leaves [× ½]

Buds [× 1]　　　Fruit [× 1]

Kamarooka Mallee

Eucalyptus froggattii

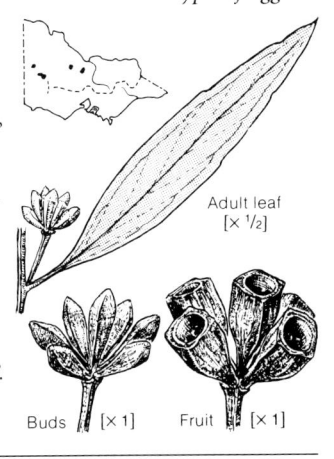

Mallee or small tree (to 9 m), with grey box-type bark on lower trunk or stems, and glossy green foliage. Endemic to Victoria, with a few isolated occurrences: e.g. Kamarooka (N of Bendigo Whipstick), NW of Charlton, W of Horsham.

BARK: Grey, scaly subfibrous to varying heights; smooth, pale green-brown above.

LEAVES: Adult—Lanceolate, thick and firm, shiny green, lateral veins hardly visible, intramarginal vein well spaced from edge. Branchlets angular in section.

　　　Juvenile—Lanceolate, green.

BUDS: *Square in section with 4 bold ribs*; clusters of 7–11 often in terminal 'panicles'.

FRUIT: In coarse clusters; *distinctively square in section*; rim thick; valves deep.

Adult leaf
[× ½]

Buds [× 1]　　　Fruit [× 1]

Wimmera Mallee-box

Eucalyptus wimmerensis

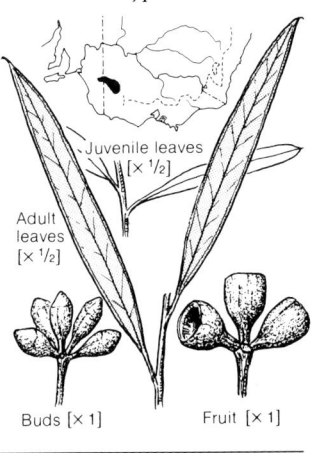

Mallee to 5 m or more (*never a tree*), apparently restricted to several Wimmera areas marginal to the Little Desert (incl. Mt Arapiles), and near Bordertown (SA). The species was described in 1990, there having been confusion with *E. odorata* (p. 91) and *E. viridis*; these, together with *E. porosa*, *E. silvestris*, *E. polybractea* and *E. froggattii* are closely related as 'mallee-boxes'.

BARK: *Smooth grey-brown almost to base.*

LEAVES: Adult—Narrow, lanceolate to oblong, *olive- to blue-green, semi-lustrous*.

　　　Juvenile—Narrow, greyish-green.

BUDS: Small, to 7(11) per cluster, on short slightly angled pedicels; caps blunt-conical.

FRUIT: Cup-shaped or ± cylindrical, tapering to short pedicels; valves enclosed.

Juvenile leaves
[× ½]

Adult leaves
[× ½]

Buds [× 1]　　　Fruit [× 1]

THE TEA-TREES (Genus *Leptospermum*)

There are about seventeen *Leptospermum* species in Victoria, but most of these are shrubs, and even the eight species described here only reach the size of small trees under particular habitat conditions. For example, Woolly Tea-tree (*L. lanigerum*) is usually a shrub in moist coastal heaths, but in wet sheltered gullies it can exceed 6 m as an erect slender tree.

Genus *Leptospermum* is included in the myrtle family Myrtaceae (together with *Eucalyptus*, *Melaleuca* and others). Leaves of its member species are small, simple, and always alternate on the stems when adult. Unlike *Eucalyptus* and *Melaleuca*, the flowers of *Leptospermum* species have petals which are conspicuous—these are five in number, rounded, and usually white (occasionally shades of pink). Within these is a ring of short stamens. The flower-base (hypanthium)—here termed a 'cup'— may be hairy or glabrous. The flowers usually appear to be solitary in leaf axils, and when fertilised develop into irregularly scattered fruit capsules. These capsules may be non-woody and fall before the next season, or woody and persistent. They open in slits on top to release copious seeds.

In all there are about 80 *Leptospermum* species, mostly Australian. The name 'tea-tree' (not 'ti-tree') originated from Captain Cook's use of the only species in New Zealand (*L. scoparium*) to brew a tea.

Coast Tea-tree (*Leptospermum laevigatum*)

Leaves, flowers and fruit of Coast Tea-tree

Coast Tea-tree

Leptospermum laevigatum

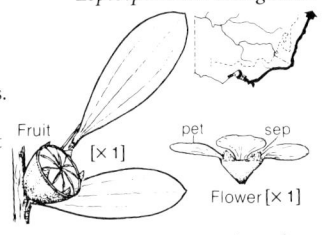

Fruit [× 1]

Flower [× 1]

Grey-green shrub to small tree, 2–8 m; stems rigid, fissured as if with 'strands'; bark flaking in thin pale strips. *Common on coastal sands*, Port Phillip area eastwards. LEAVES to 3 cm long, stiff, flat, glabrous, *dull grey-green*. FLOWERS (Sept–Nov) about 20 mm across, petals white, 'cup' without hairs. FRUIT (soon falling) non-woody, flat-topped, 6–11 cells, sepals persisting.

Paperbark Tea-tree

Leptospermum trinervium
(formerly *L. attenuatum*)

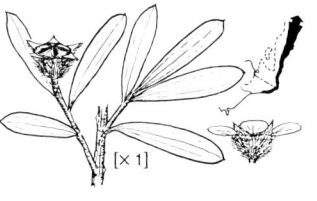

[× 1]

Rigid shrub to stout-trunked small tree (to 5 m) with pale flaky-papery bark. In East Gippsland–NSW, mostly on sands and sandstones near coast. LEAVES to 2 cm long, flat, becoming glabrous, dull green. FLOWERS (Sept–Nov) to 15 mm across, petals white, 'cup' *densely hairy*. FRUIT (soon falling) non-woody, slightly domed with 5 cells, hairs and sepals persisting.

Slender Tea-tree

Leptospermum brevipes

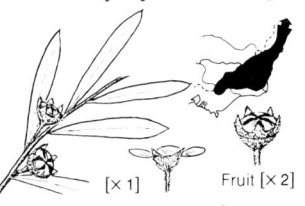

[× 1]　Fruit [× 2]

Tall shrub (to 4 m) with *slender reddish drooping branchlets*; bark close and firm. Mostly near streams at lower elevations. LEAVES becoming glabrous, green, ± flat, to 25 mm long. FLOWERS (Oct–Jan) to 10 mm across, petals white, 'cup' *silky-hairy*, pedicel slender. FRUIT (soon falling) small, non-woody, rounded top, 5 cells.

River Tea-tree

Leptospermum obovatum

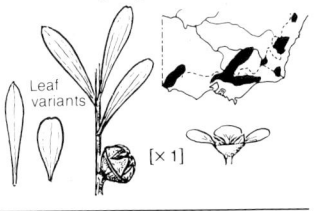

Leaf variants

[× 1]

Tall shrub (to 4 m) with close firm bark. Frequent *by streams*, especially in lowland rocky terrain. LEAVES to 15 mm, broadest towards the tip (blunt, often indented), glabrous green both sides. FLOWERS (Nov–Dec) to 12 mm across, petals creamy, 'cup' shallow and hairless. FRUIT persisting, woody, glabrous, rounded top, 5 cells.

Prickly Tea-tree

Stiff, variable shrub (to small tree of 4 m), usually erect; *pale flaky bark. Common and very widespread*, especially on poorly drained soils. LEAVES *sharp-pointed, stiff, concave above, broadest towards base, usually < 3 mm wide*, ± glabrous green. FLOWERS (Oct–Mar) 8–15 mm across, petals white, 'cup' usually hairless. FRUIT persistent, often abundant, woody, domed, 5 cells.

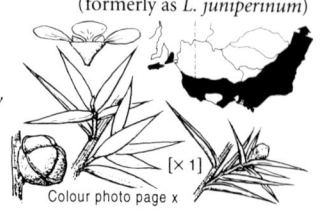

Leptospermum continentale (formerly as *L. juniperinum*)

[× 1]

Colour photo page x

Manuka

Rigid variable shrub (rarely a small tree). Main occurrences are in NZ and Tas; on mainland, only in Grampians, E Otways, E Gippsland–NSW, especially on rocky/ sandy sites near water. Generally similar to *L. continentale*—differences include: BARK closer and firmer; LEAVES *usually broader* (especially *near middle*) and some- times flatter; FRUIT sometimes larger.

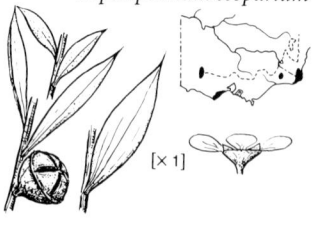

Leptospermum scoparium

[× 1]

Woolly Tea-tree

Dense shrub to erect small tree, 2–6 m; *bark compact, corky.* Widespread in *moist*, often sheltered places. LEAVES 6–15 mm × 2–5 mm, *contracting abruptly near tip*, edges turned down, *underside silvery hairy.* FLOWERS (Sept–Dec) 10–16 mm across, petals white, 'cup' *woolly.* FRUIT persistent, woody, often with hairs, 5 cells.

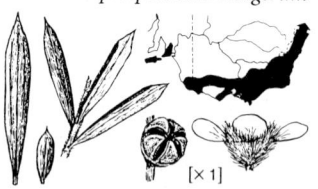

Leptospermum lanigerum

[× 1]

Mountain Tea-tree

Dense shrub, sometimes small rounded tree to 6 m; *bark flaking in thin pale strips. Mostly by cool watercourses in mountains.* LEAVES 10–35 mm × 4–10 mm, not thick, usually shiny green above and with *silvery hairs beneath.* FLOWERS 15–18 mm across, petals white, 'cup' *woolly.* FRUIT persistent, woody, often with hairs, 5 cells.

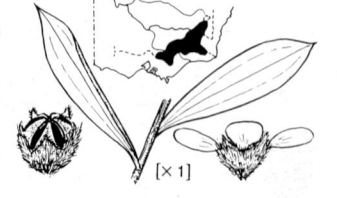

Leptospermum grandifolium

[× 1]

126

THE PAPERBARKS or HONEY-MYRTLES
(Genus *Melaleuca*)

From a distance, members of the genus *Melaleuca* can resemble tea-trees (*Leptospermum*)—they are in fact closely related in family Myrtaceae. Victoria has thirteen indigenous *Melaleuca* species; only about five reach small tree size, but the others described here can become large shrubs.

Some *Melaleuca* species are characterised by the papery bark which gives them the common name; others have a more compact corky bark.

The leaves of most *Melaleuca* species are small, narrow, and gland-dotted. For field identification it is useful to note whether the leaves are alternate on the branchlet, as for the species on page 128, or opposite and decussate (successive pairs at right-angles) as for three on page 129.

The *Melaleuca* inflorescence is distinctive—individual flowers are clustered spike- or head-like near the ends of branchlets, usually forming small soft 'bottlebrushes'. It is the stamens of the flowers which compose the 'brush'—they are up to 8 mm long and arise in five 'bundles' on each flower; the petals and sepals at their base are small and inconspicuous.

Once fertilised, each flower becomes a sessile woody capsule, so that each season's fruits, if persistent, may often be found closely clustered around the branchlet at intervals along progressively older wood.

Leaves, flowers and fruit of Swamp Paperbark

Swamp Paperbark (*Melaleuca ericifolia*)

Swamp Paperbark

Erect shrub to small tree, 2–9 m, with *pale papery bark.* Common, E Vic–NSW, often as dense scrub (esp. with Swamp Gum) *on poorly-drained soils and swampy areas,* mostly at lower elevations. LEAVES alternate (around stems), 8–15 mm long, narrow, dark green, tips bluntish. FLOWERS (Oct–Nov) creamy, in *short* 'brushes' (to 2 cm × 1.5 cm). CAPSULES in short tight clusters.

Melaleuca ericifolia

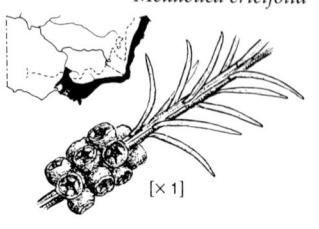
[× 1]

Melaleuca parvistaminea (meaning 'small stamens') was described in 1986 to include shrubs (rarely large) in east Vic and South Coast NSW, resembling Swamp Paperbark, but with scattered occurrences on *rockier* sites, often near streams. Other differences include more *fibrous-corky* bark, shorter leaves, longer *narrower* flower 'brushes', smaller capsules in longer clusters.

Melaleuca parvistaminea

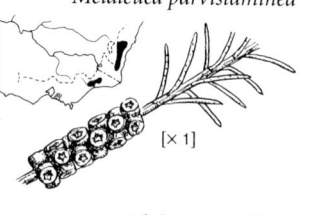
[× 1]

Giant Honey-myrtle

Large shrub or tree, 2–14 m, with *fissured firm greyish bark.* The largest *Melaleuca* of the area, occurring naturally in coastal E Gippsland–NSW, also off Wilsons Prom.; commonly planted, often along freeways. LEAVES crowded, alternate, 12–25 mm long, with *curved acute tips.* FLOWERS (Nov–Jan) usually creamy, in long 'brushes' (to 7 cm × 2.5 cm). CAPSULES in long tight clusters.

Melaleuca armillaris

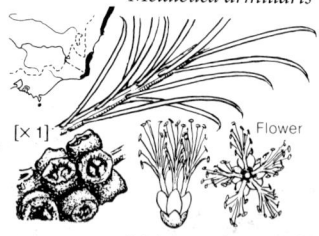
[× 1] Flower

Moonah

Dull dark-green bushy shrub or tree, 1–8 m; bark pale grey, finely fissured (not papery). Common on sandy, often *calcareous* (limy) soils, *near coast west of Western Port, and in mallee scrub.* LEAVES dark green, alternate, close, ± curving back, 5–12 mm × 1–3 mm. FLOWERS (*Feb–Apr*) in short cream 'brushes'. CAPSULES *ovoid with small opening.*

Melaleuca lanceolata

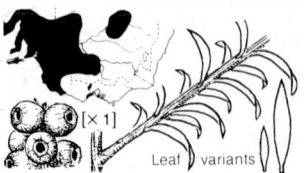
[× 1] Leaf variants

Broombush, Broom Honey-myrtle

Broom-like erect shrub, sometimes tall and mallee-like, 1–5 m. Common in NW Vic *especially in mallee scrubs on sands in 'Deserts'*. LEAVES alternate, ± *needle-like with bent tips* (but not rigid), 2–5 cm long, often brownish-green. FLOWERS (sum) in almost globular terminal clusters with pale yellow filaments. CAPSULES small, *fused into globular woody clusters* to 1 cm long.

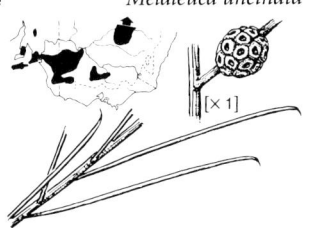

Melaleuca uncinata

[× 1]

Totem-poles

Shrub, often large, 1–4 m. Locally frequent on sands, rocky areas and near streams in C–W Vic to SA (e.g. Bendigo Whipstick, Grampians westward). LEAVES *opposite (decussate)*, bluish-green, concave above, to 15 mm long. FLOWERS (Nov–Feb) in short *pink-mauve* 'brushes'. CAPSULES *becoming embedded in thickened woody stem.*

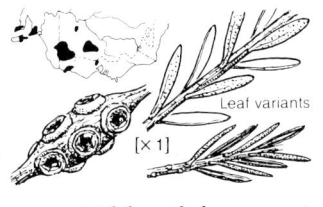

Melaleuca decussata

Leaf variants

[× 1]

Salt Paperbark

Shrub or small tree, 3–8 m; *pale papery bark.* Chiefly on brackish or muddy *saline* sites, near SA coast to *inland salt lakes in W Vic.* LEAVES *opposite (decussate)*, small (3–8 mm × 1 mm), blunt, dull green, on frequently dividing branchlets. FLOWERS (Oct–Dec) in *short* terminal whitish heads. CAPSULES cup-shaped, *very few per cluster.*

Melaleuca halmaturorum

[× 1]

Scented Paperbark

Erect shrub (or small tree to 8 m in some sheltered gullies); bark papery or corky. Often forming dense scrub (with ferns) on *dark peaty sands near swamps and sluggish stream-courses in hills*, south of Divide. LEAVES *opposite (decussate, i.e. 4-ranked)*, broad, stiff, dark green. FLOWERS (Oct–Mar) in cream-yellow terminal 'brushes' 2–4 cm long. CAPSULES with wavy orifice.

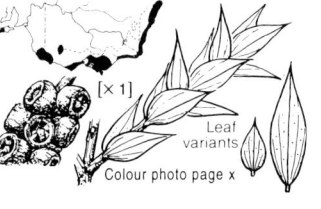

Melaleuca squarrosa

[× 1]

Leaf variants

Colour photo page x

THE WATTLES (Genus *Acacia*)

With some 950 recognised species in Australia, *Acacia* is our largest plant genus. Victoria has close to a hundred naturally occurring species, but only about a third of these are large enough to be included in this book.

Unlike *Eucalyptus*, many *Acacia* species are native to other countries around the world (especially Africa); it was from an Egyptian species that the genus was named in 1754. However, almost all the species with phyllode-type foliage are Australian in origin.

Attempts have been made in the past to subdivide the genus, but the groups most commonly used for field identification are informal ones based on foliage characters and inflorescence structure, as in this book.

Foliage

The first leaves of all wattle seedlings are a pair of compound (pinnate) leaves. For some species, *bipinnate* ('feathery') leaves develop and persist as true leaves on the adult plant; species in this group (pages 132–134) can be differentiated by checking the colour, number of pairs and size of the *pinnae* (the first leaf division) and their tiny leaflets (*pinnules*), as well as the positions of the *glands* on the central leaf axis (the *rachis*).

In the majority of our species, however, the leaf axis is soon modified (usually laterally flattened), so that on the mature plant, the adult foliage consists entirely of modified leaf-stalks which are termed *phyllodes* (see pages 135–147). Phyllodes take many forms, and may be differentiated by their colour, shape and size, by the number and pattern of veins, and by the position of a gland on the top margin (see illustrations opposite).

In a few species (e.g. *A. rubida*, *A. melanoxylon*), the transition from bipinnate leaves to phyllodes can persist on shrub-sized young plants.

Inflorescence

The tiny individual flowers of all wattles are very similar in structure, producing the numerous long soft stamens which give wattle blossom its characteristic cream to golden colours. However, the way the flowers make up an inflorescence gives rise to several different forms, identifiable even in the bud stage well before flowering. Species with their flowers in elongated cylindrical *spikes* form a definite group (pages 135–137). The others which have buds in tight round *heads* produce soft 'globules' of blossom. These heads occur either on simple stalks (*peduncles*) in the axils, or in an extended structure, as in most Victorian tree species. Time of flowering and colour of blossom can be useful for identification.

Pods and seeds

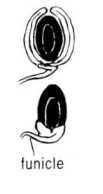

All wattles form pods, a characteristic common to genera in the family Mimosaceae (this is now commonly considered a subfamily Mimosoideae of family Fabaceae). Differences in pods can be helpful for identification. The seed attachment stalk (*funicle*) is one such diagnostic feature: in Blackwood, for example, this is red and doubly encircles the seed, whereas in Lightwood, it is white and folded at the seed base.

funicle

KEY TO GROUPS FOR FIELD IDENTIFICATION

Adult foliage always *bipinnate* ('feathery')		Page 132
Adult foliage as *phyllodes* (simple 'leaves')	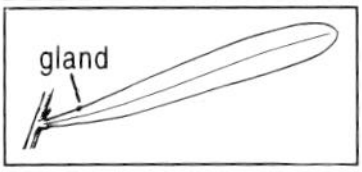	Page 135
Flowers in *cylindrical spikes*		Page 135
Flowers in *globular heads*	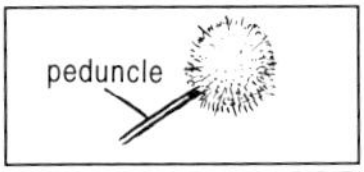	Page 138
Phyllodes with *one* main vein	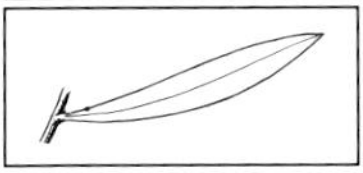	Page 138
Phyllodes with *more than one* main vein	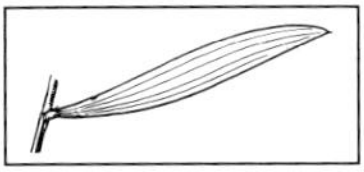	Page 143

Black Wattle

Acacia mearnsii

Dark green small tree, 5–15 m; dark bark often exuding gum. Common, widespread, in open forests and cleared areas, especially on drier shallow soils, coast to hills.

FOLIAGE: Leaves bipinnate, young shoots *yellowish*; 9–20 pairs of pinnae, each with 20–60 pairs of *short* leaflets (< 3 mm long) which *usually touch; shiny dark green above*, paler beneath; glands large and small, *irregularly spaced along the central stalk*.

FLOWERS (*Oct–Dec*): *Pale primrose yellow*; heads in extended compound inflorescence.

PODS: 6–15 cm long, ± straight, becoming dark; *constrictions between seeds*.

A. decurrens, a NSW species naturalised in places in Vic, has longer, well-separated green leaflets, earlier bright yellow flowers.

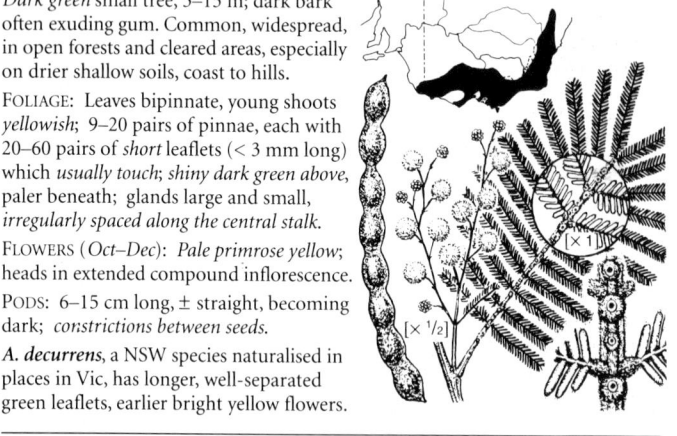

Silver Wattle

Acacia dealbata

Varies greatly from a weak shrub on poor soils, to fairly tall tree (to 25 m) in middle storey of mountain forests on deeper soils in valleys; bark often blotched pale greyish; foliage *grey-green*; young branchlets often *silvery*. Widespread from Grampians eastward (with Red Gum along inland rivers). Dense stands can develop after bushfire.

FOLIAGE: Bipinnate leaves *grey-green*, with sparse minute hairs; 10–24 pairs of pinnae, each with 20–45 pairs of leaflets 2–5 mm long, only just separated; glands on central stalk, *one at the base of each pair of pinnae*.

FLOWERS (*July–October*): *Bright yellow*; heads in extended compound inflorescence.

PODS: *Almost straight-edged*, fairly flat, light purplish-brown, 6–10 cm long.

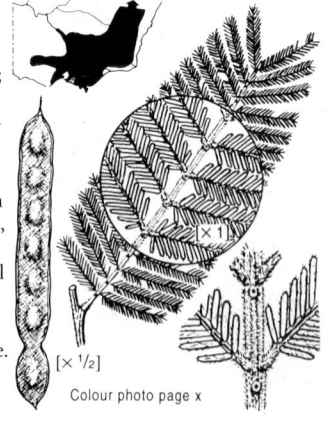

Colour photo page x

132

Dwarf Silver Wattle

Acacia nanodealbata

Straggly or bushy greyish-green shrub to small tree, 2–8 m, resembling *A. dealbata* ('*nano*' means 'dwarf'). Endemic in Vic, in central highland areas (e.g. Daylesford area, Mt Macedon area, Mt St Leonard, Warburton), also Otways.

FOLIAGE: Leaves bipinnate, greyish-green, virtually glabrous, *smaller* than in Silver Wattle; 10–20 pairs of close pinnae, each < 2 cm long, with 14–30 pairs of *short* leaflets (< 2 mm long) usually touching or overlapping; glands on central stalk, one at base of each pair of pinnae.

FLOWERS (Aug–Oct): Bright yellow; heads in extended compound inflorescence.

PODS: Almost straight, fairly flat, *wider* than in *A. dealbata* (to 6 cm × 2 cm).

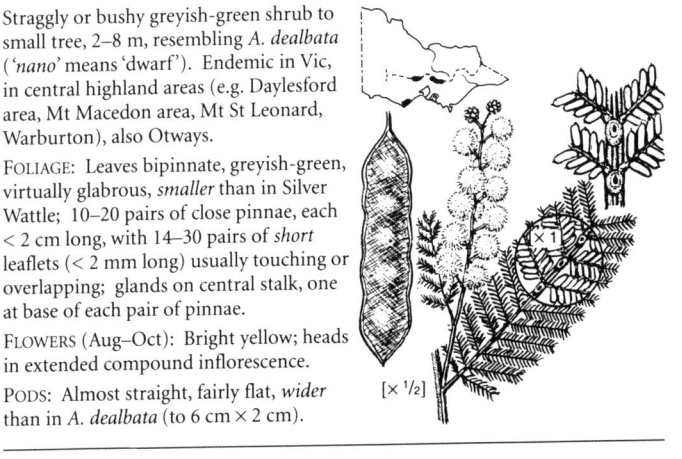

Cootamundra Wattle

Acacia baileyana

Bluish-grey large spreading shrub or small tree, 3–7 m, with smooth bark. Original natural occurrence only in West Wyalong–Cootamundra area of NSW, but now very widely planted and commonly naturalised elsewhere, including Victoria.

FOLIAGE: *Short blue-grey* bipinnate leaves, mostly with *only 3–4 pairs of pinnae* about 1.5–3 cm long, the lowest pair shorter and embracing the stem; pinnae with 12–24 pairs of narrow leaflets 4–9 mm long; a gland at base of each pair of pinnae.

FLOWERS (June–Sept): Bright yellow; heads in long slender inflorescence *extending well beyond leaves*, giving showy winter blossom.

PODS: Fairly straight and flat, to 10 cm long; brown, sometimes purplish.

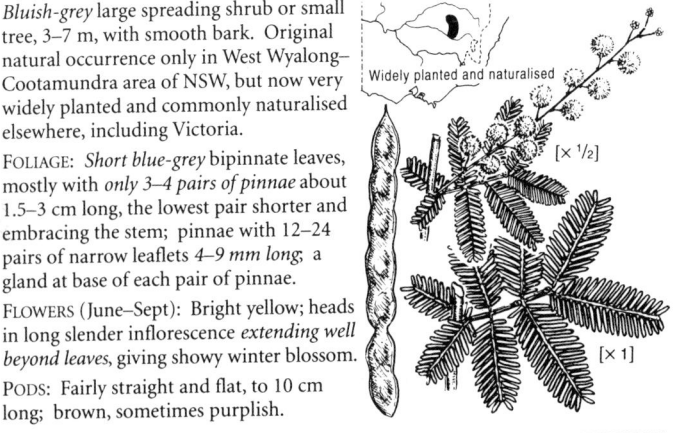

Widely planted and naturalised

Green Wattle, Deane's Wattle

Acacia deanei

Shrub or small tree, 2–9 m, foliage green (young shoots yellowish); bark smooth, grey-brown. Two subspecies recognised: [a] ssp. *deanei* mainly in C NSW; [b] ssp. *paucijuga* in Vic (e.g. Kooyoora SP area, Terricks, NE Vic, U Snowy R) and NSW, commonly in box–gum–pine woodlands.

FOLIAGE: Bipinnate leaves *green, < 10 cm long*, with relatively *few* (4–10) pairs of pinnae 2–5 cm long, each with 15–30 pairs of leaflets which are *4–11 mm* long in [b] compared with *2–4 mm* in [a]; gland at base of each pair of pinnae, others between mainly in [b].

FLOWERS (various times): Usually pale yellow; heads in extended inflorescence.

PODS: Darker and more constricted in [b].

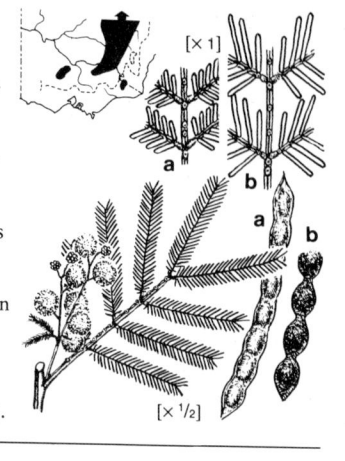

Red Wattle

Acacia silvestris

Erect tree, 7–30 m, with greyish to mid-green foliage, and ± smooth blotchy-grey bark. In Victoria, confined to *E Gippsland* (e.g. Tambo and U Snowy R areas), more abundant in ranges of NSW S Coast (e.g. Bodalla area); in dry forests, mostly on sandy or rocky sites. Regenerates to form dense stands after fire.

FOLIAGE: Bipinnate leaves with hairs; 6–18 pairs of pinnae 3–9 cm long, each with 30–40 pairs of *relatively large* leaflets (to 9 mm × 2 mm) which are broadest towards base; gland at base of each pair of pinnae and 1–3 between.

FLOWERS (July–Sept): Bright yellow; heads in extended compound inflorescence.

PODS: Fairly straight, ± flat, 6–15 cm long.

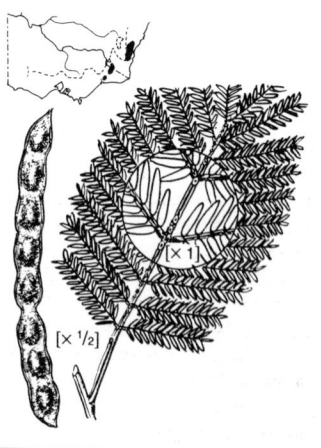

Sallow Wattle
Coast Wattle

Acacia longifolia [A]
Acacia sophorae [B]

These closely related wattles tend to inter-grade, and have been considered varieties of *A. longifolia*, but are now regarded as separate species. [A] *A. longifolia* is usually a small green tree (to 8 m), with natural occurrence in *forests* of eastern Vic–NSW. [B] *A. sophorae* is a dense spreading shrub (to 3 m) of *coastal dunes* throughout area. Intermediates are common, and tend to invade disturbed areas, becoming weeds.

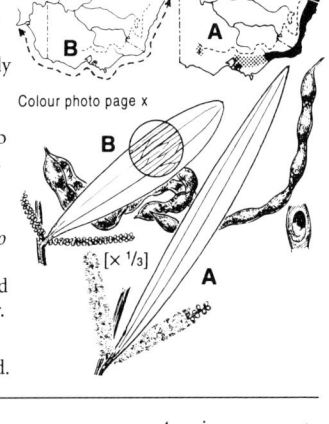

Colour photo page x

FOLIAGE: Flat green phyllodes, *spreading to erect* on stiff branches, 2(–4) main veins, gland near base. [A] longer (to 20 cm) and more pointed; [B] thicker, shorter, blunter.

FLOWERS (July–Oct): Yellow, in *spikes*.

PODS: Pale brown, often becoming twisted.

Narrow-leaved Wattle

Acacia mucronata

Large green shrub, rarely small tree, 2–8 m; bark usually smooth, greyish. Common in scrubby understoreys of forests (especially messmate stringybark), coast to ranges, mostly on and south of Vic Divide (–far SE NSW), on moderately moist soils. Can hybridize with other spike-flowered species.

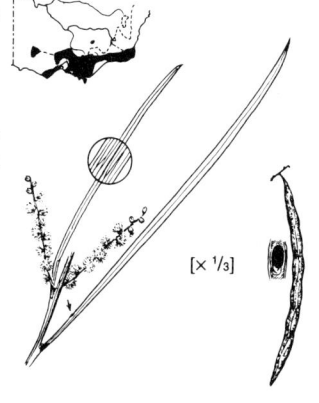

FOLIAGE: Phyllodes variable, bright to dark green, usually *long, narrow, fairly straight and spreading to erect,* sometimes bent at gland, 4–20 cm × 2–10 mm, few ± parallel raised veins, central one often stronger.

FLOWERS (Aug–Oct): Yellow, in *spikes* 2–5 cm long, *the axis visible between well-separated flowers.*

PODS: Straight or curved, 4–10 cm long, narrow, rough, light brown.

135

Spike Wattle

Acacia oxycedrus

Most commonly a stiff prickly shrub in heaths, but sometimes a small tree (to 8 m) in forests, usually on sandy soils. Can hybridize with species on previous page.

FOLIAGE: *Rigid* flat green phyllodes 2–4 cm long, slightly curved, *tapering to very sharp point*, 3–4 raised veins.

FLOWERS (July–Oct): Yellow, *crowded on axis* in *cylindrical spikes* to 3 cm long.

PODS: Sub-cylindrical, brown, to 10 cm.

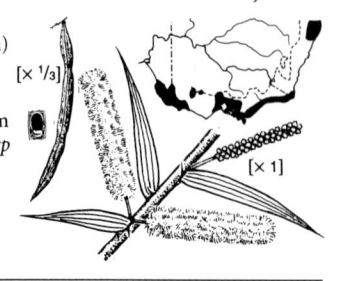

[× ¹⁄₃]

[× 1]

Prickly Moses

Acacia verticillata

Commonly a small prickly shrub in heaths, but sometimes a small light understorey tree (to 5 m) in foothill forests, favouring moister sandy sites; mostly in southern Vic.

FOLIAGE: Green phyllodes *mostly in whorls of about 6*, often *needle-like* (or flattened) with sharp point, 8–25 mm × 1–2(–5) mm.

FLOWERS (July–Oct): Bright yellow, in soft *ovoid* or cylindrical *spikes* 1–2 cm long.

PODS: Flat, almost straight, 2–7 cm long.

[× 1]

[× ¹⁄₃]

Phyllode variation

White Sallow Wattle

Acacia floribunda

Shapely dense shrub or small tree, 3–8 m, foliage green. Frequent in forests of East Gippsland and coastal NSW, mostly along rivers. Very commonly planted elsewhere.

FOLIAGE: Phyllodes crowded, *narrow, straight* (or slightly curved), 6–15 cm × 2–10 mm, green, sometimes with minute silvery hairs, numerous faint fine veins.

FLOWERS (Aug–Oct): *Pale* lemon yellow, in abundant *long loose spikes* of 3–6 cm.

PODS: Very narrow, thin-walled, 6–12 cm.

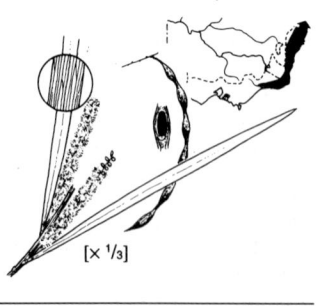

[× ¹⁄₃]

Currawang, Spearwood

Acacia doratoxylon

Tall shrub to small open tree, 3–8 m, with *dark olive-green foliage*, and *grey to brown fibrous bark*. In Vic, only in north-east (e.g. Beechworth area) and U Snowy R valley; much more extensive in NSW W Slopes; mostly in pine–gum–box formations on well-drained rocky ridges and hillslopes.

FOLIAGE: Phyllodes straight or *curved* (sickle-like), 9–20 cm × 3–8 mm, sub-glossy dark green, many faint longitudinal veins, the central one more prominent. Transitional foliage sometimes persists.

FLOWERS (Aug–Oct): Golden yellow, packed on axis in *cylindrical spikes* 2–3 cm long, often 2–3 spikes on common stalk.

PODS: Fairly straight, narrow, 5–10 cm long, brown, thin-walled.

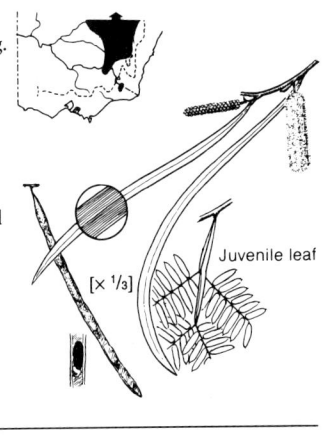

[× 1/3]

Juvenile leaf

Catkin Wattle

Acacia dallachiana

Erect spreading small tree, 4–12 m; green, but young growth often silvery-glaucous; bark fissured. *Localised in NE Vic* (e.g. Mts Buffalo and Bogong), just entering NSW in Snowy Mtns, *chiefly above 1000 m* in Alpine Ash forest on slopes and in gullies.

FOLIAGE: Phyllodes flat, gently curved, 10–16 cm × 1–3 cm, green, several distinct veins with network of finer ones between; gland near base.

FLOWERS (Oct–Dec): Yellow, in *long curving spikes* (to 6 cm) paired in axils, developing from compact catkin-like bud structures.

PODS: 6–10 cm long, thin-walled, almost straight, narrow, *constricted between widely spaced seeds*.

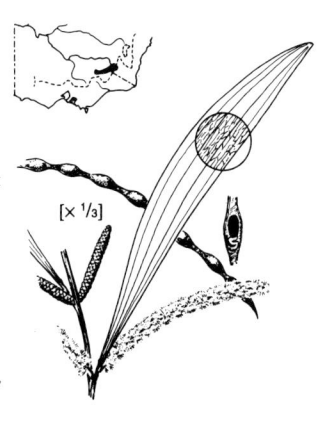

[× 1/3]

Golden Wattle

Acacia pycnantha

Erect shrub to small loosely-branched tree, 3–8 m, wholly hairless. Widespread at lower levels (often naturalised), chiefly in more open eucalypt forests, *particularly on drier shallow soils* (e.g. in box country); a paler-flowered form in mallee areas.

FOLIAGE: Leathery phyllodes 6–18 cm × 1–4 cm, *shiny dark green* (paler and duller in narrower-leaved mallee form), strong main vein and diverging lateral ones; a prominent marginal gland > 1 cm from axil. [In *A. saligna*, a similar *naturalised* WA species, the gland is *very close* to axil].

FLOWERS (Aug–Oct): In *showy golden globular heads* in extended inflorescence.

PODS: Almost straight, fairly flat, brown, to 12 cm long, funicle not encircling seed.

[× 1/3]

A. saligna

Red-stem Wattle

Acacia rubida

Shrub or small tree, 2–10 m, often slightly greyish; bipinnate juvenile leaves often persisting with phyllodes. Common in E Vic and E NSW, mostly in open forests on drier soils of hill or mountain country, also along creeks.

FOLIAGE: Phyllodes hanging, straight to curved (sickle-shaped) and *pointed*, green (sometimes glaucous), to 20 cm × 25 mm, main vein pale and margins vein-like, marginal gland prominent. Stems often red, *phyllodes becoming reddish when dried*.

FLOWERS (Aug–Oct): Yellow; globular heads in extended inflorescence.

PODS: Straight, flat, sometimes becoming dark or glaucous, 6–12 cm long; *doubled funicle encircles seed*.

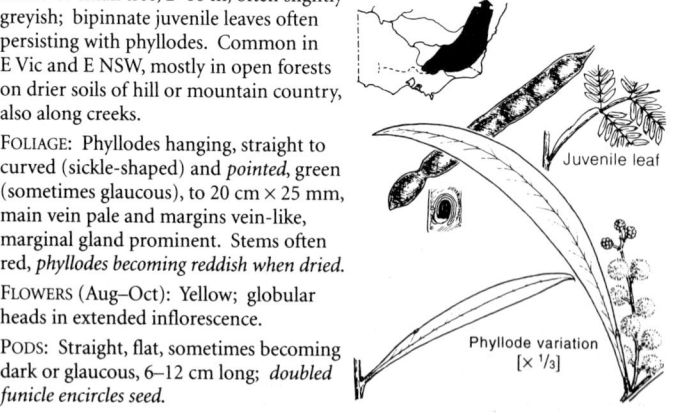

Juvenile leaf

Phyllode variation
[× 1/3]

Broad-leaved Hickory Wattle

Acacia falciformis [A]

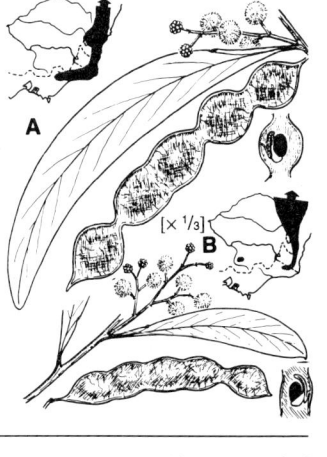

[A] *Grey-green*, often densely-foliaged tall shrub to tree, 4–12 m; bark hard, rough and sometimes *black*. Very common in eastern forests (especially with Silvertop Ash), on drier rocky soils of hilly country.

FOLIAGE: Phyllodes *large*, curved, hanging, *grey-green*, 10–20 cm × 1–3 cm, *broadest at or before middle*, main vein *central*, margins vein-like, marginal gland prominent.

FLOWERS (Aug–Jan): Pale creamy-yellow; heads in extended inflorescence (to 6 cm).

PODS: *Flat, very broad*, to 20 cm long, with *some deep constrictions between seeds.*

[B] **Hickory Wattle** (*A. penninervis*), shrub or small tree in SE NSW, has *smaller green* phyllodes (broadest beyond middle, more pointed), smaller pods (± straight-edged).

Mountain Hickory Wattle

Acacia obliquinervia [A]

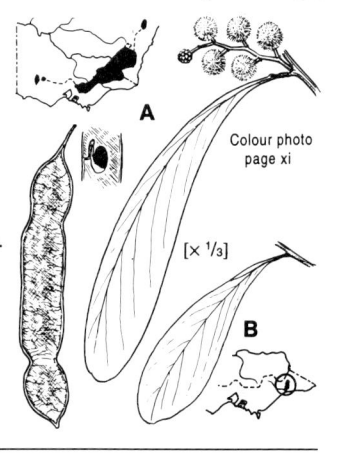

Colour photo page xi

[A] Shrub or tree, 3–15 m, usually with *fairly dense greyish foliage*. Common in eastern ranges at *higher elevations* (e.g. with Alpine Ash), also in Grampians.

FOLIAGE: Phyllodes *grey-green*, to 17 cm × 4 cm, *broadest beyond middle*, blunt or rounded at apex, curved near base, *main vein nearer upper margin*, gland at base.

FLOWERS (Aug–Nov): Bright yellow; heads in extended inflorescence (to 6 cm).

PODS: Flat, broad, to 15 cm long, brown (may be glaucous), *fairly straight-edged* (only occasional constrictions).

[B] **Buchan Blue Wattle** (*A. caerulescens,* described 1989), *only in Lakes Entrance–Buchan area*, is similar, but with *smaller very glaucous* phyllodes as illustrated.

139

Wirilda

Acacia retinodes

Two varieties are described, but marked differences suggest they are distinct species.

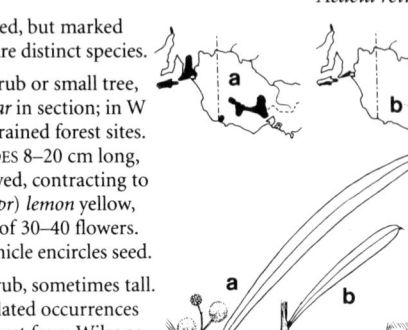

[a] Var. *retinodes* is a shrub or small tree, 3–8 m, branchlets *angular* in section; in W Vic and SA, on poorly-drained forest sites. Often planted. PHYLLODES 8–20 cm long, *ashen-green*, usually curved, contracting to point. FLOWERS (*Dec–Apr*) *lemon* yellow, 3–8 heads/raceme, each of 30–40 flowers. PODS straight-edged; funicle encircles seed.

[b] Var. *uncifolia* is a shrub, sometimes tall. Differences include: Isolated occurrences on *limy sands*, on *coast* west from Wilsons Prom.; PHYLLODES *greener*, more crowded, *smaller* (3–8 cm), tip *hooked*; FLOWERS *rich* yellow, 20–25 in *smaller but more numerous heads*; PODS with slight constrictions.

[× ¹/₃]

Hakea Wattle

Acacia hakeoides

Green, completely hairless shrub or small tree, erect or spreading, 2–8 m, bark grey-brown, smooth or fissured. Common in woodlands or open forest (e.g. box-type) and in mallee scrub, on sands and rocky ridges, *inland from Divide across the area.*

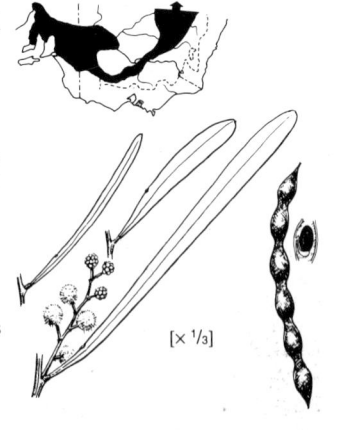

FOLIAGE: Phyllodes rather variable, green, thickish, 4–15 cm × 3–11 mm, straight or gently curved, sometimes angled at the distinct marginal gland in lower half, *always broader beyond middle*, tip blunt, central vein prominent with reticulate finer lateral veins diverging from it.

FLOWERS (July–Oct): Bright yellow; heads in extended inflorescence to 8 cm long.

[× ¹/₃]

PODS: Constricted between seeds, to 10 cm long, becoming dark.

Mountain Wattle
Acacia kettlewelliae

Large shrub or small bushy tree, 2–9 m, wholly hairless, foliage *slaty-green*, ultimate branchlets angular or flattened in section. Scattered occurrences but locally common, in montane forests (e.g. of alpine ash, or drier gum–peppermint types), and at lower elevations on valley slopes, often near streams; NE Vic to NSW Tablelands.

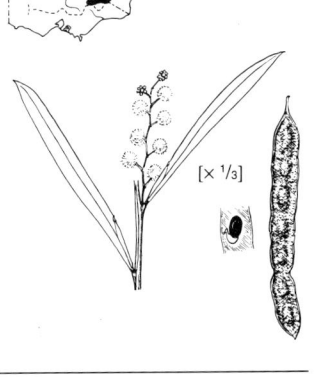

[× ⅓]

FOLIAGE: Ascending fairly thin phyllodes, 4–10 cm × 4–10 mm, apex acute with small curved point, midvein prominent and usually slightly nearer upper margin which bears a distinct *broad* gland.

FLOWERS (Sept–Nov); Bright yellow; heads in light extended inflorescence (to 7 cm).

PODS: Fairly straight, flat, to 11 cm long, becoming ashen or purplish.

Willow Wattle
Acacia salicina

Large shrub to small tree, 3–12 m, *willowy with pendulous foliage*; bark finely fissured. Scattered, *northwards from Murray River* across NSW plains, especially on heavier soils along inland waterways (e.g. with Black Box), but also on some more sandy sites with mulga, cypress-pine and others. Suckers freely, stabilising river banks.

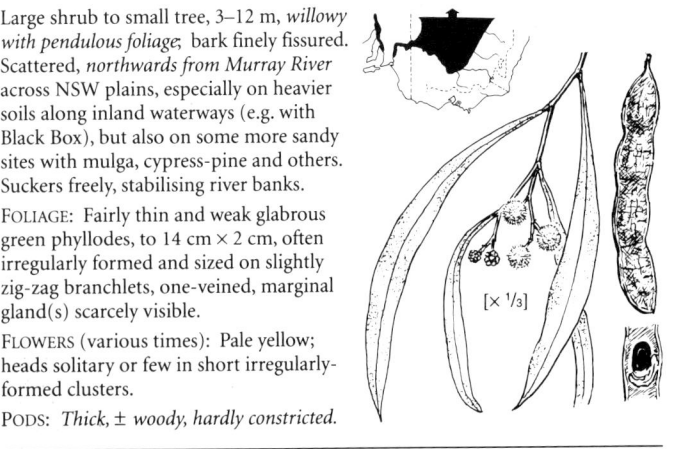

[× ⅓]

FOLIAGE: Fairly thin and weak glabrous green phyllodes, to 14 cm × 2 cm, often irregularly formed and sized on slightly zig-zag branchlets, one-veined, marginal gland(s) scarcely visible.

FLOWERS (various times): Pale yellow; heads solitary or few in short irregularly-formed clusters.

PODS: *Thick, ± woody, hardly constricted.*

141

Wallowa

Acacia calamifolia

Green or greyish rounded shrub or small tree, 2–6 m, with *many slender branches*. Common in drier rocky or sandy western and inland areas, in woodlands or mallee.

FOLIAGE: Slender phyllodes, rounded or flattened in section, 3–12 cm × 1–4 mm, appearing 1-veined, *tip always curved*.

FLOWERS (mainly spr): Bright yellow; heads on fine peduncles, often paired, sometimes in short extended clusters.

PODS: Straight or twisted, ± constricted.

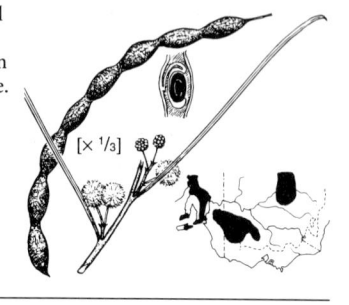

Cinnamon Wattle

Acacia leprosa

Shrub or small tree, 2–8 m, *green foliage ± sticky*, light branches often weeping. In forests (e.g. of messmate) mainly in ranges east of Melbourne. Possibly two species.

FOLIAGE: Phyllodes to 12 cm long, appearing ± 'varnished', *one main vein*. Either narrow (2–8 mm) or broad (to 30 mm).

FLOWERS (Aug–Sept): Yellow; heads 'furry' in bud, on hairy peduncles, 1–4 per axil.

PODS: Thin, brown, narrow, to 8 cm long.

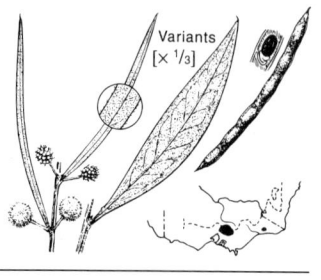

Varnish Wattle

Acacia verniciflua

Very variable shrub or small tree to 5 m, green foliage ± *sticky and usually appearing 'varnished'*. Mainly in drier forests; broad-phyllode taller form in forests of ranges.

FOLIAGE: Phyllodes thin, *variable*, usually narrower in drier inland, larger in forests; dotted with tiny glands, *two main veins*.

FLOWERS (July–Nov): Yellow; heads on sparsely hairy peduncles, 1–3 per axil.

PODS: Brown, ± sticky, to 10 cm long.

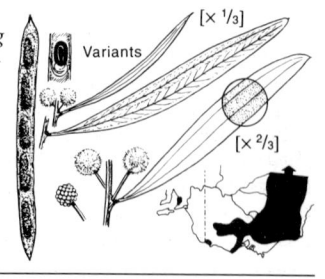

142

Sticky Wattle

Acacia howittii

Graceful rounded small tree, dark green foliage on pendulous branchlets. *Limited naturally to forests in Strzelecki Ras and U Macalister R areas* (a Gippsland endemic species); better known as a planted tree.

FOLIAGE: Thin phyllodes sticky when young, to 25 mm × 8 mm, with soft hairs on margins, several inconspicuous veins.

FLOWERS (about Oct): Lemon-yellow; heads on hairy peduncles, mostly paired.

PODS: Thin, brown, ± straight, to 6 cm.

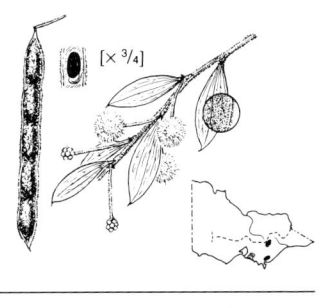

Narrow-leaved Bower Wattle

Acacia cognata

Shrub or small slender-trunked tree, 3–8 m, young foliage mid-green and *gracefully pendulous.* Common in moist gullies and on hillsides, *E Gippsland–S Coast NSW.*

FOLIAGE: Thin, *narrow* phyllodes, to 10 cm long, *1–3 mm wide*, green, often sticky, a central vein and usually two fainter ones.

FLOWERS (Sept–Oct): Pale lemon-yellow; heads on fine peduncles, mostly paired.

PODS: Very narrow, to 10 cm long, brown.

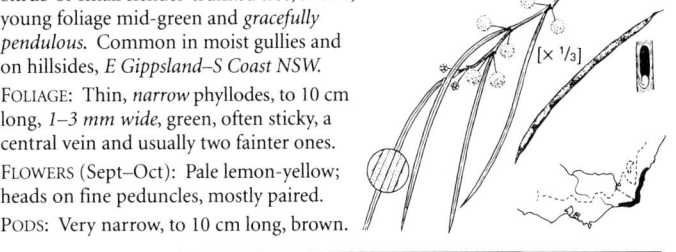

Bower Wattle

Acacia subporosa

Small tree, 4–10 m; foliage dense, dark green, sometimes willowy, usually sticky. Occurrence restricted to forests of *NSW far S Coast, just entering E Gippsland.*

FOLIAGE: Thin, flat, *dark-green* phyllodes, to 10 cm long, *4–11 mm wide*, minutely gland dotted and often sticky, *3–7 veins.*

FLOWERS (Sept–Oct): Soft pale yellow; heads on fine peduncles, 1–3 per axil.

PODS: Straight, sticky, brown, to 8 cm.

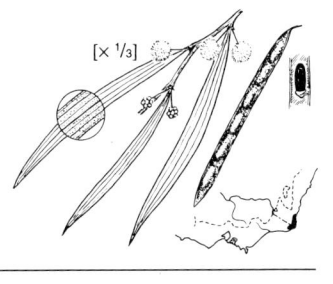

143

Blackwood

Acacia melanoxylon

Small to large tree, 6–30 m; foliage usually dense and dark green; bark dark grey, hard and fissured. Very common on a variety of sites where annual rainfall exceeds 600 mm (including basalt plains of W Vic), but best development on deep soils, especially in tall forests and eastern 'jungle' pockets.

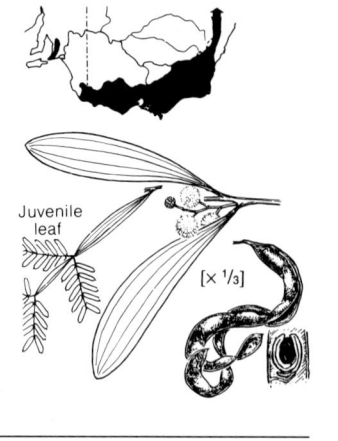

FOLIAGE: *Dark green* phyllodes, 6–14 cm × 1–3 cm, not held erect, 3–5+ veins with faint network between; *apex usually blunt* (but sometimes like Lightwood); bipinnate juvenile leaves may persist on young plants.

FLOWERS (*Aug–Oct*): Pale creamy; heads on almost glabrous peduncles, 2–8 in short extended inflorescence.

PODS: Pale brown, becoming twisted and coiled; *doubled red funicle encircles seed.*

Montane Wattle

Acacia frigescens

Large shrub to bushy tree, 3–15 m; dull green foliage *greyish* when young; bark scarcely fissured. Apparently confined to Victoria, with disjunct occurrences chiefly in *eastern montane forests* of Alpine Ash (e.g. Lake Mountain, Baw Baws, and Bonang area of East Gippsland).

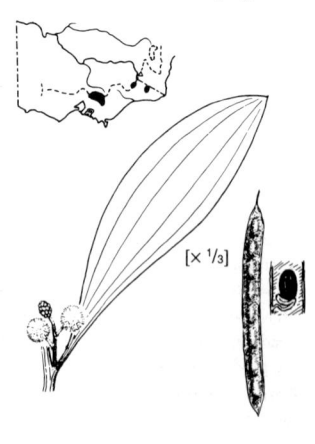

FOLIAGE: Greyish to dark green phyllodes, minutely mealy when fresh, rather stiff, 8–15 cm × 2–5 cm (broader than in Blackwood), 3–4 distinct primary veins with secondary veins and network between.

FLOWERS (Sept–Nov): Usually *bright yellow*; buds whitish; heads on *white* peduncles, few in short inflorescence.

PODS: *Almost straight* (to 10 cm), pale brown; *funicle folded under seed.*

Lightwood

Acacia implexa

Small tree, 5–15 m; crown usually fairly open with mid-green foliage; bark rough and greyish. Common and widespread, in Vic–NSW hill country, especially in *drier open forests on shallow soils.* (Other more definite differences from Blackwood are in flowering time and seed funicle.)

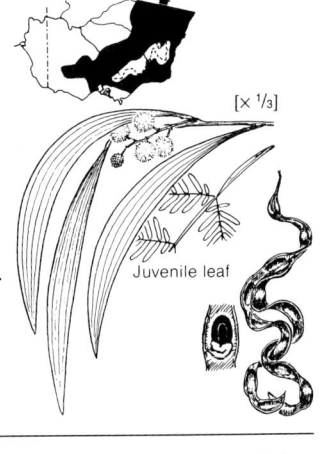

[× ¹⁄₃]

FOLIAGE: Phyllodes *green, curved (sickle-shaped), hanging,* 7–18 cm × 7–25 mm, several main veins with numerous fainter ones parallel and branching; bipinnate juvenile leaves may persist on young plants.

Juvenile leaf

FLOWERS (*Dec–Mar*): Pale creamy-yellow; heads on slender glabrous peduncles in loose extended inflorescence to 4 cm.

PODS: Narrow, to 20 cm long, becoming coiled; *white funicle folded under seed.*

Ovens Wattle

Acacia pravissima

Shrub or small tree, 3–8 m; distinctive with slender spreading or arching branches bearing ± triangular grey-green phyllodes. Locally common especially near streams and on damp sheltered sites in mountain open-forests (e.g. gum–peppermint), east Victoria (mainly north-east) to ACT in NSW. Commonly planted in gardens.

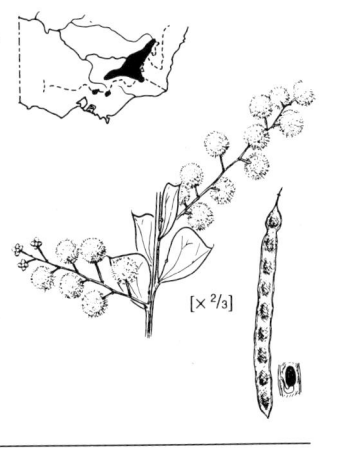

FOLIAGE: Grey-green phyllodes, *'humped' on upper margin and with sharp point,* 6–16 mm × 4–13 mm, two main veins (one stronger), marginal gland distinct.

FLOWERS (Aug–Oct): Yellow; rather small heads in inflorescences extending beyond the phyllodes, making masses of blossom.

[× ²⁄₃]

PODS: Straight or curved, flat, to 8 cm long, brown.

145

Miljee, Umbrella Wattle

Acacia oswaldii

Erect or spreading shrub or small tree, 2–6 m; dark grey bark fissured-fibrous; foliage green (sometimes silvery young). Occurs across NW Vic, extending through inland NSW and SA, in various low open forests, woodlands, mallee, or mulga scrub, on flats or rises.

FOLIAGE: Flat, thick, glabrous phyllodes, 3–8 cm × 2–9 mm (the width rather variable), straight or curved, *stiff with pungent point, many parallel fine veins*, gland right at base.

FLOWERS (Nov–Jan): Yellow; *globular heads virtually sessile*, 1–2 per axil.

PODS: Becoming distinctively *leathery or woody, strongly twisted or coiled*, 6–20 cm × 5–10 mm.

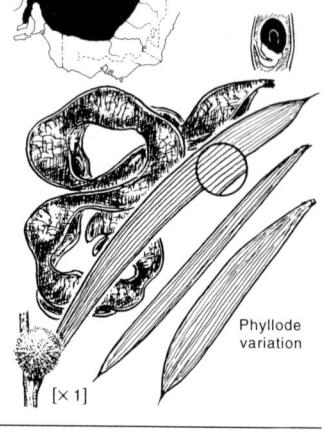

Phyllode variation

[× 1]

Eumong, River Cooba

Acacia stenophylla

Erect small tree, 4–10 m, with *weeping branches and very long phyllodes*; bark dark grey-brown and fissured. On heavy clay soils of *periodically-flooded river flats* of Murray R downstream from Echuca (e.g. Hattah Lakes), also along Lachlan–Darling R system in NSW; usually in woodlands of Red Gum and Black Box.

FOLIAGE: Phyllodes *long, narrow and strap-like*, 14–40 cm × 1–8 mm, thick, greenish, with numerous fine longitudinal veins, small gland at base.

FLOWERS (various times): Pale yellow; globular heads few (1–6) in extended axillary inflorescence to 3 cm long.

PODS: *Distinctively hard and lumpy, like a string of beads*, 10–20 cm × 1 cm, brown.

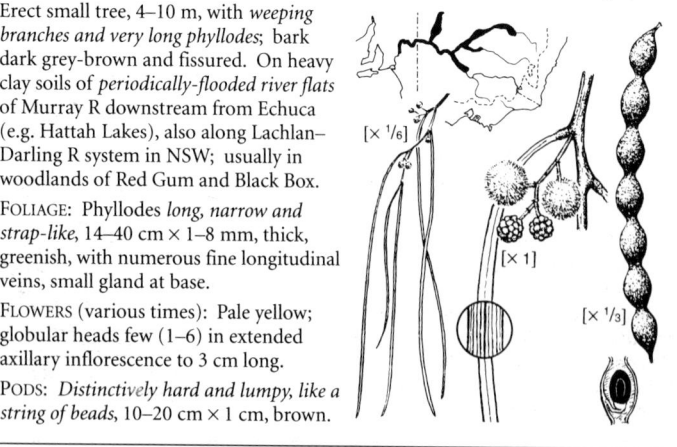

[× 1/6]

[× 1]

[× 1/3]

146

Boree, Weeping Myall

Acacia pendula

Small rough-barked tree, 5–12 m; *foliage ± silvery on willowy branchlets.* Common, often as pure stands, in NSW Riverina (rare in Vic), on *heavy black soils of alluvial flats*, especially near Black Box. Processional caterpillars build structures like birds' nests in branches, and strip foliage.

FOLIAGE: Fairly flexible smooth phyllodes, 5–12 cm × 5–10 mm, ± glaucous, usually with tiny silvery appressed hairs obscuring the 1–3 parallel veins, tip often hooked.

FLOWERS: Yellow; 2–4 *small heads of 10–20 flowers* in each short axillary inflorescence.

PODS: To 8 cm × 2 cm, flat, rather woody, *with 'wings' along edges; seeds transverse.*

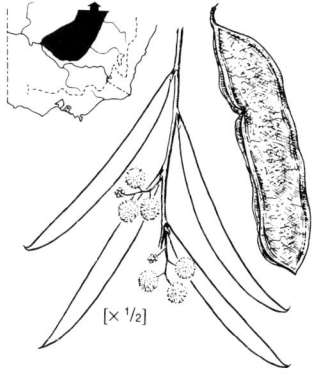

[× ¹/₂]

Yarran

Acacia omalophylla [A]
Acacia melvillei [B]

[A] *A. omalophylla* (spelt *homalophylla* in NSW) is a rough-barked tree to 7 m; near Murray R and northward, in various woodlands on reddish sandy flats and rises.

FOLIAGE: Phyllodes leathery, glabrous or slightly scurfy, ± glaucous or pale green, to 10 cm × 4–7 mm, fine veins numerous (3 apparent but the rest hardly visible).

FLOWERS: Golden; 1–3 heads (of *20–30 flowers*) in each very short inflorescence.

PODS: To 9 cm long, *narrow* (3–6 mm), ± constricted between *longitudinal* seeds.

[B] *A. melvillei*, ± glabrous tree, rare near Murray R in NW Vic, scattered on W NSW plains, is related to *A. omalophylla* and *A. pendula.* Distinguishable by usually broader phyllodes (6–12+ mm), inflorescence with 3–5 heads of *30–50 flowers,* pods to 12 mm wide, *without* edge 'wings', seeds *transverse.*

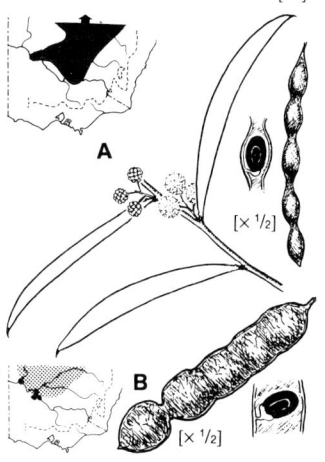

A

[× ¹/₂]

B

[× ¹/₂]

THE BANKSIAS (Genus *Banksia*)

Banksia is an almost entirely Australian genus of over seventy species. All species occurring in this book's area have been included, even though several are only of shrub size. Samples of two tree species (*B. integrifolia* and *B. serrata*) were among the first significant plant collections made at Botany Bay by the botanists Joseph Banks and Daniel Solander during Cook's first voyage in 1770; the genus was named after Banks in 1782.

The *Banksia* inflorescence consists of a mass of flowers on a central axis. The tip of each flower's style is modified with a 'pollen presenter' which picks up the flower's own pollen when it opens and projects. Birds (especially honeyeaters) and small mammals become cross-pollinating agents as they seek the nectar at the base of the flowers, so transferring pollen on their heads. Relatively few flowers develop into woody fruiting follicles in a 'cone'. In some species these follicles open spontaneously to release the two winged seeds, but for others a bushfire is needed.

The leaves of all *Banksia* species are alternate or whorled, simple, hard and rather stiff, dark green above but paler green or white beneath.

Banksia is a member of the family Proteaceae which includes other prominent Australian genera such as *Grevillea*, *Hakea*, *Telopea*, *Lomatia* and *Persoonia*—these have representatives in earlier sections of the book.

Coast Banksia (*Banksia integrifolia*)

Saw Banksia (*B. serrata*), with inflorescence and con

Coast Banksia

Usually a robust tree, 4–20 m; bark hard, grey, roughened. On *coastal sands*, Port Phillip Bay eastward. LEAVES 4–10 cm long, dark green above, whitish beneath, adult usually *entire* (i.e. without teeth), juvenile often coarsely toothed. INFLORESCENCE (Mar–June) pale yellow, to 12 cm × 7 cm. CONES with follicles opening soon after maturity; flower-remnants *not* persisting.

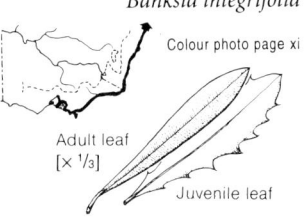

Banksia integrifolia

Colour photo page xi

Adult leaf
[× 1/3]

Juvenile leaf

Rock Banksia

Shrub on *rocky* sites in Grampians, or tree to 13 m in Wilsons Prom. forest. Described as a distinct species in 1981, the Grampians plants had previously been considered an inland form of Coast Banksia. Apart from the rocky habitat, differences are smoother thinner bark, stiffer more elliptic leaves, greyish yellow flowers (in summer), and follicles remaining closed longer.

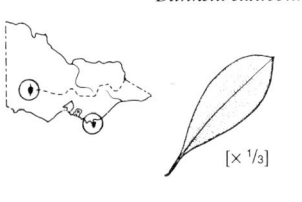

Banksia saxicola

[× 1/3]

Silver Banksia

Varies from low shrub in heaths to sturdy tree of 8 m in eastern open forests. LEAVES 3–7 cm long, with *tips ± truncate (as if cut across)* or notched, stiff, dark green above, white beneath, edges smooth when adult, ± toothed juvenile. INFLORESCENCE (Feb–June) yellow, cylindrical (to 10 cm × 6 cm); flower-remnants often persist on cone.

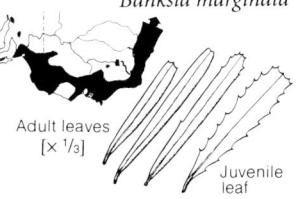

Banksia marginata

Adult leaves
[× 1/3]

Juvenile leaf

Mountain Banksia

Much-branched shrub to 3 m; sporadic but locally frequent on *rocky subalpine sites in East Gippsland* (e.g. Nunniong area), also Kybean Ra (NSW). LEAVES 3–5 cm long, green above, white beneath, *margins usually with sharp irregular spines.* INFLORESCENCE (Jan–June) pale yellow (grey-tipped early); old flowers *not* remaining on cone.

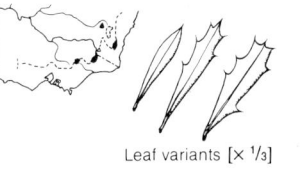

Banksia canei

Leaf variants [× 1/3]

Swamp Banksia

Many-stemmed shrub to 1.5 m, on sandy or rocky sites, often near swamps, *near-coastal NSW almost to Vic border*. LEAVES whorled, green above, whitish beneath, to 13 cm long, usually broadest towards tip, edges smooth or toothed. INFLORESCENCE (Apr–July) brown-golden, to 13 cm long, but *only 4 cm across*. Follicles usually stay closed until burnt; flower-remnants persist.

Banksia paludosa

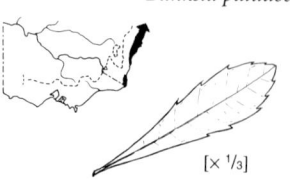

[× ⅓]

Saw Banksia

Shrub to tree, 2–12 m, often gnarled; bark thick, warty. In *near-coastal forests/heaths on sandy soils*, east from Wilsons Prom. area. LEAVES to 18 cm long, shiny green above, pale green beneath, *margins with saw-like teeth*. INFLORESCENCE grey-yellow, large (to 18 cm × 10 cm). CONES with large velvety follicles; flower-remnants persist.

Banksia serrata

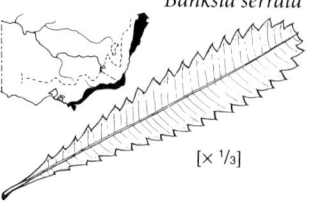

[× ⅓]

Desert Banksia

Bushy shrub to 3 m tall, common in heath-lands and mallee on *pale sands*; Grampians, 'Deserts', into SA. LEAVES *regularly toothed*, to 12 cm long, paler green beneath; young growth reddish and hairy. INFLORESCENCE (Apr–Sept) creamy, ovoid, to 11 cm long. CONES with large follicles usually opening only with fire; flower-remnants persist.

Banksia ornata

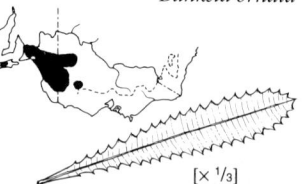

[× ⅓]

Hairpin Banksia

Shrub with two varieties in area: [a] var. *spinulosa*, usually multistemmed, in near-coastal *NSW*; [b] var. *cunninghamii*, taller (to 5 m), usually single-stemmed, scattered in *E-C Vic* hill country. LEAVES to 12 cm long, *very narrow*, edges rolled under in [a], toothed in [b]. INFLORESCENCE (Apr–July) cylindrical, to 20 cm long, golden *with stiff 'hairpin' styles* (not persisting on cone).

Banksia spinulosa

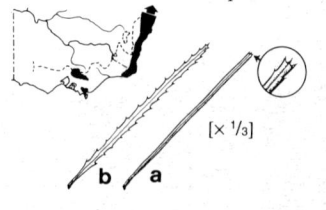

[× ⅓]

b   a

SHEOAKS and BULLOAKS
(the *Casuarina* family CASUARINACEAE)

This mainly Australian family was formerly composed of only one genus, *Casuarina*. However in 1982 it was subdivided using some differences in fruit, and now most of the fourteen Victorian species (trees and shrubs) fall into the newer genus *Allocasuarina*, with only two in *Casuarina*.

All members of this family have distinctive dark-green or grey-green slender branchlets which are modified to function as leaves (i.e. to photosynthesise)—sometimes termed cladodes. Close examination will show that they have longitudinal striations or ribs, and leaves reduced to tiny 'teeth' (scale-leaves) in whorls at regular intervals (**A**). The number of ribs and scale-leaves per whorl is consistent within a range for each species.

Most species, whether called 'sheoak' or 'bulloak/buloke', have their male and female flowers on different plants. The male flowers are pollen-bearing anthers at the extremities of branchlets (**B**), giving the male plant an orange or brown coloration at flowering time. The female flowers are small stalked heads (**C**), scattered on main branchlets, and showing only styles—these develop into the woody fruiting cones (**D**) when fertilised.

The fruiting cones open by numerous 'valves' to release seed-cases with wings (one of several wind-adaptation features in this family).

Drooping Sheoak – female (left), male flowers (right)

Drooping Sheoak (*Allocasuarina verticillata*)

Drooping Sheoak

Small tree to 10 m; bark dark grey, hard, fissured; *grey-green crown usually rounded, branchlets mostly drooping.* Widespread, on coastal cliffs, and open rocky or grassy sites inland. BRANCHLETS *long* (to 40 cm), fairly thick, visibly ribbed; teeth 9–13 in whorls 2–3 cm apart. MALE FLOWERS yellowish brown; female on different trees. CONES usually *large, barrel-shaped,* 'valves' *sharp.*

Allocasuarina verticillata (formerly *Casuarina stricta*)

[× ³/₄]   [× 4]
Branchlet

Black Sheoak

Erect dark green tree, 5–14 m, ± pine-like; bark hard, grey, closely fissured. Mostly in E Vic–NSW lighter forests, on sands and clays. BRANCHLETS dark green, *straight and fine,* mostly < 20 cm long; teeth 6–8 in whorls 5–10 mm apart. MALE FLOWERS rusty-brown; female usually on different trees. CONES ± cylindrical, 1–3 cm long.

Allocasuarina littoralis
Colour photo page xi

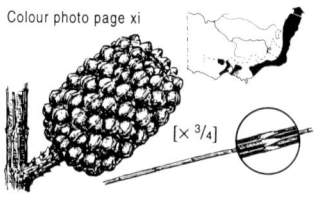

[× ³/₄]

Small Bulloak

Shrub or small tree, 1–4 m, bark usually smooth, grey. *Restricted to SA* (S Mt Lofty Ras–Kangaroo I). BRANCHLETS to 10 cm long, *curved-erect, fairly thick,* smooth; teeth 5–7 in whorls 7–15 mm apart. MALE FLOWERS golden-brown; male and female sometimes on same plant. CONES usually oblong with ± flat end, 1.5–3 cm long.

Allocasuarina striata

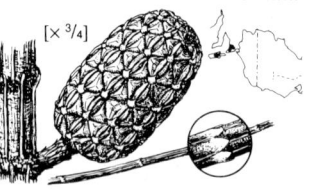

[× ³/₄]

Bulloak (Buloke)

Rough-barked erect tree, 5–15 m, with *dull green ascending branchlets.* Commonly with Grey Box and Cypress-pine in open woodlands, *northern Vic–NSW.* BRANCHLETS *wiry,* fairly thick, to 40 cm long; teeth short, 10–14 in whorls 9–20 mm apart. MALE FLOWERS yellowish; male and female on different trees. CONES *short* (broader than long), only 2–3 rows of 'valves'.

Allocasuarina luehmannii

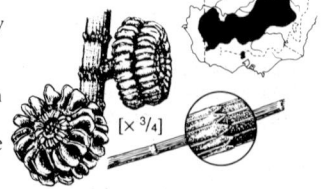

[× ³/₄]

Belah, Black Oak

Casuarina pauper

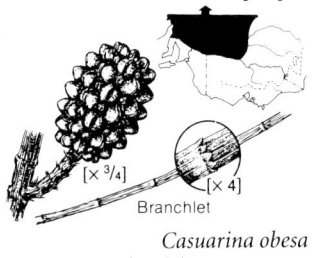

Rough-barked tree, 5–15 m. In woodlands on red-brown soils in *far NW Vic*, W NSW and SA. BRANCHLETS to 25 cm long, fairly thick, spreading or drooping, waxy, with minute hairs; teeth short, 9–13 in whorls 8–20 mm apart, sections separating easily. CONES 18–25 mm long, minutely velvety. [*C. cristata*, of C NSW, is often taller, has narrower branchlets, longer cone 'valves'.]

Branchlet

Sheoak

Casuarina obesa

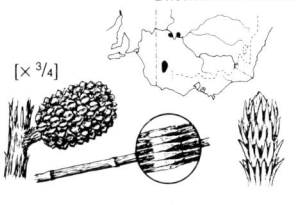

Tree 6–15 m, closely related to *C. glauca*; bark finely fissured. Mainly in WA, but a few localised occurrences in *Vic Wimmera* (e.g. near Mt Arapiles) and far NW Vic, usually near salt lakes. BRANCHLETS to 20 cm long, waxy; teeth 12–16 in whorls 8–14 mm apart (*erect* on new shoots). CONES 1–2 cm long, 'valves' small.

Swamp Sheoak

Casuarina glauca

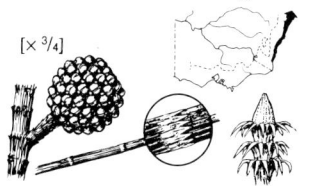

Erect dull grey-green tree to 20 m; bark finely fissured, scaly. Locally abundant in *brackish* situations, near tidal water, *near-coastal NSW south to Bermagui*. BRANCHLETS to 38 cm long, dull green, sometimes waxy; teeth 12–17 in whorls 8–20 mm apart (*long and curved back* on new shoots). CONES 9–18 mm long, 'valves' small.

River Sheoak

Casuarina cunninghamiana

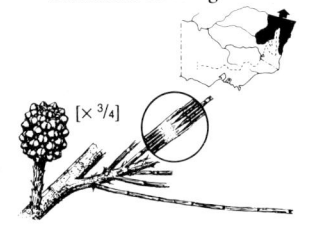

Dark green tree, sometimes tall, 15–35 m; bark finely fissured. *In E NSW*, usually in pure stands *along permanent freshwater streams*, near coast south to Bega, and west of Divide south to Tumut area. BRANCHLETS dark green, fine, straight, to 25 cm long; teeth yellow at base, 8–10 in whorls 6–9 mm apart. CONES *very small*. Hybridizes with *C. glauca* where their ranges overlap.

THE CYPRESS-PINES (Genus *Callitris*)

Apart from Mountain Plum-pine (*Podocarpus* sp., p. 31), the cypress-pines of the cypress family Cupressaceae are Victoria's only native pines. The pines common in Victorian plantations and along fencelines are not native—the main species of these, *Pinus radiata*, originally came from California, USA, and becomes a weed when it invades natural bush.

Pines are gymnosperms (meaning 'naked-seeds'). These do not have true flowers—the pollen is produced in small male cones and received on separate female cones which develop into the woody fruiting bodies. In the case of *Callitris*, these fruits are more or less rounded, and open in six segments, alternately larger and smaller, to release winged seeds.

The tiny green leaves of cypress-pines occur in whorls of three, with their bases running along the branchlets. In *C. endlicheri*, *C. muelleri* and *C. rhomboidea* (p. 156), the branchlets appear distinctly coarser than in the other species because the backs of the leaves have a 'keel' or ridge.

In Victoria, most cypress-pine occurrences are towards the more peripheral areas (Mallee, Grampians, East Gippsland and North-east), but there are a few other isolated remnants. Cypress-pines are much more extensive in NSW, particularly inland, but even there, vast areas have been cleared, the termite-resistant wood having been valued in building.

Murray Pine (*Callitris preissii*)

Callitris glaucophylla – with new and opened cones

White Cypress-pine

Single-trunked tree to 20 m, ± greyish-green. On loamy plains, rises, and some rocky outcrops; scattered trees on N Vic plains, more extensive in NSW; abundant (with White Box) in the U Snowy R area of E Gippsland; a few occurrences west of Melbourne and Geelong. BRANCHLETS rather fine (appressed leaves not keeled), usually greyish-green. CONES solitary, *mostly falling after maturity*, 15–25 mm across, never warted, segments relatively thin and *separating right to base*, rarely with tiny projection on tips.

Callitris glaucophylla
(formerly as *C. columellaris*)

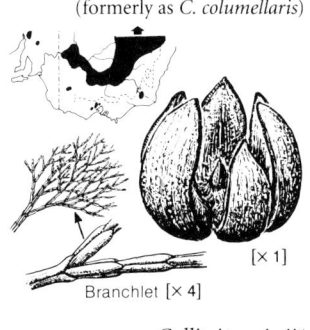

[× 1]

Branchlet [× 4]

Slender Cypress-pine, Murray Pine

Single-trunked tree to 20 m, usually dark- or olive-green. Two subspecies recognised: [a] ssp. *preissii* mainly on rocky hillsides (NSW); [b] ssp. *murrayensis* esp. on sandy rises in mallee areas (NW Vic, W NSW, SA). BRANCHLETS rather fine (appressed leaves not keeled). CONES solitary or clustered, *often persisting for years*, segments thick and *tending to adhere near base, often with scattered warts*; large (25–30 mm across); ± globular in [a], segments longer in [b]. Can hybridize with *C. glaucophylla*.

*Callitris preissii**
[*C. preissii* may be limited to WA;
populations in Vic–SA area
would become *C. gracilis*]

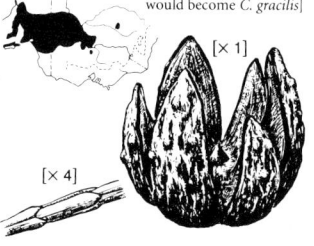

[× 1]

[× 4]

Scrub Cypress-pine, Mallee Pine

Green or grey-green shrub or small bushy tree with several trunks, 2–6 m. Common *in mallee scrub on sandy soils*, especially on pale sand-ridges in Vic–SA 'Deserts'. BRANCHLETS fine (appressed leaves not keeled), green or greyish. CONES greenish till maturity, almost spherical, about 2 cm across, *segments covered with small resinous warts* (see photo page xi). In NSW, this is considered a subspecies of *C. preissii*.

Callitris verrucosa
Colour photo
page xi

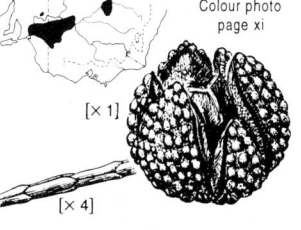

[× 1]

[× 4]

155

Cypress-pine

Callitris canescens

Shrub (or small tree) to 5 m. Scattered in mallee on sands in *Murray region of SE SA* and westward. BRANCHLETS green, fine, the short appressed leaves not keeled. CONES globular or ovoid *on stout stalks*, about 1.5 cm across, *smooth and somewhat shiny black*, segments rather *thick*, sometimes with a minute projection at each tip.

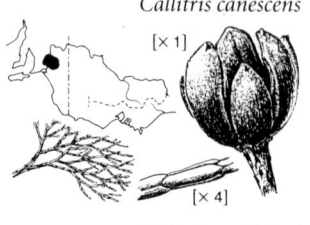

[× 1]

[× 4]

Black Cypress-pine

Callitris endlicheri

Tree, 5–15 m, foliage usually *greener* than in *C. glaucophylla*; wood is less durable. Mainly on drier rocky outcrops (especially granite), often with Blakely's Red Gum and boxes; NE Vic (e.g. Beechworth area, Pine Mountain), U Snowy R area; an isolated western occurrence in Kooyoora SP near Inglewood; more extensive in E NSW. BRANCHLETS coarser than previous species, appressed leaves *keeled* and *2–4 mm long*. CONES ± spherical, 15–20 mm across, *smooth and blackish, each segment with a small sharp projection near tip.*

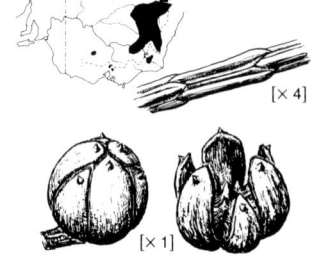

[× 4]

[× 1]

Callitris muelleri, a small tree with erect branches, mainly in Sydney region but also southwards to Eden, has cones similar to those of *C. endlicheri*, but its appressed keeled leaves are *5–10 mm long*.

[× 4]

Port Jackson Pine, Oyster Bay Pine

Callitris rhomboidea

Bushy shrub or small tree, 2–6 m, often glaucous-green. Disjunct occurrences, Mt Lofty Ras (SA), Grampians and 'Deserts', far E Gippsland–coastal NSW, on sands and sandstones. BRANCHLETS coarse with keeled leaves (often glaucous). CONES to 2 cm, *in tight persistent clusters*; smooth brown but *drying wrinkled and dark*; each segment with a *bold conical protuberance*.

[× 1]

[× 4]

Glossary and Index for Some Common Terms

alternate On either side of the stem at alternating levels (see p. 46).

axil The angle between a leaf or leaf-stalk and the branchlet (see p. 46).

bipinnate Leaf twice pinnately divided (as in some wattles; see p. 131).

calyx The sepals of a flower collectively (see p. 48 for eucalypt bud-cap).

capsule A dry fruit which opens or splits at the top to release seeds (p. 48).

concolorous/discolorous Surfaces of leaf same/different colours (shades).

corolla Petals of a flower collectively (see p. 48 for eucalypt bud-cap).

decussate Opposite (esp. of leaves) with successive pairs along the stem set at right-angles to each other (as in some *Melaleuca* species, p. 129).

drupe Fruit with seed(s) surrounded by 3 layers, one fleshy (e.g. plum).

elliptic More or less oval in outline, broadest at the middle.

exsert(ed) Projecting or protruding, e.g. valves on a capsule (see p. 48).

falcate Curved, sickle-shape, as in some eucalypt leaves.

funicle The attachment stalk of an ovule or seed (as in wattles, p. 131).

glabrous Without hairs, bristles or scales.

glaucous Bluish grey-green ('silvery') with a whitish waxy bloom.

inflorescence The flower-buds or flowers as a grouped structure.

juvenile The early (often distinctive) leaves on the young plant (p. 46).

lanceolate Lance-shape, with longer taper towards the apex (see p. 46).

montane In mountains, usually of taller forests below the subalps (p. 8).

oblique Asymmetry of leaf, particularly when 'angled' at base (see p. 46).

opposite Paired (leaves) at same level on either side of stem (see p. 46).

ovate/ovoid Egg-shape in outline, flat/solid respectively (see p. 46).

pedicel The stalk of a single bud, flower or fruit (see p. 48).

peduncle The stalk supporting a cluster of buds, flowers or fruits (p. 48).

phyllode Modified (usually flattened) leaf-stalk, acting as a leaf (p. 131).

sclerophyllous 'Hard-leaved' plant, resisting wilting, usually on poor soils.

sessile Without a stalk, seated directly on the axis (see p. 46 for leaves).

shrub Woody plant, less than 8 m, with several stems arising at base.

spike Elongated inflorescence of sessile flowers on a simple axis (p. 131).

tree Woody plant, usually with single trunk, and more than 5 m tall.

whorl Ring of leaves or flower-parts borne at same level on axis.

± Abbreviation for 'more or less', 'with or without', according to context.

Classification and Naming of Plants

Finding the best way of classifying organisms, whether plant or animal, is an on-going challenge, as new discoveries are made, and as the search continues for possible evolutionary relationships. What constitutes the 'best' classification is ultimately determined by wide acceptance.

The specialised study which deals with description, classification, and allocation of names to organisms is called **taxonomy**. To gain consistency in this whole process, there are internationally agreed codes with quite specific rules. It is sometimes because previously given names have been found to contravene these rules that they are changed by taxonomists.

Considering plants in particular, all in this book belong in a major group characterised by the production of seeds. This group is divided into the **gymnosperms** (including the cypress-pines, *Callitris*), and the **angiosperms** (flowering plants) including all the other trees in this book.

A particular type of plant which can be recognised as reasonably distinct, and which can continue to reproduce its own type, is termed a **species** (abbreviation 'sp.'). Clearly related species are grouped into a **genus** (plural **genera**). Genera are grouped into **families**, the family name being derived from a generic member, with the ending '-aceae'.

A species name always consists of two parts, identifying the genus and species respectively. As an example to explain these and other possible elements in a botanical name, consider *Eucalyptus leucoxylon* F. Muell. subsp. *connata* K. Rule. *Eucalyptus* is the generic name (abbreviated to '*E.*' only if this genus name has already been stated); *leucoxylon* (written with a small initial) identifies the particular species of *Eucalyptus*. The name (often abbreviated) of the person who formally described and named the species (in this case Ferdinand von Mueller) sometimes follows the specific name, but not in this book. A geographically distinctive form within a species may be defined as a **subspecies** ('subsp.' or 'ssp.'); the subspecies *connata* of *E. leucoxylon* was described by K. Rule in 1991. Botanists can differ in their interpretation of what actually constitutes a species, and so it is possible that in different references a particular name may be used at either species or subspecies level. To complete our example, genus *Eucalyptus* is classified in the myrtle family Myrtaceae.

For Further Information

As this book is intended as a field guide, particularly for non-specialists, explanatory detail has necessarily been limited by available space and the need for simplicity. The following books will provide more information.

Boland, D.J. & al., *Forest Trees of Australia* (4th ed.), CSIRO, Melbourne, 1984. Detailed descriptions of over 200 Australian trees of economic significance, especially for timber. Includes environmental information for each species.

Brooker, M.I.H. & Kleinig, D.A., *Field Guide to Eucalypts, Vol. 1* (South-eastern Australia), Inkata, Melbourne, 1983. Describes, with colour plates for every species, all eucalypts for NSW, Victoria, eastern SA and Tasmania, as at 1983.

Clarke, I. & Lee, H., *Name that Flower: The Identification of Flowering Plants* (5th ed.), Melbourne University Press, 1993. Explains, with illustrations, the variation in characters used in identification of Australian plants, especially types of floral structure; gives examples from major families and genera.

Costermans, L.F., *Native Trees and Shrubs of South-eastern Australia* (2nd ed.), Lansdowne, Sydney, 1983; also *Amendments and Additions,* Costermans, Melbourne, 1992. Describes, both in regions and in families, almost all trees and shrubs taller than one metre (for a wider area than in this book), with line and colour illustrations. Includes environmental introductions.

Foreman D.B. & Walsh, N.G. (eds), *Flora of Victoria, Vol. 1*, Inkata, Melbourne, (for National Herbarium of Victoria), 1993. Volume 1 is a comprehensive introduction to the Victorian environment as it affects plants; aspects treated include history, geology, climate, natural regions, soils, fire, utilisation by Koories, exotic plants. Subsequent volumes will describe all species.

Harden, G.J. (ed.), *Flora of New South Wales*, NSW University Press, Kensington, (for Royal Botanic Gardens), 1990–3. Clear systematic treatment of all NSW plants, in families, with illustrations. Volumes 1–3 include trees and shrubs.

Specific enquiries relating to plant identification and distribution, and especially taxonomic interpretation, may be directed to the government herbarium in each State or Territory (associated with each of the Botanic Gardens). In general, this book follows the taxonomic interpretations adopted at the National Herbarium, Melbourne.

Index to Species Descriptions

161

Reprinted 1994, with minor additions and amendments